Buddhism:
Philosophy, Culture and Religion

Buddhism: Philosophy, Culture and Religion

Edited by

RATAN SINGH

GLOBAL PUBLICATIONS
NEW DELHI-110 002 (INDIA)

GLOBAL PUBLICATIONS
4378/4B, G-4 JMD House
Murari Lal Street, Ansari Road
Daryaganj, New Delhi - 110 002
Phone : 23278062 (Off.)
e-mail : omega_publications@yahoo.com

Head Office :
79/23, Laxmi Garden
Near Satya Jyoti School,
Gurgaon (Haryana)
Mob : 9213562438

Buddhism : Philosophy, Culture and Religion

First Published : 2011

ISBN : 978-93-80833-22-4

PRINTED IN INDIA

Published by Ishwari Prasad Garg for Global Publications, New Delhi-110 002 and Printed at Suman Printers, Delhi

Preface

Buddhists believe the Gautama Buddha was the first to achieve enlightenment in this Buddha era and is therefore credited with the establishment of Buddhism. A Buddha era is the stretch of history during which people remember and practice the teachings of the earliest *known* Buddha. This Buddha era will end when all the knowledge, evidence and teachings of Gautama Buddha have vanished. This belief therefore maintains that many Buddha eras have started and ended throughout the course of human existence. The Gautama Buddha, then, is *the Buddha of this era,* who taught directly or indirectly to all other Buddhas in it.

In addition, Mahayana Buddhists believe there are innumerable other Buddhas in other universes. A Theravada commentary says that Buddhas arise one at a time in this world element, and not at all in others.

The idea of the decline and gradual disappearance of the teaching has been influential in East Asian Buddhism. Pure Land Buddhism holds that it has declined to the point where few, if any, are capable of following the path, so most or all must rely on the power of the Buddha Amitabha. Zen and Nichiren traditionally hold that most are incapable of following the "complicated" paths of some other schools and present what they view as a simple practice instead.

The major topics dealt in this book are : *Introduction to Buddhism; Buddhist Ethics; Buddhism and Psychology; Buddhist Philosophy and Science; History of Buddhism; Gautama Buddha;*

God in Buddhism; Buddhism and Hinduism; Buddhism and Christianity; Buddhism in Thailand; Indian Religions; Buddhist Architecture and Symbolism; etc.

No doubt, these will serve the purpose of trainees and trainers, professional and policy planners in the field. Since the sources of information are all secondary, we express our gratitude to the scholars whose works are cited or substantially made use of. We are thankful to all those who rendered ready help and cooperation while working on this project.

We express our gratitude to various scholars, teachers and friends for their assistance and guidance. Finally, we thank our publishers for bringing out this book in very limited time.

—***Editor***

Contents

1

Introduction to Buddhism

Buddhism as traditionally conceived, is a path of salvation attained through insight into the ultimate nature of reality. Buddhism encompasses a variety of traditions, beliefs and practices that are largely based on the teachings of Siddhartha Gautama, commonly known as the Buddha (Pali/Sanskrit for "The Awakened One").

Born in what is today Nepal, the Buddha lived and taught in the northeastern region of the Indian subcontinent and most likely died around 400 BCE in what is now modern India. Adherents recognize the Buddha as an awakened teacher who shared his insights to help sentient beings escape the cycle of suffering and rebirth. The Buddha's teachings provide instructions on how to understand the true nature of phenomena, end suffering, and achieve nirvana.

Buddhists use various methods to liberate themselves and others from the suffering of worldly existence. These include ethical conduct and altruism, devotional practices and ceremonies, the invocation of bodhisattvas, renunciation, meditation, the cultivation of mindfulness and wisdom, study, and physical exercises.

Two major branches of Buddhism are broadly recognized: Theravada ("The School of the Elders") and Mahayana ("The Great Vehicle"). Theravada, the oldest surviving, has a widespread following in Sri Lanka and Southeast Asia whilst Mahayana, which is found throughout East Asia, includes the traditions of Pure Land, Zen, Nichiren Buddhism,

Shingon, Tibetan Buddhism and Tendai. In some methods of classification, Vajrayana is considered a third branch. Buddhist schools disagree on the historical teachings of the Buddha and on the importance and canonicity of various scriptures. Increasingly, other forms of Modern Buddhism are encroaching upon the traditionally recognized mainstream branches. While Buddhism remains most popular within Asia, both branches are now found throughout the world. Various sources put the number of Buddhists in the world between 230 million and 500 million.

Life of the Buddha

The following information about Buddha's life comes from the Tipitaka (other scriptures, such as the Lalitavistara Sutra, give differing accounts).

Siddhartha Gautama, the founder of Buddhism, was born in the city of Lumbini around the year 563 BCE and was raised in Kapilavastu. Moments after birth, according to the scriptures, he performed the first of several miracles, taking a few steps and proclaiming, "Supreme am I in the world. Greatest am I in the world. Noblest am I in the world. This is my last birth. Never shall I be reborn."

Shortly thereafter, a wise man visited his father, King Suddhodana. The wise man said that Siddhartha would either become a great king (*chakravartin*) or a holy man (*Sadhu*) based on whether he saw life outside of the palace walls. Determined to make Siddhartha a king, Suddhodana shielded his son from the unpleasant realities of daily life. Years after this, Gautama married Yasodhara, with whom he had a son, Rahula, who later became a Buddhist monk.

At the age of 29, Siddhartha ventured outside the palace complex several times, despite his father's wishes. As a result, he discovered the suffering of his people through encounters with an old man, a diseased man, a decaying corpse, and an ascetic. These are known among Buddhists as "The Four Sights", one of the first contemplations of Siddhartha. The Four Sights eventually prompted Gautama to abandon royal life and take up a spiritual quest to free himself from suffering by living the life of a mendicant ascetic—a respectable spiritual practice at the time. He found companions with similar spiritual goals and teachers who taught him various forms of meditation, including jhâna.

Ascetics practised many forms of self-denial, including severe undereating. One day, after almost starving to death, Gautama accepted a little milk and rice from a village girl named Sujata. After this experience, he concluded that ascetic practices such as fasting, holding one's breath, and exposure to pain brought little spiritual benefit. He viewed them as counterproductive due to their reliance on self-hatred and mortification. He abandoned asceticism, concentrating instead on *anapanasati* meditation (awareness of breathing), thereby discovering what Buddhists call the Middle Way, a path of moderation between the extremes of self-indulgence and self-mortification.

At the age of 35, after discovering the Middle Way, he sat under a sacred fig tree, also known as the Bodhi tree, in the town of Bodh Gaya, India, and vowed not to rise before achieving Nirvana. After many days of meditation, he attained his goal of becoming a Buddha. After his spiritual awakening he attracted a band of followers and instituted a monastic order. He spent the rest of his life teaching the Dharma, travelling throughout the northeastern part of the Indian subcontinent. He died at the age of 80 (483 BCE) in Kushinagar, India.

Scholars are hesitant to make unqualified claims about the historical facts of Gautama Buddha's life. According to

Michael Carrithers, while there are good reasons to doubt the traditional account, "the outline of the life must be true: birth, maturity, renunciation, search, awakening and liberation, teaching, death." Most historians accept that he lived, taught and founded a monastic order, but do not consistently accept most details in his biographies.

Buddhist Concepts

Karma: Cause and Effect

Karma (from Sanskrit: action, work) is the force which drives *Samsâra,* the cycle of suffering and rebirth for each being. Good, skillful (Pâli: *kusala*) and bad, unskillful (Pâli: *akusala*) actions produce "seeds" in the mind which come to fruition either in this life or in a subsequent rebirth. The avoidance of unwholesome actions and the cultivation of positive actions is called *Úîla* (from Sanskrit: ethical conduct).

In Buddhism, Karma specifically refers to those actions (of body, speech, and mind) that spring from mental intent (Pâli: *cetana*), and which bring about a consequence (or fruit, Sanskrit: *phala*) or result (Pâli: *vipâka*). Every time a person acts there is some quality of intention at the base of the mind and it is that quality rather than the outward appearance of the action that determines its effect.

In Theravada Buddhism there can be no divine salvation or forgiveness for one's Karma, since it is a purely impersonal process that is a part of the make up of the universe. Some Mahayana traditions however hold different views. For example, the texts of certain Sutras (such as the Lotus Sutra, the Angulimaliya Sutra and the Nirvana Sutra) claim that reciting or merely hearing their texts can expunge great swathes of negative Karma. Similarly, the Japanese Pure Land teacher Genshin taught that Buddha Amitabha has the power to destroy the Karma that would otherwise bind one in Sadsâra.

Rebirth

Rebirth refers to a process whereby beings go through a succession of lifetimes as one of many possible forms of sentient life, each running from conception to death. It is important to note, however, that Buddhism rejects concepts of a permanent self or an unchanging, eternal soul, as it is called in Christianity or even Hinduism. As there ultimately is no such thing as a self (anatta), rebirth in subsequent existences must rather be understood as the continuation of a dynamic, ever-changing process of "dependent arising" (Pratîtyasamutpâda) determined by the laws of cause and effect (Karma) rather than that of one being, "jumping" from one existence to the next.

Each rebirth takes place within one of five realms, according to Theravadins, or six according to other schools. These are further subdivided into 31 planes of existence:

1. Naraka beings: those who live in one of many *Narakas* (Hells)
2. Animals: sharing some space with humans, but considered another type of life
3. Preta: Sometimes sharing some space with humans, but invisible to most people; an important variety is the hungry ghost
4. Human beings: one of the realms of rebirth in which attaining Nirvana is possible
5. Asuras: variously translated as lowly deities, demons, titans, antigods; not recognized by Theravada (Mahavihara) tradition as a separate realm.
6. Devas including Brahmas: variously translated as gods, deities, spirits, angels, or left untranslated

Rebirths in some of the higher heavens, known as the Úuddhâvâsa Worlds (Pure Abodes), can be attained only by anâgâmis (non-returners). Rebirths in the arupa-dhatu (formless realms) can be attained only by those who can meditate on the arupa-jhânas.

According to East Asian and Tibetan Buddhism, there is an intermediate state(Bardo) between one life and the next. The orthodox Theravada commentorial position rejects this, however there are passages in the Samyutta Nikaya of the Pali Canon (the collection of texts on which the Theravada tradition is based), that seem to lend support to the idea that the Buddha taught of an intermediate stage between one life and the next.

The Cycle of Samsara

Sentient beings crave pleasure and are averse to pain from birth to death. In being controlled by these attitudes, they perpetuate the cycle of conditioned existence and suffering (Samsara), and produce the causes and conditions of the next rebirth after death. Each rebirth repeats this process in an involuntary cycle, which Buddhists strive to end by eradicating these causes and conditions, applying the methods laid out by the Buddha.

Suffering: Causes and Solution

The Four Noble Truths

According to the Pali Tipitaka, the Four Noble Truths were the first teaching of Gautama Buddha after attaining Nirvana. They are sometimes considered as containing the essence of the Buddha's teachings and are presented in the manner of a medical diagnosis and remedial prescription – a style common at that time:

1. Life as we know it ultimately is or leads to suffering/uneasiness (dukkha) in one way or another.
2. Suffering is caused by craving or attachments to worldly pleasures of all kinds. This is often expressed

as a deluded clinging to a certain sense of existence, to selfhood, or to the things or phenomena that we consider the cause of happiness or unhappiness.

3. Suffering ends when craving ends, when one is freed from desire. This is achieved by eliminating all delusion, thereby reaching a liberated state of Enlightenment (bodhi);
4. Reaching this liberated state is achieved by following the path laid out by the Buddha.

Described by early Western scholars, and taught as an introduction to Buddhism by some contemporary Mahayana teachers (e.g., the Dalai Lama).

According to other interpretations by Buddhist teachers and scholars, lately recognized by some Western non-Buddhist scholars, the "truths" do not represent mere statements, but are categories or aspects that most worldly phenomena fall into, grouped in two:

1. Suffering and causes of suffering
2. Cessation and the paths towards liberation from suffering.

Thus, according to the Macmillan *Encyclopedia of Buddhism* they are

1. "The noble truth that is suffering"
2. "The noble truth that is the arising of suffering"
3. "The noble truth that is the end of suffering"
4. "The noble truth that is the way leading to the end of suffering"

The early teaching and the traditional Theravada understanding is that the Four Noble Truths are an advanced teaching for those who are ready for them. The Mahayana position is that they are a preliminary teaching for people not yet ready for the higher and more expansive Mahayana teachings. They are little known in the Far East.

The Noble Eightfold Path

The Noble Eightfold Path, the fourth of the Buddha's Noble Truths, is the way to the cessation of suffering (dukkha). It has eight sections, each starting with the word *samyak* (Sanskrit, meaning *correctly*, *properly*, or *well*, frequently translated into English as *right*), and presented in three groups (NB: Pâli transliterations appear in brackets after Sanskrit ones):

- *Prajñâ* is the wisdom that purifies the mind, allowing it to attain spiritual insight into the true nature of all things. It includes:
  1. drsti (Pâli 'ditthi'): viewing reality as it is, not just as it appears to be.
  2. samkalpa (sankappa): intention of renunciation, freedom and harmlessness.
- *Sîla* is the ethics or morality, or abstention from unwholesome deeds. It includes:
  3. vac (vâca): speaking in a truthful and non hurtful way
  4. karman (kammanta): acting in a non harmful way
  5. ajivana (âjîva): a non harmful livelihood
- *Samâdhi* is the mental discipline required to develop mastery over one's own mind. This is done through the practice of various contemplative and meditative practices, and includes:

6. vyayama (vâyâma): making an effort to improve
7. smrti (sati): awareness to see things for what they are with clear consciousness, being aware of the present reality within oneself, without any craving or aversion

8. samdhi (samâdhi): correct meditation or concentration, explained as the first 4 *dhyânas*

The practice of the Eightfold Path is understood in two ways, as requiring either simultaneous development (all eight items practiced in parallel), or as a progressive series of stages through which the practitioner moves, the culmination of one leading to the beginning of another.

In the early sources (the four main *Nikayas*) the Eightfold Path is not generally taught to laypeople, and it is little known in the Far East.

Middle Way

An important guiding principle of Buddhist practice is the Middle Way, which is said to have been discovered by Gautama Buddha prior to his enlightenment (*bodhi*). The *Middle Way* or *Middle Path* has several definitions:

1. The practice of non-extremism: a path of moderation away from the extremes of self-indulgence and self-mortification
2. The middle ground between certain metaphysical views (e.g., that things ultimately either do or do not exist)
3. An explanation of Nirvana (perfect enlightenment), a state wherein it becomes clear that all dualities apparent in the world are delusory
4. Another term for emptiness, the ultimate nature of all phenomena (in the Mahayana branch), lack of inherent existence, which avoids the extremes of permanence and nihilism or inherent existence and nothingness

The Nature of Reality

Buddhist scholars have produced a prodigious quantity of intellectual theories, philosophies and world view concepts.

Some schools of Buddhism discourage doctrinal study, some regard it as essential, but most regard it as having a place, at least for some people at some stages. The concept of Liberation (Nirvana), the goal of the Buddhist path, is closely related to the correct perception of reality. In awakening to the true nature of the self and all phenomena one is liberated from the cycle of suffering (Dukkha) and involuntary rebirths (Samsara).

Impermanence, Suffering and Non-Self

Impermanence is one of the *Three Marks of Existence.* The term expresses the Buddhist notion that all compounded or conditioned phenomena (things and experiences) are inconstant, unsteady, and impermanent. Everything we can experience through our senses is made up of parts, and its existence is dependent on external conditions. Everything is in constant flux, and so conditions and the thing itself are constantly changing. Things are constantly coming into being, and ceasing to be. Nothing lasts.

According to the impermanence doctrine, human life embodies this flux in the aging process, the cycle of rebirth (samsara), and in any experience of loss. The doctrine further asserts that because things are impermanent, attachment to them is futile and leads to suffering (dukkha).

Suffering or Dukkha is a central concept in Buddhism, the word roughly corresponding to a number of terms in English including suffering, pain, unsatisfactoriness, sorrow, affliction, anxiety, dissatisfaction, discomfort, anguish, stress, misery, and frustration.

Although dukkha is often translated as "suffering", its philosophical meaning is more analogous to "disquietude" as in the condition of being disturbed. As such, "suffering" is too narrow a translation with "negative emotional connotations" (Jeffrey Po), which can give the impression that the Buddhist view is one of pessimism, but Buddhism is neither pessimistic nor optimistic, but realistic. Thus in English-language Buddhist literature *dukkha* is often left untranslated, so as to encompass its full range of meaning.

Anatta (Pâli) or *anâtman* (Sanskrit) refers to the notion of "not-self". In Indian philosophy, the concept of a self is called âtman (that is, "soul" or metaphysical self), which refers to an unchanging, permanent essence conceived by virtue of existence. This concept and the related concept of Brahman, the Vedantic monistic ideal, which was regarded as an ultimate âtman for all beings, were indispensable for mainstream Indian metaphysics, logic, and science; for all apparent things there had to be an underlying and persistent reality, akin to a Platonic form. Buddhists reject all these concepts of âtman, emphasizing not permanence, but changeability. Therefore all concepts of a substantial personal self are incorrect and formed in the realm of ignorance.

In the Nikayas, anatta is not meant as a metaphysical assertion, but as an approach for gaining release from suffering. In fact, the Buddha rejected both of the metaphysical assertions "I have a Self" and "I have no Self" as ontological views that bind one to suffering. By analyzing the constantly changing physical and mental constituents ("skandhas") of a person or object, the practitioner comes to the conclusion that neither the respective parts nor the person as a whole comprise a Self.

Dependent Arising

The doctrine of pratîtyasamutpâda, often translated as "Dependent Arising," is an important part of Buddhist metaphysics. It states that phenomena arise together in a mutually interdependent web of cause and effect. It is variously rendered into English as "dependent origination", "conditioned genesis", "dependent co-arising", "interdependent arising", or "contingency".

The best-known application of the concept of Pratîtyasamutpâda is the scheme of Twelve Nidânas (from Pali *nidâna* "cause, foundation, source or origin"), which explain the continuation of the cycle of suffering and rebirth (Samsara) in detail.

The Twelve Nidânas describe a causal connection between the subsequent characteristics/conditions of cyclic existence, each giving rise to the next:

1. Avidyâ: ignorance, specifically spiritual
2. Sadskâras: literally formations, explained as referring to Karma.
3. Vijñâna: consciousness, specifically discriminative
4. Nâmarûpa: literally name and form, referring to mind and body
5. baâyatana: the six sense bases: eye, ear, nose, tongue, body and mind-organ
6. Sparœa: variously translated contact, impression, stimulation (by a sense object)
7. Vedanâ: usually translated feeling: this is the "hedonic tone", i.e. whether something is pleasant, unpleasant or neutral
8. Ticnâ: literally thirst, but in Buddhism nearly always used to mean craving
9. Upâdâna: clinging or grasping; the word also means fuel, which feeds the continuing cycle of rebirth
10. Bhava: literally being (existence) or becoming. (The Theravada explains this as having two meanings: karma, which produces a new existence, and the existence itself.)
11. Jâti: literally birth, but life is understood as starting at conception

12. Jarâmarana (old age and death) and also œokaparidevadu%khadaurmanasyopâyâsa (sorrow, lamentation, pain, sadness, and misery)

Sentient beings always suffer throughout samsara, until they free themselves from this suffering by attaining Nirvana. Then the absence of the first Nidâna, ignorance, leads to the absence of the others.

Emptiness

Mahâyâna Buddhism received significant theoretical grounding from Nâgârjuna (perhaps c.150–250 CE), arguably the most influential scholar within the Mahâyâna tradition. Nâgârjuna asserted the nature of the dharmas, i.e. all *phenomena* or *constituent factors of human experience*, to be úûnya (void or empty), bringing together other key Buddhist doctrines, particularly anâtman (no-self) and pratîtyasamutpâda (dependent arising). His school of thought is known as the Mâdhyamaka. Some of the writings attributed to Nâgârjuna made explicit references to Mahâyâna texts, but his philosophy was argued within the parameters set out by the agamas.He may have arrived at his positions from a desire to achieve a consistent exegesis of the Buddha's doctrine as recorded in the Canon. In the eyes of Nâgârjuna the Buddha was not merely a forerunner, but the very founder of the Mâdhyamaka system.

Sarvâstivâda teachings, which were criticized by Nâgârjuna, were reformulated by scholars such as Vasubandhu and Asanga and were adapted into the Yogâcâra (Sanskrit: yoga practice) school. While the Mâdhyamaka school held that asserting the existence or non-existence of any ultimately real thing was inappropriate, some exponents of Yogâcâra asserted that the mind and only the mind is ultimately real (cittamatra). Not all Yogâcârins asserted that mind was truly existent, Vasubandhu and Asanga in particular did not. These two schools of thought, in opposition or synthesis, form the basis of subsequent Mahâyâna metaphysics in the Indo-Tibetan tradition.

Besides emptiness (úûnyatâ), Mahâyâna schools often place emphasis on the notions of perfected spiritual insight (prajñâpâramitâ) and Buddha-nature (tathâgatagarbha). According to the tathâgatagarbha sutras, the Buddha revealed the reality of the deathless Buddha-nature (tathâgatagarbha - which means 'Buddha embryo' or 'Buddha-matrix'), which is said to be inherent in all sentient beings and enables them all eventually to reach complete enlightenment, i.e. Buddhahood. Buddha-nature is stated in the Mahâyâna *Angulimaliya Sutra* and Mahaparinirvana Sutra *not* to be úûnya, but to be replete with eternal Buddhic virtues. In the tathâgatagarbha sutras the Buddha is portrayed proclaiming that the teaching of the tathâgatagarbha constitutes the "absolutely final culmination" of his Dharma—the highest presentation of truth (other sûtras make similar statements about other teachings) and it has traditionally been regarded as the highest teaching in East Asian Buddhism. However, in modern China all doctrines are regarded as equally valid. The Mahâyâna can also on occasion communicate a vision of the Buddha or Dharma which amounts to mysticism and gives expression to a form of mentalist panentheism (God in Buddhism).

Speculation versus Direct Experience: Buddhist Epistemology

Decisive in distinguishing Buddhism from other schools of Indian philosophy is the issue of epistemological justification (from *epistemology*, Greek: theory of knowledge). While all schools of Indian logic recognize various sets of valid justifications for knowledge, or *pramana*, Buddhism recognizes a smaller set than do the others. All accept perception and inference, for example, but for some schools of Buddhism the received textual tradition is an equally valid epistemological category.

According to the scriptures, during his lifetime the Buddha remained silent when asked several metaphysical questions. These regarded issues such as whether the universe is eternal or non-eternal (or whether it is finite or infinite), the unity or separation of the body and the self, the complete inexistence of a person after nirvana and death, and others. One explanation for this silence is that such questions distract from activity that is practical to realizing enlightenment and bring about the danger of substituting the experience of liberation by conceptual understanding of the doctrine or by religious faith. Another explanation is that both affirmative and negative positions regarding these questions are based on attachment to and misunderstanding of the aggregates and senses. That is, when one sees these things for what they are, the idea of forming positions on such metaphysical questions simply does not occur to one. Another closely related explanation is that reality is devoid of designations, or *empty*, and therefore language itself is a priori inadequate.

Thus, the Buddha's silence does not indicate misology or disdain for philosophy. Rather, it indicates that he viewed these questions as not leading to true knowledge. Dependent arising is, according to some, one of the Buddha's great contributions to philosophy, and provides a framework for analysis of reality that is not based on metaphysical assumptions regarding existence or non-existence, but instead on direct cognition of phenomena as they are presented to the mind. This informs and supports the Buddhist approach to liberation via ethical and meditative training known as the Noble Eightfold Path.

Accordingly, most Buddhists agree that, to a greater or lesser extent, words are inadequate to describe the goal of the Buddhist path, but concerning the usefulness of words in the path itself, schools differ radically.

In the Pali Canon and numerous Mahayana Sutras and Tantras, the Buddha is portrayed stressing that Dharma (in the sense of *truth*) cannot truly be understood with the ordinary rational mind or logic—reality transcends all worldly concepts.

In the Mahayana Mahaparinirvana Sutra's self-styled "Uttara-Tantra", the Buddha insists that, while pondering upon Dharma is vital, one must then relinquish fixation on words and letters, as these are utterly divorced from liberation and the Buddha-nature. The Tantra entitled the "All-Creating King" (Kunjed Gyalpo Tantra, a scripture of Tibetan Buddhism) also emphasizes how Buddhist truth lies beyond the range of discursive/verbal thought and is ultimately mysterious. The Supreme Buddha, Samantabhadra, states there: "The mind of perfect purity ... is beyond thinking and inexplicable ...." Also later, the famous Indian Buddhist practitioner (yogi) and teacher, mahasiddha Tilopa discouraged any intellectual activity in his six words of advice.

Speaking from the Mahayana perspective of the inconceivable, universal and non-discursive nature of the knowledge gained through Awakening or Enlightenment (Bodhi), Professor C. D. Sebastian states:

> "*Bodhi* is the final goal of a Bodhisattva's career and it is indicated by such words as *buddha-jnana* (knowledge of Buddha), *sarvjnata* (omniscience), *sarvakarajnata* (the quality of knowing things as they are), ... and *acintyam jnanam* (inconceivable knowledge) ... *Bodhi* is pure universal and immediate knowledge, which extends over all time, all universes, all beings and elements, conditioned and unconditioned. It is absolute and identical with Reality and thus it is Tathata. *Bodhi* is immaculate and non-conceptual, and it, being not an outer object, cannot be understood by discursive thought. It has neither beginning, nor middle nor end and it is indivisbile. It is non-dual (*advayam*)... The only possible way to comprehend it is through sạmadhi by the yogin"

Mahayana often adopts a pragmatic concept of truth: doctrines are "true" in the sense of being spiritually beneficial.

In modern Chinese Buddhism, all doctrinal traditions are regarded as equally valid.

Theravâda promotes the concept of Vibhajjavada (Pali), literally "Teaching of Analysis". This doctrine says that insight must come from the aspirant's experience, critical investigation, and reasoning instead of by blind faith. As the Buddha said according to the canonical scriptures:

> Do not accept anything by mere tradition ... Do not accept anything just because it accords with your scriptures ... Do not accept anything merely because it agrees with your pre-conceived notions ... But when you know for yourselves—these things are moral, these things are blameless, these things are praised by the wise, these things, when performed and undertaken, conduce to well-being and happiness—then do you live acting accordingly.

Liberation

Nirvana

Nirvana (Sanskrit; Pali "Nibbana") means "cessation", "extinction" (of craving and ignorance and therefore suffering and the cycle of involuntary rebirths Samsara), "extinguished", "quieted", "calmed"; it's also known as "Awakening" or "Enlightenment" in the West. Buddhists believe that anybody who has achieved nirvana is in fact a Buddha.

Bodhi is a term applied to the experience of Awakening of arahants. Bodhi literally means "awakening", but is more commonly referred to as "enlightenment". In Early Buddhism, bodhi carried a meaning synonymous to nirvana, using only some different metaphors to describe the experience, which implies the extinction of *raga* (greed, craving), *dosa* (hate, aversion) and *moha* (delusion). In the later school of Mahayana Buddhism, the status of nirvana was downgraded in some scriptures, coming to refer only to the extinction of greed and hate, implying that delusion was still present in one who attained nirvana, and that one needed to attain bodhi to eradicate delusion:

> An important development in the Mahayana that it came to separate nirvana from bodhi ('awakening' to the truth, Enlightenment), and to put a lower value on the former (Gombrich, 1992d). Originally nirvana and bodhi refer to the same thing; they merely use different metaphors for the experience. But the Mahayana tradition separated them and considered that nirvana referred only to the extinction of craving (passion and hatred), with the resultant escape from the cycle of rebirth. This interpretation ignores the third fire, delusion: the extinction of delusion is of course in the early texts identical with what can be positively expressed as gnosis, Enlightenment.
>
> —Richard F. Gombrich, *How Buddhism Began*

Therefore, according to Mahayana Buddhism, the arahant has attained only nirvana, thus still being subject to delusion, while the bodhisattva not only achieves nirvana but full liberation from delusion as well. He thus attains bodhi and becomes a buddha. In Theravada Buddhism, bodhi and nirvana carry the same meaning, that of being freed from greed, hate and delusion.

The term, parinirvana, is also encountered in Buddhism, and this generally refers to the complete nirvana attained by the arhat at the moment of death, when the physical body expires.

Buddhas

Theravada

In Theravada doctrine, a person may awaken from the "sleep of ignorance" by directly realizing the true nature of reality; such people are called arahants and occasionally buddhas. After numerous lifetimes of spiritual striving, they have reached the end of the cycle of rebirth, no longer reincarnating as human, animal, ghost, or other being. The commentaries to the Pali Canon classify these awakened beings into three types:

- Sammasambuddha, usually just called Buddha, who discovers the truth by himself and teaches the path to awakening to others
- Paccekabuddha, who discovers the truth by himself but lacks the skill to teach others
- Savakabuddha, who receive the truth directly or indirectly from a Sammasambuddha

Bodhi and *nirvana* carry the same meaning, that of being freed from craving, hate, and delusion. In attaining bodhi, the arahant has overcome these obstacles. As a further distinction, the extinction of only hatred and greed (in the sensory context) with some residue of delusion, is called anagami.

Mahayana

In the Mahayana, the Buddha tends not to be viewed as merely human, but as the earthly projection of a beginningless and endless, omnipresent being (see *Dharmakaya*) beyond the range and reach of thought. Moreover, in certain Mahayana sutras, the Buddha, Dharma and Sangha are viewed essentially as One: all three are seen as the eternal Buddha himself.

Celestial Buddhas are individuals who no longer exist on the material plane of existence, but who still aid in the enlightenment of all beings.

Nirvana came to refer only to the extinction of greed and hate, implying that delusion was still present in one who attained Nirvana. Bodhi became a higher attainment that eradicate delusion entirely. Thus, the Arahant attains Nirvana but not Bodhi, thus still being subject to delusion, while the Buddha attains Bodhi.

The method of self-exertion or "self-power" – without reliance on an external force or being – stands in contrast to another major form of Buddhism, Pure Land, which is characterised by utmost trust in the salvific "other-power" of Amitabha Buddha. Pure Land Buddhism is a very widespread and perhaps the most faith-orientated manifestation of Buddhism and centres upon the conviction that faith in Amitabha Buddha and the chanting of homage to his name will liberate one at death into the "happy land" or "pure land" of Amitabha Buddha. This Buddhic realm is variously construed as a foretaste of Nirvana, or as essentially Nirvana itself. The great vow of Amitabha Buddha to rescue all beings from samsaric suffering is viewed within Pure Land Buddhism as universally efficacious, if only one has faith in the power of that vow or chants his name.

Nearly all Chinese Buddhists accept that the chances of attaining sufficient enlightenment by one's own efforts are very slim, so that Pure Land practice is essential as an "insurance policy" even if one practises something else.

Buddha Eras

Buddhists believe the Gautama Buddha was the first to achieve enlightenment in this Buddha era and is therefore credited with the establishment of Buddhism. A Buddha era is the stretch of history during which people remember and practice the teachings of the earliest *known* Buddha. This Buddha era will end when all the knowledge, evidence and teachings of Gautama Buddha have vanished. This belief therefore maintains that many Buddha eras have started and ended throughout the course of human existence. The Gautama Buddha, then, is *the Buddha of this era,* who taught directly or indirectly to all other Buddhas in it.

In addition, Mahayana Buddhists believe there are innumerable other Buddhas in other universes. A Theravada commentary says that Buddhas arise one at a time in this world element, and not at all in others.

The idea of the decline and gradual disappearance of the teaching has been influential in East Asian Buddhism. Pure Land Buddhism holds that it has declined to the point where few, if any, are capable of following the path, so most or all must rely on the power of the Buddha Amitabha. Zen and Nichiren traditionally hold that most are incapable of following the "complicated" paths of some other schools and present what they view as a simple practice instead.

BODHISATTVAS

Mahayana Buddhism puts great emphasis and, in fact, encourages anybody to follow the path of a Bodhisattva.

Bodhisattva means either "enlightened (bodhi) existence (sattva)" or "enlightenment-being" or, given the variant Sanskrit spelling *satva* rather than *sattva,* "heroic-minded one (satva) for enlightenment (bodhi)". Another translation is "Wisdom-Being".

The various divisions of Buddhism understand the word Bodhisattva in different ways. Theravada and some Mahayana sources consider a Bodhisattva as someone on the path to Buddhahood, while other Mahayana sources speak of Bodhisattvas renouncing Buddhahood, but especially in Mahayana Buddhism, it mainly refers to a being that compassionately refrains from entering nirvana in order to save others. So the Bodhisattva is a person who already has a considerable degree of enlightenment and seeks to use their wisdom to help other sentient beings to become liberated themselves.

While Theravada regards it as an option, Mahayana encourages everyone to follow a Bodhisattva path and to take the Bodhisattva vows. With these vows, one makes the promise to work for the complete enlightenment of all sentient beings.

A famous saying by the 8th-century Indian Buddhist scholar-saint Shantideva, which the Dalai Lama often cites as his favourite verse, summarizes the Bodhisattva's intention (Bodhicitta) as follows: "For as long as space endures, and for as long as living beings remain, until then may I too abide to dispel the misery of the world."

According to the Mahayana, a Bodhisattva practices in the six perfections: giving, morality, patience, joyous effort, concentration and wisdom.

Practice

Devotion

Devotion is an important part of the practice of most Buddhists. Devotional practices include bowing, offerings, pilgrimage, chanting. In Pure Land Buddhism, devotion to the Buddha Amitabha is the main practice. In Nichiren Buddhism, devotion to the Lotus Sutra is the main practice.

Refuge in the Three Jewels

Traditionally, the first step in most Buddhist schools requires taking refuge in the Three Jewels (Sanskrit: *tri-ratna,* Pâli: *ti-ratana*) as the foundation of one's religious practice. The practice of taking refuge on behalf of young or even unborn children is mentioned in the Majjhima Nikaya, recognized by most scholars as an early text (cf. Infant baptism). Tibetan Buddhism sometimes adds a fourth refuge, in the *lama*. In Mahayana, the person who chooses the bodhisattva path makes a vow or pledge, considered the ultimate expression of compassion. In Mahayana, too, the Three Jewels are perceived as possessed of an eternal and unchanging essence and irreversible effect: 'The Three Jewels have the quality of excellence. Just as real jewels never change their faculty and goodness, whether praised or reviled, so are the Three Jewels

(Refuges), because they have an eternal and immutable essence. These Three Jewels bring a fruition that is changeless, for once one has reached Buddhahood, there is no possibility of falling back to suffering.'

The Three Jewels are:

- The Buddha. This is a title for those who have attained Nirvana. The Buddha could also be represented as a concept instead of a specific person: the perfect wisdom that understands Dharma and sees reality in its true form. In Mahayana Buddhism, the Buddha can be viewed as the supreme Refuge: 'Buddha is the Unique Absolute Refuge. Buddha is the Imperishable, Eternal, Indestructible and Absolute Refuge.'
- The *Dharma*. The teachings or law of nature as expounded by the Gautama Buddha. It can also, especially in Mahayana, connote the ultimate and sustaining Reality which is inseparable from the Buddha.
- The *Sangha*. Those who have attained to any of the Four stages of enlightenment, or simply the congregation of monastic practitioners.

According to the scriptures, Gautama Buddha presented himself as a model. The Dharma offers a refuge by providing guidelines for the alleviation of suffering and the attainment of Nirvana. The Sangha is considered to provide a refuge by preserving the authentic teachings of the Buddha and providing further examples that the truth of the Buddha's teachings is attainable.

BUDDHIST ETHICS

Sîla (Sanskrit) or *sîla* (Pâli) is usually translated into English as "virtuous behavior", "morality", "ethics" or "precept". It is an action committed through the body, speech, or mind, and involves an intentional effort. It is one of the *three practices* (*sila, samadhi,* and *panya*) and the second *pâramitâ*. It refers to moral purity of thought, word, and deed. The four conditions of *sîla* are chastity, calmness, quiet, and extinguishment.

Sîla is the foundation of *Samadhi/Bhâvana* (Meditative cultivation) or mind cultivation. Keeping the precepts promotes not only the peace of mind of the cultivator, which is internal, but also peace in the community, which is external. According to the Law of Karma, keeping the precepts are meritorious and it acts as causes which would bring about peaceful and happy effects. Keeping these precepts keeps the cultivator from rebirth in the four woeful realms of existence.

Sîla refers to overall principles of ethical behavior. There are several levels of *sila*, which correspond to "basic morality" (five precepts), "basic morality with asceticism" (eight precepts), "novice monkhood" (ten precepts) and "monkhood" (*Vinaya* or *Patimokkha*). Lay people generally undertake to live by the five precepts, which are common to all Buddhist schools. If they wish, they can choose to undertake the eight precepts, which add basic asceticism.

The five precepts are training rules in order to live a better life in which one is happy, without worries, and can meditate well:

1. To refrain from taking life (non-violence towards sentient life forms)
2. To refrain from taking that which is not given (not committing theft)
3. To refrain from sensual (including sexual) misconduct
4. To refrain from lying (speaking truth always)
5. To refrain from intoxicants which lead to loss of mindfulness (specifically, drugs and alcohol)

The precepts are not formulated as imperatives, but as training rules that laypeople undertake voluntarily to facilitate practice. In Buddhist thought, the cultivation of dana and ethical conduct will themselves refine consciousness to such a level that rebirth in one of the lower heavens is likely, even if there is no further Buddhist practice. There is nothing improper or un-Buddhist about limiting one's aims to this level of attainment.

In the eight precepts, the third precept on sexual misconduct is made more strict, and becomes a precept of celibacy. The three additional precepts are:

6. To refrain from eating at the wrong time (only eat from sunrise to noon)
7. To refrain from dancing and playing music, wearing jewelry and cosmetics, attending shows and other performances
8. To refrain from using high or luxurious seats and bedding

Monastic Life

Vinaya is the specific moral code for monks and nuns. It includes the Patimokkha, a set of 227 rules for monks in the Theravadin recension. The precise content of the vinayapitaka (scriptures on Vinaya) differ slightly according to different schools, and different schools or subschools set different standards for the degree of adherence to Vinaya. Novice-monks use the ten precepts, which are the basic precepts for monastics.

Regarding the monastic rules, the Buddha constantly reminds his hearers that it is the spirit that counts. On the other hand, the rules themselves are designed to assure a satisfying life, and provide a perfect springboard for the higher attainments. Monastics are instructed by the Buddha to live as "islands unto themselves". In this sense, living life as the vinaya prescribes it is, as one scholar puts it: "more than merely a means to an end: it is very nearly the end in itself."

In Eastern Buddhism, there is also a distinctive Vinaya and ethics contained within the Mahayana Brahmajala Sutra (not to be confused with the Pali text of that name) for Bodhisattvas, where, for example, the eating of meat is frowned upon and vegetarianism is actively encouraged. In Japan, this has almost completely displaced the monastic vinaya, and allows clergy to marry.

Meditation

Buddhist meditation is fundamentally concerned with two themes: transforming the mind and using it to explore itself and other phenomena. According to Theravada Buddhism the Buddha taught two types of meditation, *samatha* meditation (Sanskrit: *samatha*) and *vipassanâ* meditation (Sanskrit: *vipaúyanâ*). In Chinese Buddhism, these exist (translated *chih kuan*), but Chan (Zen) meditation is more popular. According to Peter Harvey, whenever Buddhism has been healthy, not only monks, nuns, and married lamas, but also more committed lay people have practiced meditation. According to Routledge's Encyclopedia of Buddhism, in contrast, throughout most of Buddhist history before modern times, serious meditation by lay people has been unusual. The evidence of the early texts suggests that at the time of the Buddha, many male and female lay practitioners did practice meditation, some even to the point of proficiency in all eight jhânas.

Samâdhi (Meditative Cultivation): Samatha Meditation

In the language of the Noble Eightfold Path, *samyaksamâdhi* is "right concentration". The primary means of cultivating *samâdhi* is meditation. Upon development of *samâdhi,* one's mind becomes purified of defilement, calm, tranquil, and luminous.

Once the meditator achieves a strong and powerful concentration, his mind is ready to penetrate and gain insight (vipassanâ) into the ultimate nature of reality, eventually obtaining release from all suffering. The cultivation of mindfulness is essential to mental concentration, which is needed to achieve insight.

Samatha Meditation starts from being mindful of an object or idea, which is expanded to one's body, mind and entire surroundings, leading to a state of total concentration and tranquility (*jhâna*) There are many variations in the style of meditation, from sitting cross-legged or kneeling to chanting or walking. The most common method of meditation is to concentrate on one's breath (anapanasati), because this practice can lead to both *samatha* and *vipassana'*.

In Buddhist practice, it is said that while *samatha* meditation can calm the mind, only *vipassanâ* meditation can reveal how the mind was disturbed to start with, which is what leads to knowledge (*jñâna*; Pâli *ñana*) and understanding (*prajñâ* Pâli *paññâ*), and thus can lead to *nirvâna* (Pâli *nibbâna*). When one is in jhana, all defilements are suppressed temporarily. Only understanding (*prajñâ* or *vipassana*) eradicates the defilements completely. Jhanas are also states which *Arahants* abide in order to rest.

In Theravâda

In Theravâda Buddhism, the cause of human existence and suffering is identified as craving, which carries with it the various defilements. These various defilements are traditionally summed up as greed, hatred and delusion. These are believed to be deeply rooted afflictions of the mind that create suffering and stress. In order to be free from suffering and stress, these defilements need to be permanently uprooted through internal investigation, analyzing, experiencing, and understanding of the true nature of those defilements by using *jhâna*, a technique which is part of the Noble Eightfold Path. It will then lead the meditator to realize the Four Noble Truths, Enlightenment and *Nibbana*. Nibbana is the ultimate goal of Theravadins.

Prajñâ (Wisdom): Vipassana Meditation

Prajñâ (Sanskrit) or *paññâ* (Pâli) means wisdom that is based on a realization of dependent origination, The Four Noble Truths and the three marks of existence. *Prajñâ* is the wisdom that is able to extinguish afflictions and bring about *bodhi*. It is spoken of as the principal means of attaining *nirvna*, through its revelation of the true nature of all things as *dukkha* (unsatisfactoriness), *anicca* (impermanence) and *anatta* (not-self). *Prajñâ* is also listed as the sixth of the six *pâramitâs* of the Mahayana.

Initially, *prajñâ* is attained at a conceptual level by means of listening to sermons (dharma talks), reading, studying, and sometimes reciting Buddhist texts and engaging in discourse. Once the conceptual understanding is attained, it is applied to daily life so that each Buddhist can verify the truth of the Buddha's teaching at a practical level. Notably, one could in theory attain Nirvana at any point of practice, whether deep in meditation, listening to a sermon, conducting the business of one's daily life, or any other activity.

Zen

Zen Buddhism, pronounced *Ch'an* in Chinese or *Zen* in Japanese (derived from the Sanskrit term *dhyana*, meaning "meditation") is a form of Buddhism that became popular in China and Japan and that lays special emphasis on meditation. Zen places less emphasis on scriptures than some other forms of Buddhism and prefers to focus on direct spiritual breakthroughs to truth.

Zen Buddhism is divided into two main schools: Rinzai and Soto, the former greatly favouring the use in meditation on the koan (a meditative riddle or puzzle) as a device for spiritual break-through, and the latter (while certainly employing koans) focusing more on *shikantaza* or "just sitting".

Zen Buddhist teaching is often full of paradox, in order to loosen the grip of the ego and to facilitate the penetration into the realm of the True Self or Formless Self, which is equated with the Buddha himself. According to Zen master, Kosho Uchiyama, when thoughts and fixation on the little 'I' are transcended, an Awakening to a universal, non-dual Self occurs: ' When we let go of thoughts and wake up to the reality of life that is working beyond them, we discover the Self that is living universal non-dual life (before the separation into two) that pervades all living creatures and all existence.'. Thinking and thought must therefore not be allowed to confine and bind one. Nevertheless, Zen does not neglect the scriptures.

Vajrayana and Tantra

Though based upon Mahayana, Tibeto-Mongolian Buddhism is one of the schools that practice *Vajrayâna* or "Diamond Vehicle" (also referred to as Mantrayâna, Tantrayâna, Tantric Buddhism, or esoteric Buddhism). It accepts all the basic concepts of Mahâyâna, but also includes a vast array of spiritual and physical techniques designed to enhance Buddhist practice. Tantric Buddhism is largely concerned with ritual and meditative practices. One component of the Vajrayâna is harnessing psycho-physical energy through ritual, visualization, physical exercises, and meditation as a means of developing the mind. Using these techniques, it is claimed that a practitioner can achieve Buddhahood in one lifetime, or even as little as three years. In the Tibetan tradition, these practices can include sexual yoga, though only for some very advanced practitioners.

Philosophical Roots

Historically, the roots of Buddhism lie in the religious thought of Ancient India during the second half of the first millennium BC. That was a period of social and religious turmoil, as there was significant discontent with the sacrifices and rituals of Vedic Brahmanism. It was challenged by numerous new ascetic religious and philosophical groups and teachings that broke with the Brahmanic tradition and rejected the authority of the Vedas and the Brahmans. These groups, whose members were known as shramanas, were a continuation of a non-Vedic strand of Indian thought distinct from Indo-Aryan Brahmanism. Scholars have reasons to believe that ideas such as samsara, karma (in the sense of the influence of morality on rebirth), and moksha originated in the shramanas, and were later adopted by Brahmin orthodoxy. At the same time, they were influenced by, and in some respects continued, earlier philosophical thought within the Vedic tradition as reflected e.g. in the Upanishads. These movements included, besides Buddhism, various skeptics (such as Sanjaya Belatthiputta), atomists (such as Pakudha Kaccayana), materialists (such as Ajita Kesakambali), antinomians (such as Purana Kassapa); the most important ones in the 5th century BC were the Ajivikas, who emphasized the rule of fate, the Lokayata (materialists), the Ajnanas (agnostics) and the Jains, who stressed that the soul must be freed from matter. Many of these new movements shared the same conceptual vocabulary - atman ("Self"), buddha ("awakened one"), dhamma ("rule" or "law"), karma ("action"), nirvana ("extinguishing"), samsara ("eternal recurrence") and yoga ("spiritual practice"). The shramanas rejected the Veda, and the authority of the brahmans, who claimed to be in possession of revealed truths not knowable by any ordinary human means; moreover, they declared that the entire Brahmanical system was fraudulent: a conspiracy of the brahmans to enrich themselves by charging exorbitant fees for the performance of bogus rites and the giving of futile advice. A particular criticism of the Buddha's was Vedic animal sacrifice. Their leaders, including Buddha, were often known as sramanas. The Buddha declared that priests reciting the Vedas were like blind leading the blind. According to him, those priests who had memorized the Vedas really knew nothing. He also mocked the Vedic "hymn of the cosmic man". He declared that the primary goal of Upanishadic thought, the Atman, was in fact non-existent,, and, having explained that Brahminical attempts to achieve liberation at death were futile, proposed his new idea of liberation in life.

At the same time, the traditional Brahminical religion itself gradually underwent profound changes, transforming it into what is recognized as early Hinduism. In particular, the brahmans thus developed "philosophical systems of their own, meeting the new ideas with adaptations of their doctrines".

Indian Buddhism

The history of Indian Buddhism may be divided into the following five periods:

1. Early Buddhism (occasionally called Pre-sectarian Buddhism)
2. Nikaya Buddhism or Sectarian Buddhism: The period of the Early Buddhist schools
3. Early Mahayana Buddhism
4. Later Mahayana Buddhism
5. Esoteric Buddhism (also called Vajrayana Buddhism)

Pre-Sectarian Buddhism

Pre-sectarian Buddhism is the earliest phase of Buddhism, recognized by nearly all scholars. Its main scriptures are the Vinaya Pitaka and the four principal Nikayas or Agamas.

Certain basic teachings appear in many places throughout the early texts, so most scholars conclude that Gautama Buddha must have taught something similar to the following:

- the three characteristics
- the five aggregates

- dependent arising
- karma and rebirth
- the four noble truths
- the eightfold path
- nirvana

Some scholars disagree, and have proposed many other theories.

Early Buddhist Schools

According to the scriptures, soon after the parinirvga (from Sanskrit: "highest extinguishment") of Gautama Buddha, the first Buddhist council was held. As with any ancient Indian tradition, transmission of teaching was done orally. The primary purpose of the assembly was to collectively recite the teachings to ensure that no errors occurred in oral transmission. In the first council, Ânanda, a cousin of the Buddha and his personal attendant, was called upon to recite the discourses (*sûtras*, Pâli *sutta*s) of the Buddha, and, according to some sources, the abhidhamma. Upâli, another disciple, recited the monastic rules (*vinaya*). Scholars regard the traditional accounts of the council as greatly exaggerated if not entirely fictitious.

According to most scholars, at some period after the Second Council the *Sangha* began to break into separate factions. The various accounts differ as to when the actual schisms occurred. According to the *Dipavamsa* of the Pâli tradition, they started immediately after the Second Council, the Puggalavada tradition places it in 137 AN, the Sarvastivada tradition of Vasumitra says it was in the time of Asoka and the Mahasanghika tradition places it much later, nearly 100 BCE.

The root schism was between the Sthaviras and the Mahâsânghikas. The fortunate survival of accounts from both sides of the dispute reveals disparate traditions. The

Sthavira group offers two quite distinct reasons for the schism. The Dipavamsa of the Theravâda says that the losing party in the Second Council dispute broke away in protest and formed the Mahasanghika. This contradicts the Mahasanghikas' own *vinaya*, which shows them as on the same, winning side. The Mahâsânghikas argued that the Sthaviras were trying to expand the *vinaya* and may also have challenged what they perceived to be excessive claims or inhumanly high criteria for arhatship. Both parties, therefore, appealed to tradition.

The Sthaviras gave rise to several schools, one of which was the Theravâda school. Originally, these schisms were caused by disputes over vinaya, and monks following different schools of thought seem to have lived happily together in the same monasteries, but eventually, by about 100 CE if not earlier, schisms were being caused by doctrinal disagreements too.

Following (or leading up to) the schisms, each Samgha started to accumulate an Abhidharma, a detailed scholastic reworking of doctrinal material appearing in the Suttas, according to schematic classifications. These Abhidharma texts do not contain systematic philosophical treatises, but summaries or numerical lists. Scholars generally date these texts to around the 3rd century BCE, 100 to 200 years after the death of the Buddha. Therefore the seven Abhidharma works are generally claimed not to represent the words of the Buddha himself, but those of disciples and great scholars. Every school had its own version of the Adhidharma, with different theories and different texts. The different Adhidharmas of the various schools did not agree with each other. Scholars disagree on whether the Mahasanghika school had an Abhidhamma Pitaka or not.

Early Mahayana Buddhism

The period of Early Mahayana Buddhism concerns the origins of Mahayana and the contents of early Mahayana

Sutras. The development of the various Early Buddhist Schools and the arising of Mahayana were not always consecutive. For example, the early schools continued to exist alongside Mahayana.

Origins of Mahayana

The commonly expressed misconception that Mahayana started as a lay-inspired movement is based on a selective reading of a very tiny sample of extant Mahayana Sutra literature. Currently scholars have moved away from this limited corpus, and have started to examine early Mahayana literature, which is very ascetic and expounds the ideal of the monks' life in the forest. A scholarly consensus about the origin of the Mahayana has not yet been reached, but it has been suggested that when Mahayana became popular, in the 5th century CE, it had become something it had previously objected to: a landed monastic institution with a lay orientation. Prior to this, the movement may well have been either a marginalized ascetic group of monks living in the forest, or a group of conservatives embedded in mainstream, socially engaged early Buddhist monasteries. Most scholars conclude that Mahayana remained a marginal movement until the 5th century AD.

Earliest Mahayana Sutras

The earliest Mahayana Sutras are called the Proto-Mahayana Sutras such as the Ajitasena Sutra which contains a mixture of Mahayana and pre-Mahayana ideas. It occurs in a world where monasticism is the norm, which is typical of the Pali Suttas; there is none of the usual antagonism towards the followers of the Early Buddhist Schools or the notion of Arahantship, which is typical of many Mahayana Sutras such as the White Lotus, or Vimalakirti Nirdesha. However, the sutra also has an Arahant seeing all the Buddha fields, it is said that reciting the name of the sutra will save beings from suffering and the hell realms, and a meditative practice is described which allows the practitioner to see with the eyes of a Buddha, and to receive teachings from them that are very much typical of Mahayana Sutras. Some early Mahayana Sutras are Ratnagunasamcayagatha and the Astasaharika.

Some scholars contend that the Mahayana sutras were mainly composed in the south of India, and that later the activity of writing additional scriptures was continued in the east and north of India.

Late Mahayana Buddhism

During the period of Late Mahayana Buddhism, four major types of thought developed: Madhyamaka, Yogacara, Tathagatagarbha, and Buddhist Logic as the last and most recent. In India, the two main philosophical schools of the Mahayana were the Madhyamaka and the later Yogacara. According to Dan Lusthaus, Madhyamaka and Yogacara have a great deal in common, and the commonality stems from early Buddhism. There were no great Indian teachers associated with tathagatagarbha thought.

Vajrayana (Esoteric Buddhism)

Scholarly research concerning Esoteric Buddhism is still in its early stages and has a number of problems which make research difficult:

1. Vajrayana Buddhism was influenced by Hinduism, and therefore the research has to include research on Hinduism as well.
2. The scriptures of Vajrayana have not yet been put in any kind of order.
3. Ritual has to be examined as well, not just doctrine.

The Early Spread of Buddhism

Buddhism may have spread only slowly in India until the time of the Mauryan emperor Ashoka, who was a public supporter of the religion. The support of Aúoka and his descendants led to the construction of more stûpas (Buddhist religious memorials) and to efforts to spread Buddhism throughout the enlarged Maurya empire and even into neighboring lands – particularly to the Iranian-speaking regions of Afghanistan and Central Asia, beyond the Mauryas' northwest border, and to the island of Sri Lanka south of India. These two missions, in opposite directions, would ultimately lead, in the first case to the spread of Buddhism into China, and in the second case, to the emergence of Theravâda Buddhism and its spread from Sri Lanka to the coastal lands of Southeast Asia.

This period marks the first known spread of Buddhism beyond India. According to the edicts of Aœoka, emissaries were sent to various countries west of India in order to spread Buddhism (Dharma), particularly in eastern provinces of the neighboring Seleucid Empire, and even farther to Hellenistic kingdoms of the Mediterranean. This led, a century later, to the emergence of Greek-speaking Buddhist monarchs in the Indo-Greek Kingdom, and to the development of the Greco-Buddhist art of Gandhâra. During this period Buddhism was exposed to a variety of influences, from Persian and Greek civilization, and from changing trends in non-Buddhist Indian religions – themselves influenced by Buddhism. It is a matter of disagreement among scholars whether or not these emissaries were accompanied by Buddhist missionaries.

The Theravada school spread south from India in the 3rd century BC, to Sri Lanka and Thailand and Burma and later also Indonesia. The Dharmagupta school spread (also in 3rd century BC) north to Kashmir, Gandhara and Bactria (Afghanistan). In the 2nd century AD, Mahayana Sutras spread from that general area to China, and then to Korea and Japan, and were translated into Chinese. During the Indian period of Esoteric Buddhism (from 8th century onwards), Buddhism spread from India to Tibet and Mongolia.

Buddhism Today

By the late Middle Ages, Buddhism had become virtually extinct in India, and although it continued to exist in surrounding countries, its influence was no longer expanding. It is now again gaining strength in India and elsewhere. Estimates of the number of Buddhist followers by scholars range from 230 million to 500 million, with most around 350 million. Most scholars classify similar numbers of people under a category they call "Chinese folk" or "traditional" religion, an amalgam of various traditions that includes Buddhism. One Buddhist organization claims the total could be as much as 1.691 billion.

Formal membership varies between communities, but basic lay adherence is often defined in terms of a traditional formula in which the practitioner takes refuge in The Three Jewels: the *Buddha*, the *Dharma* (the teachings of the Buddha), and the *Sangha* (the Buddhist community).

Estimates are uncertain for several reasons:

- difficulties in defining who counts as a Buddhist;
- syncretism among the Eastern religions. Buddhism is practiced by adherents alongside many other religious traditions- including Taoism, Confucianism, Shinto, traditional religions, shamanism, and animism- throughout East and Southeast Asia.
- difficulties in estimating the number of Buddhists who do not have congregational memberships and often do not participate in public ceremonies;
- official policies on religion in several historically Buddhist countries that make accurate assessments of religious adherence more difficult; most notably China, Vietnam and North Korea. In many current and former Communist governments in Asia, government

policies may discourage adherents from reporting their religious identity, or may encourage official counts to underestimate religious adherence.

According to one analysis, Buddhism is the fourth-largest religion in the world behind Christianity, Islam, and Hinduism. The monks' order (Sangha), which began during the lifetime of the Buddha, is among the oldest organizations on earth.

- Theravâda Buddhism, using Pâli as its scriptural language, is the dominant form of Buddhism in Cambodia, Laos, Thailand, Sri Lanka, and Burma. The Dalit Buddhist movement in India (inspired by B. R. Ambedkar) also practices Theravada. Approximately 124 million adherents.
- East Asian forms of Mahayana Buddhism that use scriptures in Chinese are dominant in most of China, Japan, Korea, Taiwan, Singapore and Vietnam as well as within Chinese and Japanese communities within Indochina, Southeast Asia and the West. Approximately 185 million adherents.
- Tibetan Buddhism is found in Tibet, Bhutan, Mongolia, surrounding areas in India, China, Nepal, and the Russian Federation, and Kalmykia. Approximately 20 million adherents.

Most Buddhist groups in the West are at least nominally affiliated with one of these three traditions.

At the present time, the teachings of all three branches of Buddhism have spread throughout the world, and Buddhist texts are increasingly translated into local languages. While, in the West, Buddhism is often seen as exotic and progressive, in the East, Buddhism is regarded as familiar and traditional. Buddhists in Asia are frequently well organized and well funded. In a number of countries, it is recognized as an official religion and receives state support. In the West, Buddhism is recognized as one of the growing spiritual influences. Modern influences increasingly lead to new forms of Buddhism that significantly depart from traditional beliefs and practices.

Overall there is an overwhelming diversity of recent forms of Buddhism.

SCHOOLS AND TRADITIONS

Buddhists generally classify themselves as either Theravada or Mahayana. This classification is also used by some scholars and is the one ordinarily used in the English language. An alternative scheme used by some scholars divides Buddhism into the following three traditions or geographical or cultural areas: Theravada, East Asian Buddhism and Tibetan Buddhism. Some scholars use other schemes. Buddhists themselves have a variety of other schemes. Hinayana (literally "lesser vehicle") is used by Mahayana followers to name the family of early philosophical schools and traditions from which contemporary Theravada emerged, but as this term is rooted in the Mahayana viewpoint and can be considered derogatory, a variety of other terms are increasingly used instead, including Úrâvakayâna, Nikaya Buddhism, early Buddhist schools, sectarian Buddhism, conservative Buddhism, mainstream Buddhism and non-Mahayana Buddhism.

Not all traditions of Buddhism share the same philosophical outlook, or treat the same concepts as central. Each tradition, however, does have its own core concepts, and some comparisons can be drawn between them.

Mahayana Buddhism shows a great deal of doctrinal variation and development over time, and even more variation in terms of practice. While there is much agreement on general principles, there is disagreement over which texts are more authoritative.

Despite some differences among the Theravada and Mahayana schools, there are, e.g. according to one Buddhist ecumenical organization, several concepts common to both major Buddhist branches:

- Both accept the Buddha as their teacher.
- Both accept the Middle way, Dependent origination, the Four Noble Truths, the Noble Eightfold Path and the Three marks of existence, in theory, though in practice these have little or no importance in some traditions.
- Both accept that members of the laity and of the sangha can pursue the path toward enlightenment (bodhi).
- Both consider buddhahood to be the highest attainment; however Theravadins consider the nirvana (nibbana to the Theravadins) attained by arahants as identical to that attained by the Buddha himself, as there is only one type of nirvana. According to Theravadins, a buddha is someone who has discovered the path all by himself and taught it to others.

Theravâda

Theravâda ("Doctrine of the Elders", or "Ancient Doctrine") is the oldest surviving Buddhist school. It is relatively conservative, and *generally* closest to early Buddhism. This school is derived from the Vibhajjavâda grouping which emerged amongst the older Sthavira group at the time of the Third Buddhist Council (c. 250 BCE). This school gradually declined on the Indian subcontinent, but its branch in Sri Lanka and South East Asia continues to survive.

The Theravada school bases its practice and doctrine exclusively on the Pâli Canon and its commentaries. After being orally transmitted for a few centuries, its scriptures, the Pali Canon, were finally committed to writing in the last century BCE, in Sri Lanka, at what the Theravada usually reckon as the fourth council. It is also one of the first Buddhist schools to commit the complete set of its canon into writing. The Sutta collections and Vinaya texts of the Pâli Canon (and the corresponding texts in other versions of the Tripitaka), are generally considered by modern scholars to be the earliest Buddhist literature, and they are accepted as authentic in every branch of Buddhism.

Theravâda is primarily practiced today in Sri Lanka, Burma, Laos, Thailand, Cambodia as well as small portions of China, Vietnam, Malaysia and Bangladesh. It has a growing presence in Europe and America.

Mahayana

Mahayana Buddhism flourished in India from the fifth century AD onwards, during the dynasty of the Guptas. Mahâyâna centres of learning were established, the most important one being the Nâlandâ University in north-eastern India.

Mahayana schools recognize all or part of the Mahayana Sutras. Some of these sutras became for Mahayanists a manifestation of the Buddha himself, and faith in and veneration of those texts are stated in some sutras (e.g. the Lotus Sutra and the Mahaparinirvana Sutra) to lay the foundations for the later attainment of Buddhahood itself.

Native Eastern Buddhism is practiced today in China, Japan, Korea, Singapore, parts of Russia and most of Vietnam. The Buddhism practiced in Tibet, the Himalayan regions, and Mongolia is also Mahayana in origin, but will be discussed below under the heading of Northern Buddhism. There are a variety of strands in Eastern Buddhism, which in most of this area are fused into a single unified form of Buddhism. However, in Japan they form separate denominations. The five major ones are the following.

- Nichiren, peculiar to Japan
- Pure Land

- Shingon, a form of Vajrayana
- Tendai
- Chan/Zen

In Korea, nearly all Buddhists belong to the Chogye school, which is officially Son (Zen), but with substantial elements from other traditions.

Vajrayâna

The Vajrayana school of Buddhism spread both to China and Tibet. In Tibet, Vajrayana has always been a main component of Tibetan Buddhism while in China, it formed a separate sect. However, Vajrayana Buddhism became extinct in China but survived in Japan as Shingon sect and Tendai sect, which incorporated Vajrayana element into their practice.

There are differing views as to just when Vajrayâna and its tantric practice started. In the Tibetan tradition, it is claimed that the historical Úâkyamuni Buddha taught tantra, but as these are esoteric teachings, they were written down long after the Buddha's other teachings. Nâlandâ University became a center for the development of Vajrayâna theory and continued as the source of leading-edge Vajrayâna practices up through the 11th century. These practices, scriptures and theory were transmitted to China, Tibet, Indochina and Southeast Asia. China generally received Indian transmission up to the 11th century including tantric practice, while a vast amount of what is considered to be Tibetan Buddhism (Vajrayâna) stems from the late (9th–12th century) Nâlandâ tradition.

In one of the first major contemporary academic treatises on the subject, Fairfield University professor Ronald M. Davidson argues that the rise of Vajrayana was in part a reaction to the changing political climate in India at the time. With the fall of the Gupta dynasty, in an increasingly fractious political environment, institutional Buddhism had difficulty attracting patronage, and the folk movement led by siddhas became more prominent. After perhaps two hundred years, it had begun to get integrated into the monastic establishment.

Vajrayana combined and developed a variety of elements, a number of which had already existed for centuries. In addition to the Mahâyâna scriptures, Vajrayâna Buddhists recognise a large body of Buddhist Tantras, some of which are also included in Chinese and Japanese collections of Buddhist literature, and versions of a few even in the Pali Canon.

Buddhist Texts

Buddhist scriptures and other texts exist in great variety. Different schools of Buddhism place varying levels of value on learning the various texts. Some schools venerate certain texts as religious objects in themselves, while others take a more scholastic approach. Buddhist scriptures are written in these languages: Pâli, Tibetan, Mongolian, Chinese, along with some texts that still exist in Sanskrit and Buddhist Hybrid Sanskrit.

Unlike many religions, Buddhism has no single central text that is universally referred to by all traditions. However, some scholars have referred to the Vinaya Pitaka and the first four Nikayas of the Sutta Pitaka as the common core of all Buddhist traditions. However, this could be considered misleading, as Mahâyâna considers these merely a preliminary, and not a core, teaching, the Tibetan Buddhists have not even translated most of the âgamas, though theoretically they recognize them, and they play no part in the religious life of either clergy or laity in China and Japan. Other scholars say there is no universally accepted common core. The size and complexity of the Buddhist canons have been seen by some (including Buddhist social reformer Babasaheb Ambedkar) as presenting barriers to the wider understanding of Buddhist philosophy.

The followers of Theravâda Buddhism take the scriptures known as the Pâli Canon as definitive and authoritative, while the followers of Mahâyâna Buddhism base their faith and philosophy primarily on the Mahâyâna sûtras and their own *vinaya*. The Pâli sutras, along with other, closely related scriptures, are known to the other schools as the *âgamas*.

Over the years, various attempts have been made to synthesize a single Buddhist text that can encompass all of the major principles of Buddhism. In the Theravada tradition, condensed 'study texts' were created that combined popular or influential scriptures into single volumes that could be studied by novice monks. Later in Sri Lanka, the Dhammapada was championed as a unifying scripture.

Dwight Goddard collected a sample of Buddhist scriptures, with the emphasis on Zen, along with other classics of Eastern philosophy, such as the Tao Te Ching, into his 'Buddhist Bible' in the 1920s. More recently, Dr. Babasaheb Ambedkar attempted to create a single, combined document of Buddhist principles in "The Buddha and His Dhamma". Other such efforts have persisted to present day, but currently there is no single text that represents all Buddhist traditions.

Pâli Tipitaka

The Pâli Tipitaka, which means "three baskets", refers to its three main:

- The *Vinaya Pitaka* contains disciplinary rules for the Buddhist monks and nuns, as well as explanations of why and how these rules were instituted, supporting material, and doctrinal clarification.
- The *Sutta Pitaka* contains discourses ascribed to Gautama Buddha.

- The *Abhidhamma Pitaka* contains material often described as systematic expositions of the Gautama Buddha's teachings.

The Pâli Tipitaka is the only early Tipitaka (Sanskrit: *Tripimaka*) to survive intact in its original language, but a number of early schools had their own recensions of the Tipitaka featuring much of the same material. We have portions of the Tipitakas of the Sârvâstivâda, Dharmaguptaka, Sammitya, Mahâsanghika, Kâsyapîya, and Mahîsâsaka schools, most of which survive in Chinese translation only. According to some sources, some early schools of Buddhism had five or seven pitakas.

According to the scriptures, soon after the death of the Buddha, the first Buddhist council was held; a monk named Mahâkâsyapa (Pâli: Mahâkassapa) presided. The goal of the council was to record the Buddha's teachings. Upâli recited the *vinaya*. Ânanda, the Buddha's personal attendant, was called upon to recite the dhamma. These became the basis of the Tripitaka. However, this record was initially transmitted orally in form of chanting, and was committed to text in the last century BCE. Both the sûtras and the *vinaya* of every Buddhist school contain a wide variety of elements including discourses on the Dharma, commentaries on other teachings, cosmological and cosmogonical texts, stories of the Gautama Buddha's previous lives, and various other subjects.

Much of the material in the Canon is not specifically "Theravadin", but is instead the collection of teachings that this school preserved from the early, non-sectarian body of teachings. According to Peter Harvey, it contains material which is at odds with later Theravadin orthodoxy. He states:

The Theravadins, then, may have *added* texts to the Canon for some time, but they do not appear to have tampered with what they already had from an earlier period.

Mahayana Sutras

The Mahayana sutras are a very broad genre of Buddhist scriptures that the Mahayana Buddhist tradition holds are original teachings of the Buddha. The adherents of Mahayana accept both the early teachings and the Mahayana sutras as authentic teachings of Gautama Buddha, and claim they were designed for different types of persons and different levels of spiritual understanding.

The Mahayana sutras often claim to articulate the Buddha's deeper, more advanced doctrines, reserved for those who follow the bodhisattva path. That path is explained as being built upon the motivation to liberate all living beings from unhappiness. Hence the name *Mahâyâna* (lit., *the Great Vehicle*).

According to Mahayana tradition, the Mahayana sutras were transmitted in secret, came from other Buddhas or Bodhisattvas, or were preserved in non-human worlds because human beings at the time couldn't understand them:

> Some of our sources maintain the authenticity of certain other texts not found in the canons of these schools (the early schools). These texts are those held genuine by the later school, not one of the eighteen, which arrogated to itself the title of Mahayana, 'Great Vehicle'. According to the Mahayana historians these texts were admittedly unknown to the early schools of Buddhists. However, they had all been promulgated by the Buddha. [The Buddha's] followers on earth, the sravakas ('pupils'), had not been sufficiently advanced to understand them, and hence were not given them to remember, but they were taught to various supernatural beings and then preserved in such places as the Dragon World.
>
> —*Indian Buddhism*

Approximately six hundred Mahayana sutras have survived in Sanskrit or in Chinese or Tibetan translations. In addition, East Asian Buddhism recognizes some sutras regarded by scholars to be of Chinese rather than Indian origin.

Generally, scholars conclude that the Mahayana scriptures were composed from the first century CE onwards: "Large numbers of Mahayana sutras were being composed in the period between the beginning of the common era and the fifth century." five centuries after the historical Gautama Buddha, with some of them having their roots in other scriptures, composed in the first century BCE. It was not until after the fifth century CE that the Mahayana sutras started to influence the behavior of mainstream Buddhists in India: "But outside of texts, at least in India, at exactly the same period, very different—in fact seemingly older—ideas and aspirations appear to be motivating actual behavior, and old and established Hinnayana groups appear to be the only ones that are patronized and supported." These texts were apparently not universally accepted among Indian Buddhists when they appeared; the pejorative label 'Hinayana' was applied by Mahayana supporters to those who rejected the Mahayana sutras.

Only the Theravada school does not include the Mahayana scriptures in its canon. As the modern Theravada school is descended from a branch of Buddhism that diverged and established itself in Sri Lanka prior to the emergence of the Mahayana texts, debate exists as to whether the Theravada were historically included in the 'hinayana' designation; in the modern era, this label is seen as in any case derogatory, and generally avoided.

Comparative Studies

Buddhism provides many opportunities for comparative study with a diverse range of subjects. For example, dependent origination can be considered one of Buddhism's contributions to metaphysics. Additionally, Buddhism's emphasis on the Middle way not only provides a unique guideline for ethics but has also allowed Buddhism to peacefully coexist with various differing beliefs, customs and institutions in countries in which it has resided throughout its history. Also, Its moral and spiritual parallels with other systems of thought—for example, with various tenets of Christianity—have been subjects of close study.

●●

2
Buddhist Ethics

Ethics in Buddhism are traditionally based on what Buddhists view as the enlightened perspective of the Buddha, or other enlightened beings who followed him. Moral instructions are included in Buddhist scriptures or handed down through tradition. Most scholars of Buddhist ethics thus rely on the examination of Buddhist scriptures, and the use of anthropological evidence from traditional Buddhist societies, to justify claims about the nature of Buddhist ethics. For more on the academic discussion of Buddhist ethics, and its contested relationship to Western ethics.

According to traditional Buddhism, the foundation of Buddhist ethics for laypeople is the Pancasila: no killing, stealing, lying, sexual misconduct, or intoxicants. In becoming a Buddhist, or affirming one's commitment to Buddhism, a layperson is encouraged to vow to abstain from these negative actions. The precepts are not formulated as imperatives, but as training rules that laypeople undertake voluntarily to facilitate practice. In Buddhist thought, the cultivation of dana and ethical conduct will themselves refine consciousness to such a level that rebirth in one of the lower heavens is likely, even if there is no further Buddhist practice. There is nothing improper or un-Buddhist about limiting one's aims to this level of attainment. Buddhist monks and nuns take hundreds more such vows.

The Buddha provided some basic guidelines for acceptable behavior that are part of the Eightfold path. The initial precept is non-injury or non-violence to all living creatures from the lowest insect to humans. This precept defines a non-violent attitude toward every living thing. The Buddhist practice of this does not extend to the extremes exhibited by Jainism, but from both the Buddhist and Jain perspectives, non-violence suggests an intimate involvement with, and relationship to, all living things.

KILLING, CAUSING OTHERS TO KILL

Abortion

There is no single Buddhist view concerning abortion although traditional Buddhism rejects abortion because it involves the deliberate destroying of a life and regards life as starting at conception. Those practicing in Japan and the United States are said to be more tolerant of abortion than those who live elsewhere. In Japan, women sometimes participate in Mizuko kuyo after an induced abortion or an abortion as the result of a miscarriage. The Dalai Lama has said that abortion is "negative," but there are exceptions. He said, "I think abortion should be approved or disapproved according to each circumstance."

Death Penalty

As a religion Buddhism places great emphasis on the sanctity of life. However there is disagreement among Buddhists as to whether or not Buddhism forbids the death penalty. The first of the Five Precepts (Panca-sila) is to abstain from destruction of life. Chapter 10 of the Dhammapada states:

Everyone fears punishment; everyone fears death, just as you do. Therefore do not kill or cause to kill. Everyone fears punishment; everyone loves life, as you do. Therefore do not kill or cause to kill.

Chapter 26, the final chapter of the Dhammapada, states "Him I call a brahmin who has put aside weapons and renounced violence toward all creatures. He neither kills nor helps others to kill". These sentences are interpreted by many Buddhists (especially in the West) as an injunction against supporting any legal measure which might lead to the death penalty. However, as is often the case with the interpretation of scripture, there is dispute on this matter. Thailand, where Buddhism is the official religion, practices the death penalty, as do many other countries where the majority of the population are Buddhist, such as Sri Lanka, Japan, Korea and Taiwan. Moreover, almost throughout history, countries where Buddhism has been the official religion (which have included most of the Far East and Indochina) have practiced the death penalty. One exception is the abolition of the death penalty by the Emperor Saga of Japan abolished in 818. This lasted until 1165, although in private manors executions conducted as a form of retaliation continued to be conducted.

In the Jataka, which tell stories of the past lives of the Buddha, Bodhisattva (a previous incarnation of the Buddha) actually kills someone to save another person's life, though because of this action, he was no longer able to achieve enlightenment in that particular life. Therefore, few (if any) Buddhist groups issue blanket decrees against Buddhists being soldiers, police officers or farmers (which in Buddhism is classified as a profession involved in destruction of life), and some argue that the death penalty is permissible in certain circumstances. In general, Buddhist groups in secular countries such as Japan, Korea and Taiwan tend to take anti-death penalty stance while those in Thailand, Sri Lanka and Bhutan where Buddhism has strong political influence, the opposite is true. Almost all Buddhist groups, however, oppose the use of the death penalty as a means of retribution.

Euthanasia

In Theravada Buddhism, for a monk to praise the advantages of death including simply telling a person of the miseries of life or the bliss of dying and going to heaven in such a way that he/she might feel inspired to commit suicide or simply pine away to death is explicitly stated as a breach in one of highest vinaya code regarding prohibition of harming life, hence it will result in automatic expulsion from Sangha. In caring for the terminally ill, no one should subject a patient to treatment designed to bring on death faster than it would if the disease were simply allowed to run its course.

Vegetarianism

The first precept of Buddhism focuses mainly on direct participation in the destruction of life. This is one reason that the Buddha made a distinction between killing animals and eating meat, and refused to introduce vegetarianism into monastic practice.

Many Buddhists, especially in East Asia, believe that Buddhism advocates or promotes vegetarianism. While Buddhist theory tends to equate killing animals with killing people (and avoids the conclusion that killing can sometimes be ethical, e.g. defense of others), as a practical matter most Buddhists do eat meat outside of the Chinese and Vietnamese monastic tradition. There is some controversy surrounding whether or not the Buddha himself died from eating rancid pork . While most Chinese and Vietnamese monastics are vegetarian , vegetarian Tibetans are rare indeed (and not only for lack of vegetables in Tibet, since Tibetan exile monks in India actually consume *more* meat). The same applies to the scarcity of Japanese Buddhist vegetarians . The Dalai Lama (who himself tried to become a vegetarian but caught Hepatitis B and was advised by doctors to switch to a high animal-protein diet) once engaged in an amusing ethical discussion with some Theravadan Buddhists who believed that as long as one was determined to eat meat, seafood was preferable to red meat. The Dalai Lama responded that one bowl of shrimp would kill multitudes of sentient beings, but one sheep or cow would feed many people. The Dalai Lama eats vegetarian every second day, so is effectively vegetarian for 6 months of the year.

The first lay precept in Buddhism is usually translated as "I undertake the precept to refrain from destroying living creatures." Many see this as implying that Buddhists should not eat the meat of animals. However, this is not necessarily the case. There is a divergence of views within Buddhism on the need for vegetarianism, with some schools of Buddhism rejecting such a claimed need and with most Buddhists in fact eating meat. Many Mahayana Buddhists - especially the Chinese and Vietnamese traditions - strongly oppose meat-eating on scriptural grounds.

In the Pali version of the Tripitaka, there are number of occasions in which the Buddha ate meat as well as recommending certain types of meat as a cure for medical conditions. On one occasion, a general sent a servant to purchase meat specifically to feed the Buddha. The Buddha declared that

> meat should not be eaten under three circumstances: when it is seen or heard or suspected (that a living being has been purposely slaughtered for the eater); these, Jivaka, are the three circumstances in which meat should not be eaten, Jivaka! I declare there are three circumstances in which meat can be eaten: when it is not seen or heard or suspected (that a living being has been purposely slaughtered for the eater); Jivaka, I say these are the three circumstances in which meat can be eaten.
>
> — Jivaka Sutta

The Buddha, on one particular occasion, specifically refused suggestions by a monk to institute vegetarianism in Sangha. According to Kassapa Buddha (a previous Buddha of legend not Shakyamuni Buddha) "aking life, beating, wounding, binding, stealing, lying, deceiving, worthless knowledge, adultery; this is stench. Not the eating of meat." (Amagandha Sutta). There were, however, rules prohibiting consumption of 10 types of meat. Those are humans, elephants, horses, dogs, snakes, lions, tigers, leopards, bears and hyenas because these animals can be provoked by the smell of the flesh of their own kind.

Theravada commentaries explain the Buddha was making distinction between direct destruction of life and eating of already dead meat. Moreover, they point out that any act of consumption would involve proxy killing, including the farming of crops, so the idea that meat eating amounted to proxy killing while eating vegetables does not is ignorance. For this reason, they discourage gluttony or any other act of craving which lead to over consumption. However, some Therevadan monks suggest that it is possible to make some case for vegetarianism starting from brahmavihara. Interestingly, this, in addition to their Mahayana scriptural sources, is how many Mahayana Buddhists make the case for vegetarianism,

While there is no mention of Buddha endorsing or repudiating vegetarianism in surviving portions of Pali Tripitaka and no Mahayana sutras explicitly declare that meat eating violates the first precept, certain Mahayana sutras vigorously and unreservedly denounce the eating of meat, mainly on the ground that such an act violates the bodhisattva's compassion. The sutras which inveigh against meat-eating include the Mahayana version of the *Nirvana Sutra,* the *Shurangama Sutra,* the *Brahmajala Sutra,* the *Angulimaliya Sutra,* the *Mahamegha Sutra,* and the *Lankavatara Sutra,* as well as the Buddha's comments on the negative karmic effects of meat consumption in the *Karma Sutra*. In the Mahayana Mahaparinirvana Sutra, which presents itself as the final elucidatory and definitive Mahayana teachings of the Buddha on the very eve of his death, the Buddha states that "the eating of meat extinguishes the seed of Great Kindness", adding that all and every kind of meat and fish consumption (even of animals found already dead) is prohibited by him. He specifically rejects the idea that monks who go out begging and receive meat from a donor should eat it: ". . . it should be rejected . . . I say that even meat, fish, game, dried hooves and scraps of meat left over by others constitutes an infraction . . . I teach the harm arising from meat-eating." The Buddha also predicts in this sutra that later monks will "hold spurious writings to be the authentic Dharma" and will concoct their own sutras and lyingly claim that the Buddha allows the eating of meat, whereas in fact he says he does not. A long passage in the Lankavatara Sutra shows the Buddha speaking out very forcefully against meat consumption and unequivocally in favor of vegetarianism, since the eating of the flesh of fellow sentient beings is said by him to be incompatible with the compassion that a Bodhisattva should strive to cultivate. In several other Mahayana scriptures, too (e.g., the Mahayana jatakas), the Buddha is seen clearly to indicate that meat-eating is undesirable and karmically unwholesome.

Sexual Misconduct

The Third (or sometimes Fourth) of the Five Precepts of Buddhism states that one is to refrain from "sexual misconduct". Buddhist teachings are usually disdainful towards sexuality and distrustful of sensual enjoyment and desire in general. Buddhist monks and nuns of most traditions are not only expected to refrain from all sexual activity but take vows of celibacy.

Homosexuality

Among the manifold Buddhist traditions there is a vast diversity of opinion about homosexuality and in interpreting the precedents which define "sexual misconduct". Though there is no explicit condemnation of homosexuality in Buddhist scripture be it Theravada, Mahayana or Mantrayana, societal and community attitudes and the historical view of practitioners have established precedents. Some sangha equate homosexuality with scriptural sexual misconduct prohibited by the Five Precepts. Other sangha hold that if sexuality is compassionate and/or consensual and does not contravene vows, then there is no dharmic infraction irrespective of whether it is same-sex or not.

VEGETARIANISM AND RELIGION

Vegetarianism and religion are strongly linked in a number of religions that originated in ancient India (Hinduism, Jainism and Buddhism). In Jainism vegetarianism is mandatory for everyone, in Hinduism and Mahayana Buddhism it is advocated by some influential scriptures and religious authorities. Comparatively, in the Abrahamic religions (Judaism, Christianity and Islam) and in Sikhism, vegetarianism is not promoted by mainstream authorities. In Christianity and Sikhism, however, there are groups promoting vegetarianism on religious grounds.

Religions of Indian Origin

Hinduism

Vegetarianism plays a strong role in Hindu tradition, although there are a wide variety of practices and beliefs that have changed over time. It is estimated some 30% of all Hindus are vegetarian. Other sects of Hindus do not observe vegetarianism.

Nonviolence

The principle of nonviolence applied to animals is connected with the intention to avoid negative karmic influences which result from violence. The suffering of all beings is believed to arise from craving and desire, conditioned by the karmic effects of both animal and human action. The violence of slaughtering animals for food, and its source in craving, reveal flesh eating as one mode in which humans enslave themselves to suffering. Hinduism holds that such influences affect he who permits the slaughter of an animal, he who cuts it up, he who kills it, he who buys or sells meat, he who cooks it, he who serves it up, and he who eats it. They must all be considered the slayers of the animal. The question of religious duties towards the animals and of negative Karma incurred from violence (*himsa*) against them is discussed in detail in Hindu scriptures and religious law books.

Hindu scriptures belong or refer to the Vedic period which lasted till about 500 BCE according to the chronological division by modern historians. In the historical Vedic religion, the predecessor of Hinduism, meat eating was not banned in principle, but was restricted by specific rules. Several highly authoritative scriptures bar violence against domestic animals except in the case of ritual sacrifice. This view is clearly expressed in the Mahabharata (3.199.11-12; 13.115; 13.116.26; 13.148.17), the Bhagavata Purana (11.5.13-14), and the Chandogya Upanishad (8.15.1). It is also reflected in the Manu Smriti (5.27-44), a particularly renowned traditional Hindu law book (Dharmaúâstra). These texts strongly condemn the slaughter of animals and meat eating unless it happens in the context of the appropriate sacrifice ritual administered by priests. The Mahabharata allows people who are warriors by profession (Kshatriyas) to hunt and to eat meat "acquired by expenditure of prowess" (13.115.59-60; 13.116.15-18), but opposes such activities in the case of hermits who must be strictly nonviolent.

The Mahabharata (12.260; 13.115-116; 14.28) and the Manu Smriti (5.27-55) contain lengthy discussions about the legitimacy of ritual slaughter and subsequent consumption of the meat. In the Mahabharata both meat eaters and vegetarians present various arguments to substantiate their viewpoints. Apart from the debates about domestic animals, there is also a long discourse by a hunter in defence of hunting and meat eating. These texts show that both ritual slaughter and hunting were challenged by advocates of universal non-violence and their acceptability was doubtful and a matter of dispute. In modern Hinduism slaughter according to the rituals permitted in the Vedic scriptures has virtually disappeared.

Spiritual Aspects

In some traditions, especially within Vaishnavism, it is essential that devotees offer all their food to their chosen deity before eating it as prasad. This rule is strictly observed by the disciples of the schools of Bhakti Yoga, especially the Gaudiya Vaishnavas. They worship Vishnu or Krishna, and according to the scriptural injunctions they obey, only vegetarian food is acceptable as prasad.

Vegetarianism is also mandatory for the practitioners of Hatha Yoga. They follow the advice of scriptures such as the Bhagavad Gita to eat only high-quality food, because they are convinced that food shapes the personality, mood and mind. Meat is said to promote sloth and ignorance and an undesirable mental state known as *tamas,* while a vegetarian diet is considered to promote the desirable *sattvic* qualities essential for spiritual progress.

Essential Scriptural Evidence

> "What need there be said of those innocent and healthy creatures endued with love of life, when they are sought to be slain by sinful wretches subsisting by slaughter? For this reason, O monarch, know that the discarding of meat is the highest refuge of religion, of heaven, and of happiness. Abstention from injury is the highest religion. It is, again, the highest penance. It is also the highest truths from which all duty proceeds. Flesh cannot be had from grass or wood or stone. Unless a living

creature is slain, it cannot be had. Hence is the fault in eating flesh. ... That man who abstains from meat, is never put in fear, O king, by any creature. All creatures seek his protection. He never causes any anxiety in others, and himself has never to become anxious. If there were nobody who ate flesh there would then be nobody to kill living creatures. The man who kills living creatures kill them for the sake of the person who eats flesh. If flesh were regarded as inedible, there would then be no slaughter of living creatures. It is for the sake of the eater that the slaughter of living creatures goes on in the world. Since, O thou of great splendour, the period of life is shortened of persons who slaughter living creatures or cause them to be slaughtered, it is clear that the person who wishes his own good should give up meat entirely. ... The purchaser of flesh performs *himsa* [violence] by his wealth; he who eats flesh does so by enjoying its taste; the killer does *himsa* by actually tying and killing the animal. Thus, there are three forms of killing. He who brings flesh or sends for it, he who cuts off the limbs of an animal, and he who purchases, sells, or cooks flesh and eats it - all of these are to be considered meat-eaters." (Mahabharata 13.115)

"Those sinful persons who are ignorant of actual religious principles, yet consider themselves to be completely pious, without compunction commit violence against innocent animals who are fully trusting in them. In their next lives, such sinful persons will be eaten by the same creatures they have killed in this world." (Bhagavata Purana 11.5.14)

"A person fully aware of religious principles should never offer anything like meat, eggs or fish in the Sraddha ceremony, and even if one is a Ksatriya (warrior), he himself should not eat such things." (Bhagavata Purana 7.15.7)

Current Situation

In modern India the food habits of Hindus vary according to their community or caste and according to regional traditions. Hindu vegetarians usually eschew eggs but consume milk and dairy products, so they are lacto-vegetarians.

According to a survey of 2006, vegetarianism is weak in coastal states and strong in landlocked northern and western states and among Brahmins in general, 55 percent of whom are vegetarians. Many coastal habitants are fish eaters. In particular Bengali Hindus have romanticized fishermen and the consumption of fish through poetry, literature and music.

In India, latest reports indicate that meat consumption is actually going up .

Buddhism

The first lay precept in Buddhism prohibits killing. Unlike the Biblical commandment (Thou Shalt Not Kill), which Jewish and Christian authorities have typically applied only to human beings, the First Precept has always been held to apply to animals as well as humans. Many see this as implying that Buddhists should not eat the meat of animals. There are however differing points of view. The Buddha made distinction between killing an animal and consumption of meat, stressing that it is immoral conduct that makes one impure, not the food one eats. At one point the Buddha specifically refused to institute vegetarianism. There were, however, rules prohibiting certain types of meat, such as human, leopard or elephant. Monks are also prohibited from consuming meat if they witnessed the animal's death or know it was killed specifically for them.

On the other hand, the Buddha in certain Mahayana sutras strongly denounces the eating of meat. In the Mahayana

Mahaparinirvana Sutra, the Buddha states that "the eating of meat extinguishes the seed of great compassion", adding that all and every kind of meat and fish consumption (even of animals already found dead) is prohibited by him. The Buddha goes on to emphasize that meat-eating cannot coexist with the great compassion and calls for not just a vegetarian, but a vegan lifestyle. The Buddha also predicts in this sutra that later monks will "hold spurious writings to be the authentic Dharma" and will concoct their own sutras and mendaciously claim that the Buddha allows the eating of meat, whereas in fact (he says) he does not.· The Lankavatara Sutra (a Mahayana scripture), in particular, devotes an entire chapter to the Buddha's response to the request of a disciple named Mahamati to "teach us as to the merit and vice of meat-eating". A long passage in the Lankavatara Sutra shows the Buddha weighing strongly in favor of vegetarianism, since the eating of the flesh of fellow sentient beings is said by him to be incompatible with the compassion a Bodhisattva should strive to cultivate. Several other Mahayana sutras also emphatically prohibit the consumption of meat.

A solution to this problem arose when monks from the Indian sphere of influence migrated to China, as of the year 65 CE. There they met followers who provided them with money instead of food. From those days onwards Chinese monastics, and others who came to inhabit northern countries, cultivated their own vegetable plots and bought everything else they needed in terms of food in the market.

In the modern Buddhist world, attitudes toward vegetarianism vary by location. on China and Vietnam, monks typically eat no meat (and with other restrictions as well – see Buddhist cuisine). In Japan or Korea some schools do not eat meat, while most do. Theravadins in Sri Lanka and South-east Asia do not practice vegetarianism. All Buddhists however, including monks, are allowed to practice vegetarianism if they wish to do so. Experts have estimated that worldwide about half of all Buddhists are vegetarian.

Sikhism

Followers of Sikhism do not have a preference for meat or vegetarian consumption. There are two views on initiated or "Amritdhari Sikhs" and meat consumption. "Amritdhari" Sikhs (i.e. those that follow the Sikh Rehat Maryada (the Official Sikh Code of Conduct) can eat meat (provided it is not Kutha meat)."Amritdharis" that belong to some Sikh sects (eg Akhand Kirtani Jatha, Namdhari, Rarionwalay, etc.) are vehemently against the consumption of meat and eggs.

In the case of meat, the Sikh Gurus have indicated their preference for a simple diet, which could include meat or be vegetarian. Passages from the Guru Granth Sahib (the holy book of Sikhs, also known as the Adi Granth) say that fools argue over this issue. Guru Nanak said that any consumption of food involves a drain on the Earth's resources and thus on life. The tenth guru, Guru Gobind Singh, prohibited the Sikhs from the consumption of halal or Kutha (any ritually slaughtered meat) meat because of the Sikh belief that sacrificing an animal in the name of God is mere ritualism (something to be avoided).

Jainism

Vegetarianism in Jainism is based on the principle of nonviolence (ahimsa) like in Hinduism, but it is stricter than in the main Hindu traditions and mandatory for everyone. Jains are either lacto-vegetarians or vegans. No use or consumption of products obtained from dead animals is allowed. Moreover Jains try to avoid unnecessary injury to plants and *suksma jiva* (Sanskrit for *subtle life forms*; minuscule organisms). The goal is to cause as little violence to living things as possible, hence they avoid eating roots, tubers and anything that involves uprooting (and thus eventually killing) a plant to obtain food.

Abrahamic Religions

Judaic, Christian, and Muslim traditions (Abrahamic religions) all have strong connections to the biblical ideal of the Garden of Eden, which includes references to a diet similar to fruitarianism (see Genesis 1:29, 9:2-4; Isaiah 11:6-9). However, only minorities within these populations actually practice and advocate such strict diets, since the same book of the Bible, Genesis, later gives permission to Noah (and presumably his descendants) to consume animal flesh due to an emergency lack of food situation.

Judaism

Rabbinical Judaism discourages ascetic practices in general, and encourages one to enjoy the bounty of this world in a proper fashion. With respect to food, this teaching may be summarized by the Talmudic statement, "Man will have to account for everything he saw but did not eat." (This refers to permissible or kosher foods only, not to forbidden animal species such as pork.) On the other hand, the Talmud discourages indulgence and states that it is preferable that one's diet consist mostly of non-meat products. To Jewish vegetarians wishing to remain consistent with this teaching, vegetarianism is not a form of self-deprivation, because the vegetarian does not desire to eat meat and believes it is healthier not to eat meat.

Several passages in the Old Testament encourages eating animal flesh such as Genesis 9:3 which states "Every moving thing that liveth shall be meat for you."

> Genesis 1:29 states "And God said: Behold, I have given you every herb yielding seed which is upon the face of all the earth, and every tree that has seed-yielding fruit - to you it shall be for food." According to some classical Jewish Bible commentators this means that God's original plan was for mankind to be vegetarian, and

that God only later gave permission for man to eat meat because of man's weak nature.· As the ideal images of the Torah are vegetarian, it is natural to similarly see the laws of kashrut as actually designed to wean us away from meat eating towards the vegetarian ideal. The rituals of kashrut remind us of the magnitude of what we do each time we kill a living being. Other commentators argue that people may eat animals because God gave Adam and Eve dominion over them.

Generally speaking, Judaism has not promoted vegetarianism. However, some prominent rabbis have promoted vegetarian lifestyle, among them the first Chief Rabbi of Palestine, Abraham Isaac Kook, his student David Cohen (known as "Ha-Nazir"), and Chief Rabbi of Israel Shlomo Goren. Rabbi Isaac ha-Levi Herzog said:

> "Jews will move increasingly to vegetarianism out of their own deepening knowledge of what their tradition commands... A whole galaxy of central rabbinic and spiritual leaders...has been affirming vegetarianism as the ultimate meaning of Jewish moral teaching."
>
> "Man ideally should not eat meat, for to eat meat a life must be taken, an animal must be put to death."

Rabbi Milgrom regards the commandment against blood as a law that permits man to "indulge in his lust for meat and not be brutalized in the process."

Some Orthodox authorities have ruled that it is forbidden for an individual to become a vegetarian if they do so because they believe in animal rights; however, they have ruled that vegetarianism is allowed for pragmatic reasons (if kosher meat is expensive or hard to come by in their area), health concerns, or for reasons of personal taste (if someone finds meat unpalatable). Some believe that halakha encourages the eating of meat at the Sabbath and Festival meals, thus some

Orthodox Jews who are otherwise vegetarian will nevertheless consume meat at these meals.

There are several arguments from Judaism used by Jewish vegetarians. For the Jewish vegetarian there are three main components which prove vegetarianism to be an ethical mitzvah: tsar baalei haim, pikuah nefesh and bal tashchit. Tsaar Baalei Haim is the injunction not to cause 'pain to living creatures'. Pikkuah Nefesh is not only the regard for human life which is in immediate danger. Bal Tashchit is the law which prohibits waste. Another argument is that, since Adam and Eve were not allowed to eat meat and that, according to some opinions, in the Messianic era, the whole world will be vegetarian, not eating meat is something that brings the world closer to that ideal. In his booklet summarizing many of Rav Kook's teachings, Joseph Green, a 20th-century South African Jewish vegetarian writer, concludes that Jewish religious ethical vegetarians are pioneers of the messianic era; they are leading lives that make the coming of the Messiah more likely. The Jewish tradition asserts that one way to speed the coming of the Messiah is to start practicing the ways that will prevail in the messianic time. A second one is that the laws of shechita are meant to prevent the suffering of animals and today, with factory farming and high-speed, mechanized slaughterhouses, even kosher slaughterhouses are considered by some authorities not to fulfill enough of the requirements to render the meat kosher. A third one is that the Sages only mandated eating an olive's bulk of meat during festivals, but even then, this was because in Talmudic times, meat was considered essential for one's diet (whereas a vegetarian will probably be of the opinion that current science has shown otherwise).

Christianity

Several Christian monastic groups, including the Desert Fathers, Trappists, Benedictines and Carthusians, and also

Christian esoteric groups, such as the Rosicrucian Fellowship, have encouraged vegetarianism. Some Christian groups, such as Seventh-day Adventists and Christian anarchists, take a literal interpretation of the Biblical prophecies of universal vegetarianism and encourage vegetarianism as a preferred, though not required, lifestyle. However, most evangelical groups are unaware of the existence of any such prophecies, and point instead to the explicit prophecies of temple sacrifices in the Messianic Kingdom, e.g. Ezekiel 46:12 where peace offerings and freewill offerings will be offered, and Leviticus 7:15-20 where it states that such offerings are eaten. Some Christian vegetarians argue that Jesus himself was a vegetarian. There is one argument that Jesus was an Essene (vegetarian inhabitants of the Dead Sea community at Qumran). The present academic consensus is that Jesus was not an Essene. There is no historical record of Jesus' precise attitudes to animals, but there is a strand in his ethical teaching about the primacy of mercy to the weak, the powerless and the oppressed, which Walters and Portmess argue can also refer to captive animals. St. Augustine and Saint David became vegetarians for ascetic reasons, not necessarily because of a religious edict to that effect. In the 19th century, members of the Bible Christian sect established the first vegetarian groups in England and the United States.

In the Book of Genesis by the Garden of Eden, there is no description of suffering, exploitation, or violence at all. People and animals may have been vegetarians, since Genesis 1:29 reads: "God said, 'See, I have given you every plant yielding seed that is upon the face of all the Earth, and every tree with seed in its fruit; you shall have them for food'". Immediately after the world in this state, God describes it as "very good." This is the only time in the narrative that God calls creation "very good" instead of merely "good" – and this immediately follows God's command with regard to vegetarianism.

However, it has been argued that the anthropocentric viewpoint of the Bible encourages human exploitation of animals and meat eating. Genesis 1:26-28 has been interpreted to condemn vegetarianism. The Bible says: "..And God said, Let us make man in our image, and after our likeness: and let him have dominion over the fish of the sea, and over the fowl of the air, and over the cattle, and over all the earth, and over every creeping thing that creepeth upon the earth." In addition, Genesis 1:28 states "God blessed them and said to them, "Be fruitful and increase in number; fill the earth and subdue it. Rule over the fish of the sea and the birds of the air and over every living creature that moves on the ground.". In Genesis 1:30: "And to every beast of the earth, and to every fowl of the air, and to every thing that creepeth upon the earth, wherein there is life, I have given every green herb for meat: and it was so." Continuing into Genesis 1:31, the Bible says: "And God saw every thing that he had made, and, behold, it was very good. And the evening and the morning were the sixth day."

In Romans 14:2 St. Paul may explicitly discourage vegetarianism, since he writes "For one believeth that he may eat all things: another, who is weak, eateth herbs."

> Non-vegetarian Christians sometimes cite Numbers 11:31-32: "And there went forth a wind from the LORD, and brought quails from the sea, and let them fall by the camp, as it were a day's journey on this side, and as it were a day's journey on the other side, round about the camp, and as it were two cubits high upon the face of the earth. And the people stood up all that day, and all that night, and all the next day, and they gathered the quails: he that gathered least gathered ten homers: and they spread them all abroad for themselves round about the camp." But the next verse says, "And while the flesh was yet between their teeth, ere it was chewed, the wrath of the LORD was kindled against the people, and the LORD smote the people with a very great plague."

Islam

Islam explicitly prohibits eating of some kinds of meat, especially pork. However, one of the most important Islamic celebrations, *Eid ul-Adha,* involves animal sacrifices. Muslims who can afford to do so sacrifice their best domestic animals (usually sheep, but also camels, cows, and goats). According to the Quran a large portion of the meat has to be given towards the poor and hungry people so they can all join in the feast on Eid-ul-Adha. The remainder is cooked for the family celebration meal in which relatives and friends are invited to share. The regular charitable practices of the Muslim community are demonstrated during Eid ul-Adha by the concerted effort to see that no impoverished Muslim is left without sacrificial food during these days. Since these practices are justified by Koran, advocacy of vegetarianism by implying that God ordained diet to be immoral could be seen as contrary to Islam. Certain Islamic orders are mainly vegetarian; many Sufis maintain a vegetarian diet, as do the Druze of Lebanon, who, for instance, often frown upon the consumption of port.

Rastafari

Rastafarians generally follow a diet called "I-tal", which eschews the eating of food that has been artificially preserved, flavoured, or chemically altered in any way. Many Rastafarians consider it to also forbid the eating of meat.

Bahá'í Faith

While there are no dietary restrictions in the Bahá'í Faith, 'Abdu'l-Bahá, the son of the founder of the religion, noted that a vegetarian diet consisting of fruits and grains was desirable, except for people with a weak constitution or those that are sick. He stated that there are no requirements that Bahá'ís become vegetarian, but that a future society would gradually become vegetarian. 'Abdu'l-Bahá also stated that killing animals was somewhat contrary to compassion. While Shoghi Effendi, the Guardian of the Bahá'í Faith stated that a purely vegetarian diet would be preferable since it avoided killing animals, both he and the Universal House of Justice, the governing body of the Bahá'ís have stated that these teachings do not constitute a Bahá'í practice and that Bahá'ís can choose to eat whatever they wish, but to be respectful of others beliefs.

Other Religions

Taoism

In Chinese societies, "simple eating" refers to a particular restricted diet associated with Taoist monks, and sometimes practiced by members of the general population during Taoist festivals. It is referred to by the English word "vegetarian"; however, though it rejects meat, eggs, and milk, this diet does include oysters and oyster products.

Zoroastrianism

One of the main precepts in Zoroastrianism is respect and kindness towards all living things, condemnation of cruelty against animals and the sacrifice of animals.

Neopaganism

There is no set teaching on vegetarianism within the diverse neopagan communities, however many do follow a vegetarian diet often connected to ecological concerns as well as the welfare and rights of animals. Vegetarian practitioners of Wicca will often see their standpoint as a natural extension of the Wiccan Rede and Odinists of Odinism. Organisations like SERV refer to the historic figures of Porphyry, Pythagoras and Iamblichus as sources for the Pagan view of vegetarianism. During the 1970s the publication Earth Religion News, focused on articles related to neopaganism and vegetarianism, it was edited by the author Herman Slater. ●●

3

Buddhism and Psychology

Buddhism and psychology overlap in theory and in practice. Over the last century, three strands of interplay have evolved:

- Descriptive phenomenology: Western and Buddhist scholars have found in Buddhist teachings a detailed introspective phenomenological psychology (particularly in the *Abhidhamma*).
- Psychotherapeutic meaning: Humanistic psychotherapists have found in Buddhism's non-dualistic approach and enlightenment experiences (such as in Zen *kensho*) the potential for transformation, healing and finding existential meaning.
- Clinical utility: Contemporary mental-health practitioners increasingly find ancient Buddhist practices (such as the development of mindfulness) of empirically proven therapeutic value.

Mindstream

Psychology is the study of the Psyche often rendered in English as mind. The principal and central teaching of Buddha Dharma is the 'consciousness continuum' or the Mindstream. As Mañjuúrîmitra states in Verse 62 of the *Bodhicittabhavana,* a seminal early text of Ati Yoga, here rendered into English by Kunpal Tulku (1995: unpaginated):

Yet no phenomena exists for either ordinary people or for enlightened Saints other than the continuum (santana) of their own mind (citta).

In human experience, a particular station of sentient beings, all phenomena or dharmas are mediated through and by the mind[stream]. Importantly, mind as embodied in the cartesian dualism of mind and body does not exist in the Buddha Dharma and instead is replaced with the mindstream which may be conveyed in a traditional metaphorical relationship where the mindstream is the flame of the candle of the skandha: where in exegetical commentary, the flame never touches the wick of the candle.

Buddhism's Phenomenological Psychology

The establishment of Buddhism predates the field of psychology by over two millennia; thus, any assessment of Buddhism in terms of psychology is necessarily a modern invention. One of the first such assessments occurred when British Indologists started translating Theravada Buddhism's *Abhidhamma* from Pali and Sanskrit texts. Long-term efforts to juxtapose abhidhammic psychology with Western empirical sciences have been carried out by such Vajrayana leaders as Chogyam Trungpa Rinpoche and the 14th Dalai Lama.

Overview of the Abhidhamma

The earliest Buddhist writings are preserved in the three-part *Tipitaka* (Pali; Skt. *Tripitaka*). The third part (or *pitaka,* literally "basket") is known as the *Abhidhamma* (Pali; Skt. *Abhidharma*). Ven. Bhikkhu Bodhi, president of the Buddhist Publication Society, has synopsized the Abhidhamma as follows:

> "The system that the Abhidhamma Pitaka articulates is simultaneously a philosophy, a psychology, and an ethics, all integrated into the framework of a program for liberation.... The Abhidhamma's attempt to comprehend the nature of reality, contrary to that of classical science in the West, does not proceed from the standpoint of a neutral observer looking outwards

> towards the external world. The primary concern of the Abhidhamma is to understand the nature of experience, and thus the reality on which it focuses is conscious reality.... For this reason the philosophical enterprise of the Abhidhamma shades off into a phenomenological psychology. To facilitate the understanding of experienced reality, the Abhidhamma embarks upon an elaborate analysis of the mind as it presents itself to introspective meditation. It classifies consciousness into a variety of types, specifies the factors and functions of each type, correlates them with their objects and physiological bases, and shows how the different types of consciousness link up with each other and with material phenomena to constitute the ongoing process of experience." (Bodhi, 2000, pp. 3-4.)

Western recognition of the phenomenological-psychological aspect of the Abhidhamma started over a century ago with the work of British Indologists.

Rhys Davids' Early Scholarship (1900)

In 1900, Indologist Caroline A. F. Rhys Davids published through the Pali Text Society a translation of the Theravada Abhidhamma's first book, the Dhamma Sangani, and entitled the translation, "Buddhist Manual of Psychological Ethics" (Rhys Davids, 2003). In the introduction to this seminal work, Rhys Davids writes:

> "... Buddhist philosophy is ethical first and last. This is beyond dispute. But among ethical systems there is a world of difference in the degree of importance attached to the psychological prolegomena of ethics.... he Buddhists were, in a way, more advanced in the psychology of their ethics than Aristotle — in a way, that is, which would now be called scientific. Rejecting the assumption of a psyche and of its higher manifestations ..., they were content to resolve the

consciousness of the Ethical Man, *as they found it,* into a complex continuum of subjective phenomena.... The distinguishable groups of dhammâ — of states or mental psychoses — 'arise' in every case in consciousness, in obedience to certain laws of causation, physical and moral — that is, ultimately, as the outcome of antecedent states of consciousness.... It postulated other percipients as Berkeley did, together with, not a Divine cause or source of precepts, but the implicit Monism of early thought veiled by a deliberate Agnosticism.... o Buddhism, from a quite early stage of its development, set itself to analyze and classify mental processes with remarkable insight and sagacity...." (Rhys Davids, 1900, pp. xvi-xvii.)

Buddhism's psychological orientation is a theme Rhys Davids pursued for decades as evidenced by Rhys Davids (1914) and Rhys Davids (1936).

Trungpa Rinpoche and the Naropa Institute (1974)

"Buddhism will
come to the West
as a psychology."

- *Chogyam Trungpa, 1974*

In his introduction to his 1975 book, *Glimpses of the Abhidharma,* Chogyam Trungpa Rinpoche wrote:

"Many modern psychologists have found that the discoveries and explanations of the abhidharma coincide with their own recent discoveries and new ideas; as though the abhidharma, which was taught 2,500 years ago, had been redeveloped in the modern idiom." (Trungpa, 1975, p.2.)

Trungpa Rinpoche's book goes on to describe the nanosecond phenomenological sequence by which a sensation becomes conscious using the Buddhist concepts of the "five aggregates."

In 1974, Trungpa Rinpoche founded the Naropa Institute, now called Naropa University. Since 1975, this accredited university has offered degrees in "contemplative psychology."

The Dalai Lama and the Mind and Life Dialogues (1987)

Every two years, since 1987, the Dalai Lama has convened "Mind and Life" gatherings of Buddhists and scientists. Reflecting on one Mind and Life session in March 2000, psychologist Daniel Goleman notes:

> "Since the time of Gautama Buddha in the fifth century BC, an analysis of the mind and its workings has been central to the practices of his followers. This analysis was codified during the first millennium after his death within the system called, in the Pali language of Buddha's day, Abhidhamma (or Abhidharma in Sanskrit), which means 'ultimate doctrine'.... Every branch of Buddhism today has a version of these basic psychological teachings on the mind, as well as its own refinements" (Goleman, 2004, pp. 72-73).

Psychotherapy and Enlightenment

British barrister Christmas Humphreys has referred to mid-twentieth century collaborations between psychoanalysts and Buddhist scholars as a meeting between "two of the most powerful forces operating in the Western mind today." Ever since, a variety of renowned teachers, clinicians and writers such as D.T. Suzuki, Carl Jung, Erich Fromm, Alan Watts and Jack Kornfield have attempted to bridge and integrate psychology and Buddhism in a manner that offers meaning, inspiration and healing. More recently, some traditional Buddhist practitioners have expressed concern that attempts to view Buddhism through the lens of Western psychology diminishes the Buddha's liberating message.

Suzuki & Jung (1948)

A number of psychologists have identified a pivotal collaboration between Buddhism and psychology was when psychoanalyst Carl Jung wrote the foreword to Zen scholar Daisetz Teitaro Suzuki's *Introduction to Zen Buddhism,* first published together in 1948. In his foreword, Jung highlights the enlightenment experience of *satori* as the unsurpassed transformation to wholeness for Zen practitioners. And while acknowledging the inadequacy of Westerners' attempts to comprehend *satori* through the lens of Western intellectualism, Jung nonetheless contends:

> "The only movement within our culture which partly has, and partly should have, some understanding of these aspirations [for such enlightenment] is psychotherapy. It is therefore not a matter of chance that this foreword is written by a psychotherapist.... Taken basically, psychotherapy is a dialectic relationship between the doctor and the patient.... The goal is transformation...." (Suzuki & Jung, 1948, p. 25).

Suzuki & Fromm (1957)

Referencing Jung and Suzuki's collaboration as well as the efforts of others, humanistic philosopher and psychoanalyst Erich Fromm noted:

> "...here is an unmistakable and increasing interest in Zen Buddhism among psychoanalysts" (Fromm *et al.*, 1960, pp. 77-78).

Suzuki, Fromm and other psychoanalysts collaborated at a 1957 workshop on "Zen Buddhism and Psychoanalysis" in Cuernavaca, Mexico. In his contribution to this workshop, Fromm declares: "Psychoanalysis is a characteristic expression of Western man's spiritual crisis, and an attempt to find a solution" (Fromm *et al.*, 1960, p. 80). Fromm contends that, at the turn of the twentieth century, most psychotherapeutic patients sought treatment due to medical-like symptoms that hindered their social functioning. However, by mid-century, the majority of psychoanalytic patients lacked overt symptoms and functioned well but instead suffered from an "inner deadness":

> "The common suffering is the alienation from oneself, from one's fellow man, and from nature; the awareness that life runs out of one's hand like sand, and that one will die without having lived; that one lives in the midst of plenty and yet is joyless" (Fromm *et al.* pp. 85-86).

Paraphrasing Suzuki broadly, Fromm continues:

> "Zen is the art of *seeing into the nature of one's being;* it is a way *from bondage to freedom;* it *liberates our natural energies;* ... and it impels us to express our faculty for *happiness and love* (p. 115).
>
> "...hat can be said with more certainty is that the knowledge of Zen, and a concern with it, can have a most fertile and clarifying influence on the theory and technique of psychoanalysis. Zen, different as it is in its method from psychoanalysis, can sharpen the focus, throw new light on the nature of insight, and heighten the sense of what it is to see, what it is to be creative, what it is to overcome the affective contaminations and false intellectualizations which are the necessary results of experience based on the subject-object split" (p. 140).

Mainstream Teachers and Popularizers

In 1961, Philosopher and Orientalist Alan Watts wrote:

> "If we look deeply into such ways of life as Buddhism and Taoism, Vedanta and Yoga, we do not find either philosophy or religion as these are understood in the West. We find something more nearly resembling psychotherapy.... The main resemblance between these

Eastern ways of life and Western psychotherapy is in the concern of both with bringing about changes of consciousness, changes in our ways of feeling our own existence and our relation to human society and the natural world. The psychotherapist has, for the most part, been interested in changing the consciousness of peculiarly disturbed individuals. The disciplines of Buddhism and Taoism are, however, concerned with changing the consciousness of normal, socially adjusted people." (Watts, 1975, pp. 3-4.)

Since Watts's early observations and musings, there have been many other important contributors to the contemporary popularization of the integration of Buddhist meditation with psychology including Kornfield (1993), Joseph Goldstein, Tara Brach, Epstein (1995) and Nhat Hanh (1998).

Caveats Regarding "Romantic Buddhism"

Tracing the roots of modern Western spiritual ideals from German Romantic Era philosopher Immanuel Kant through American psychologist and philosopher William James, Jung and humanistic psychologist Abraham Maslow, Thanissaro Bhikkhu (*undated*) identifies broad commonalities between "Romantic/humanistic psychology" and early Buddhism: beliefs in human (versus divine) intervention with an approach that is experiential, pragmatic and therapeutic. However, Thanissaro asserts that there are also core differences between Romantic/humanistic psychology and Buddhism. These are summarized in the table to the right. Thanissaro implicitly deems those who impose Romantic/humanistic goals on the Buddha's message as "Buddhist Romantics."

Recognizing the widespread alienation and social fragmentation of modern life, Thanissaro Bhikkhu writes:

"When Buddhist Romanticism speaks to these needs, it opens the gate to areas of dharma [the Buddha's teachings] that can help many people find the solace they're looking for. In doing so, it augments the work of psychotherapy....

"However, Buddhist Romanticism also helps close the gate to areas of the dharma that would challenge people in their hope for an ultimate happiness based on interconnectedness. Traditional dharma calls for renunciation and sacrifice, on the grounds that all interconnectedness is essentially unstable, and any happiness based on this instability is an invitation to suffering. True happiness has to go beyond interdependence and interconnectedness to the unconditioned. ... he gate [of Buddhist Romanticism] closes off radical areas of the dharma designed to address levels of suffering remaining even when a sense of wholeness has been mastered." (Thanissaro, *undated.*)

Buddhist Techniques in Clinical Settings

For over a millennium, throughout the world, Buddhist practices have been used for non-Buddhist ends. More recently, Western clinical psychologists, theorists and researchers have incorporated Buddhist practices in widespread formalized psychotherapies. Buddhist mindfulness practices have been explicitly incorporated into a variety of psychological treatments. More tangentially, psychotherapies dealing with cognitive restructuring share core principles with ancient Buddhist antidotes to personal suffering.

Mindfulness Practices

Fromm (2002, pp. 49–52) distinguishes between two types of meditative techniques that have been used in psychotherapy:

1. auto-suggestion used to induce relaxation; and,
2. meditation "to achieve a higher degree of non-attachment, of non-greed, and of non-illusion; briefly, those that serve to reach a higher level of being".

Fromm attributes techniques associated with the latter to Buddhist mindfulness practices.

Two increasingly popular therapeutic practices using Buddhist mindfulness techniques are Jon Kabat-Zinn's Mindfulness-based Stress Reduction (MBSR) and Marsha M. Linehan's Dialectical Behavioral Therapy (DBT). Other prominent therapies that use mindfulness include Steven C. Hayes' Acceptance and Commitment Therapy (ACT) and, based on MBSR, Mindfulness-based Cognitive Therapy (MBCT) (Segal *et al.*, 2002).

Mindfulness Based Stress Reduction (MBSR):

Kabat-Zinn developed the eight-week MBSR program over a ten year period with over four thousand patients at the University of Massachusetts Medical Center (Kabat-Zinn, 1990, p. 1). Describing the MBSR program, Kabat-Zinn writes:

> "This 'work' involves above all the regular, disciplined practice of moment-to-moment awareness or *mindfulness,* the complete 'owning' of each moment of your experience, good, bad, or ugly. This is the essence of full catastrophe living." (p. 11)

Kabat-Zinn, a one-time Zen practitioner, goes on to write:

> "Although at this time mindfulness meditation is most commonly taught and practiced within the context of Buddhism, its essence is universal.... Yet it is no accident that mindfulness comes out of Buddhism, which has as its overriding concerns the relief of suffering and the dispelling of illusions." (pp. 12-13)

Not surprisingly, in terms of clinical diagnoses, MBSR has proven beneficial for people with depression and anxiety disorders; however, the program is meant to serve anyone experiencing significant stress.

Dialectical Behavioral Therapy (DBT):

In writing about DBT, Zen practitioner Linehan (1993a, p. 19) states:

> "As its name suggests, its overriding characteristic is an emphasis on 'dialectics' – that is, the reconciliation of opposites in a continual process of synthesis.... This emphasis on acceptance as a balance to change flows directly from the integration of a perspective drawn from Eastern (Zen) practice with Western psychological practice."

Similarly, Linehan (1993b, p. 63) writes:

> "Mindfulness skills are central to DBT.... They are the first skills taught and are [reviewed] ... every week.... The skills are psychological and behavioral versions of meditation practices from Eastern spiritual training. I have drawn most heavily from the practice of Zen...."

Controlled clinical studies have demonstrated DBT's effectiveness for people with borderline personality disorder.

Cognitive Restructuring

Dr. Albert Ellis, considered the "grandfather of cognitive-behavioral therapy" (CBT), has written:

> "Many of the principles incorporated in the theory of rational-emotive psychotherapy are not new; some of them, in fact, were originally stated several thousands of years ago, especially by the Greek and Roman Stoic philosophers (such as Epictetus and Marcus Aurelius) and by some of the ancient Taoist and Buddhist thinkers (see Suzuki, 1956, and Watts, 1959, 1960)." (Ellis, 1991, p. 35.)

To give but one example, Buddhism identifies anger and ill-will as basic hindrances to spiritual development (see, for instance, the Five Hindrances, Ten Fetters and *kilesas*). A common Buddhist antidote for anger is the use of active contemplation of loving thoughts (see, for instance, *metta*). This is similar to using a CBT technique known as "emotional training" which Ellis (1997, pp. 86–87) describes in the following manner:

> "Think of an intensely pleasant experience you have had with the person with whom you now feel angry. When you have fantasized such a pleasant experience and have actually given yourself unusually good, intensely warm feelings toward that person as a result of this remembrance, continue the process. Recall pleasant experiences and good feelings, and try to make these feelings paramount over your feelings of hostility."

●●

4

Buddhist Philosophy and Science

Buddhist philosophy deals extensively with problems in metaphysics, phenomenology, ethics, and epistemology.

The Buddha's general outlook has been described as neither ontological nor metaphysical, but empirical. He assumed an unsympathetic attitude toward speculative and religious thought in general. A basic idea of the Buddha is that the world must be thought of in procedural terms, not in terms of things or substances. The Buddha advised viewing reality as comprised of dependently originated phenomena; Buddhists view this approach to experience as avoiding the two extremes of reification and nihilism.

Particular points of Buddhist philosophy have often been the subject of disputes between different schools of Buddhism. While theory for its own sake is not valued in Buddhism, theory pursued in the interest of enlightenment is consistent with Buddhist values and ethics.

Philosophy

Historical Context

Early Buddhism displays a strong streak of skepticism; the Buddha cautioned his followers to stay aloof from intellectual disputation for its own sake, saying that this is fruitless and distracts from the practices leading to enlightenment. However, the Buddha's doctrine did have an important philosophical component: it negated the major claims of rival positions while building upon them at a new philosophical and religious level.

In a skeptical vein, he asserted the insubstantiality of the ego, and in doing so countered those Upanishadic sages who sought knowledge of an unchanging ultimate self. The Buddha created a new position in opposition to their theories, and held that attachment to a permanent self in this world of change is the cause of suffering and the main obstacle to liberation. The same skeptical approach negates the existence of any high god or spiritual substance, and undercuts both traditional and iconoclastic spiritual goals. He broke new ground by going on to explain the source for the apparent ego: it is merely the result of the aggregates (*skandhas*) which make up experience.

In this breaking down into constituent elements, the Buddha was heir to earlier element philosophies which had sought to characterize existing things as made up of a set of basic elements. The Buddha, however, eliminated mythological rhetoric, systematized world components into five groups, and used this approach not to characterize a substantial object, but to explain a delusion. He coordinated material components with psychological ones. The Buddha criticized the religious sages' theories of an Absolute as yet another reification, instead giving a path to self-perfection as a means of transcending the world of name and form.

Epistemology

Decisive in distinguishing Buddhism from what is commonly called Hinduism is the issue of epistemological justification. All schools of Indian logic recognize various sets of valid justifications for knowledge, or *pramana* – Buddhism recognizes a set that is smaller than the others'. All accept perception and inference, for example, but for some schools of Hinduism and Buddhism the received textual tradition is an epistemological category equal to perception and inference (although this is not necessarily true for some other schools).

Thus, in the Hindu schools, if a claim was made that could not be substantiated by appeal to the textual canon, it would be considered as ridiculous as a claim that the sky was green and, conversely, a claim which could not be substantiated via conventional means might still be justified through textual reference, differentiating this from the epistemology of hard science.

Some schools of Buddhism, on the other hand, rejected an inflexible reverence of accepted doctrine. As the Buddha said, according to the canonical scriptures:

> Do not accept anything by mere tradition ... Do not accept anything just because it accords with your scriptures ... Do not accept anything merely because it agrees with your pre-conceived notions ... But when you know for yourselves – these things are moral, these things are blameless, these things are praised by the wise, these things, when performed and undertaken, conduce to well-being and happiness – then do you live acting accordingly.

Early Buddhist philosophers and exegetes of one particular early school (as opposed to Mahayana), the Sarvastivadins, created a pluralist metaphysical and phenomenological system, in which all experiences of people, things and events can be broken down into smaller and smaller perceptual or perceptual-ontological units called *dharmas*. Other schools incorporated some parts of this theory and criticized others. The Sautrantikas, another early school, and the Theravadins, the only surviving early Buddhist school, criticized the realist standpoint of the Sarvastivadins.

The Mahayanist Nagarjuna, one of the most influential Buddhist thinkers, promoted classical Buddhist emphasis on phenomena and attacked Sarvastivada realism and Sautrantika nominalism in his magnum opus The Fundamental Verses on the Middle Way.

Dependent Origination

What some consider the original positive Buddhist contribution to the field of metaphysics is *pratîtyasamutpâda*. It states that events are not predetermined, nor are they random, and it rejects notions of direct causation, which are necessarily undergirded by a substantialist metaphysics. Instead, it posits the arising of events under certain conditions which are inextricable, such that the processes in question at no time are considered to be entities.

Pratitya-samutpada goes on to posit that certain specific events, concepts, or realities are always dependent on other specific things. Craving, for example, is always dependent on, and caused by, emotion. Emotion is always dependent on contact with our surroundings. This chain of causation purports to show that the cessation of decay, death, and sorrow is indirectly dependent on the cessation of craving.

Nâgârjuna asserted a direct connection between, even identity of, dependent origination, anatta, and úûnyatâ. He pointed out that implicit in the early Buddhist concept of dependent origination is the lack of any substantial being (anätta) underlying the participants in origination, so that they have no independent existence, a state identified as emptiness (úûnyatâ), or emptiness of a nature or essence (svabhâva).

Interpenetration

'Interpenetration' or 'coalescence'. This doctrine comes from the Avatamsaka Sutra, a Mahayana scripture, and its associated schools. It holds that all 'phenomena' (Sanskrit: dharmas) are intimately connected (and mutually arising). Two images are used to convey this idea. The first is known as Indra's net. The net is set with jewels which have the extraordinary property that they reflect all of the other jewels. The second image is that of the 'world text'. This image portrays the world as consisting of an enormous text which is as large as the Universe itself. The 'words' of the text are composed of the phenomena that make up the world. However, every atom of the world contains the whole text within it. It is the work of a Buddha to let out the text so that beings can be liberated from suffering. The upaya doctrine of interpenetration influenced the Japanese monk Kûkai, who founded the Shingon school of Buddhism. The upaya doctrine of interpenetration is iconographically represented by Yab-yum. Interpenetration and Essence-Function are mutually informing in the East Asian Buddhist traditions, especially the Korean Buddhist tradition.

ETHICS

Although there are many ethical tenets in Buddhism that differ depending on whether one is a monk or a layman, and depending on individual schools, the Buddhist system of ethics can be summed up in the Eightfold Path.

And this, monks, is the noble truth of the way of practice leading to the cessation of suffering — precisely this Noble Eightfold Path – right view, right resolve, right speech, right action, right livelihood, right effort, right mindfulness, right concentration.

The purpose of living an ethical life is to escape the suffering inherent in *samsara.* Skillful actions condition the mind in a positive way and lead to future happiness, while the opposite is true for unskillful actions. Ethical discipline also provides the mental stability and freedom to embark upon mental cultivation via meditation.

Philosophy or Religion

Buddhism can be regarded as either a practical philosophy or a belief-based religion. In the South and East Asian cultures in which Buddhism developed, the distinction between philosophy and religion is not always strongly present. As such, the need to classify Buddhism as one or the other may be a mere semantic problem.

Proponents of the view that Buddhism is a philosophy argue (a) that Buddhism is non-theistic, having no particular use for the existence or non-existence of a god or gods; and (b) that religion entails theism. However, both prongs of this argument are contested by proponents of the alternative view, that Buddhism is a religion. Namely, (a) in the Mahayana branch a vast pantheon of Buddhas and Bodhisattvas serve as the object of prayer and worship and (b) the Tathagatagarbha doctrine may be interpreted in a theistic sense. Another argument for Buddhism as a philosophy is that Buddhism does not have doctrines in the same sense as other religions; instead, Buddhism offers specific methods for applying its philosophical principles, although this too is contentious.

Regardless of its formal classification, Buddhism is a religion rich with philosophical content. Lama Anagorika Govinda expressed it as follows in *A Living Buddhism for the West*:

> Thus we could say that the Buddha's Dharma is,
>
> - as experience and as a way to practical realisation, a religion;
> - as the intellectual formulation of this experience, a philosophy;
> - and as a result of self-observation and analysis, a psychology.

Whoever treads this path acquires a norm of behavior that is not dictated from without, but is the result of an inner process of maturation and that we – regarding it from without – can call morality.

History

Early Development

Certain basic teachings appear in many places throughout the early texts, so most scholars conclude that the Buddha must at least have taught something of the kind:

- the three characteristics
- the five aggregates
- dependent arising
- karma and rebirth
- the four noble truths
- the eightfold path
- nirvana

Some scholars disagree, and have proposed many other theories. According to such scholars, there was something they variously call Earliest Buddhism, original Buddhism or pre-canonical Buddhism. The Buddha rejected certain precepts of Indian philosophy that were prominent during his lifetime. According to some scholars, the philosophical outlook of Earliest Buddhism was primarily negative, in the sense that it focused on what doctrines to *reject* more than on what doctrines to *accept*. This dimension is also found in the Madhyamaka school. It includes critical rejections of all views, which is a form of philosophy, but it is reluctant to posit its own.

Only knowledge that is useful in achieving enlightenment is valued. According to this theory, the cycle of philosophical upheavals that in part drove the diversification of Buddhism into its many schools and sects only began once Buddhists began attempting to make explicit the implicit philosophy of the Buddha and the early Suttas. Other scholars reject this theory. After the death of the Buddha, attempts were made to gather his teachings and transmit them in a commonly agreed form, first orally, then also in writing (The Tripitaka).

Later Developments

The main Buddhist philosophical schools are the Abhidharma schools, (particularly Theravada and Sarvastivada), and the Mahayana schools (the latter includes the Madhyamika, Yogacara, Huayan, and Tiantai schools).

Cataphatic Presentations

The Tathagatagarbha doctrine of some schools of Mahayana Buddhism, the Theravada doctrine of bhavanga, and the Yogachara store consciousness were all identified at some point with the "luminous mind" of the Nikayas.

The Tathagatagarbha sutras, in a depature from mainstream Buddhist language, insist that the true self lies at the very heart of the Buddha himself and of nirvana, as well as being concealed within the mass of mental and moral contaminants that blight all beings. Such doctrines saw a shift from a largely apophatic (negative) philosophical trend within Buddhism to a decidedly more cataphatic (positive) modus. The tathagatagarbha (or Buddha-nature) does not, according to some scholars, represent a substantial self; rather, it is a positive language expression of "sunyata" and represents the potentiality to realize Buddhahood through Buddhist practices. In this interpretation, the intention of the teaching of tathagatagarbha is soteriological rather than theoretical. The word "atman" is used in a way idionsyncratic to these sutras; the "true self" is described as the perfection of the wisdom of not-self in the Buddha-Nature Treatise, for example. Language that had previously been used by essentialist non-Buddhist philosophers was now adopted, with new definitions, by Buddhists to promote orthodox teachings.

Prior to the period of these scriptures, Mahayana metaphysics had been dominated by teachings on emptiness in the form of Madhyamaka philosophy. The language used by this approach is primarily negative, and the Tathagatagarbha genre of sutras can be seen as an attempt to state orthodox Buddhist teachings of dependent origination using positive language instead, to prevent people from being turned away from Buddhism by a false impression of nihilism. In these sutras the perfection of the wisdom of not-self is stated to be the true self; the ultimate goal of the path is then characterized using a range of positive language that had been used in Indian philosophy previously by essentialist philosophers, but which was now transmuted into a new Buddhist vocabulary to describe a being who has successfully completed the Buddhist path.

Comparison with Other Philosophies

Baruch Spinoza, though he argued for the existence of a permanent reality, asserts that all phenomenal existence is transitory. In his opinion sorrow is conquered "by finding an object of knowledge which is not transient, not ephemeral, but is immutable, permanent, everlasting." Buddhism teaches that such a quest is bound to fail. David Hume, after a relentless analysis of the mind, concluded that consciousness consists of fleeting mental states. Hume's Bundle theory is a very similar concept to the Buddhist skandhas, though his denial of causation lead him to opposite conclusions in other areas. Arthur Schopenhauer's philosophy had some parallels in Buddhism.

Ludwig Wittgenstein's "word games" map closely to the warning of intellectual speculation as a red herring to understanding, such as the *Parable of the Poison Arrow*. Friedrich Nietzsche, although himself dismissive of Buddhism as yet another nihilism, developed his philosophy of accepting life-as-it-exists and self-cultivation as extremely similar to

Buddhism as better understood in the West. Heidegger's ideas on Being and nothingness have been held by some to be similar to Buddhism today.

An alternative approach to the comparison of Buddhist thought with Western philosophy is to use the concept of the Middle Way in Buddhism as a critical tool for the assessment of Western philosophies. In this way Western philosophies can be classified in Buddhist terms as eternalist or nihilist.

BUDDHISM AND SCIENCE

Buddhism and science have increasingly been discussed as compatible, and Buddhism has increasingly entered into the ongoing science and religion dialog. The case is made that the philosophic and psychological teachings within Buddhism share commonalities with modern scientific and philosophic thought.

For example, Buddhism encourages the impartial investigation of Nature (an activity referred to as *Dhamma-Vicaya* in the Pali Canon) - the principal object of study being oneself.

With a special focus on the nature of mind and its implications for the concept of reality, Buddhism offers explanations for metaphysical issues within psychology and studies of consciousness. Some popular conceptions of Buddhism connect it to discourse regarding evolution, quantum theory, and cosmology, though most scientists see a separation between the religious and metaphysical statements of Buddhism and the methodology of science.

Buddhism has been described as rational and non-dogmatic, and there is evidence that this has been the case from the earliest period of its history , though some have suggested this aspect is given greater emphasis in modern times and is in part a reinterpretation. Not all forms of Buddhism eschew dogmatism, remain neutral on the subject of the supernatural, or are open to scientific discoveries.

Buddhism is a varied tradition and aspects include fundamentalism, devotional traditions, supplication to local spirits, and various superstitions. Nevertheless, certain commonalities have been cited between scientific investigation and Buddhist thought. Tenzin Gyatso, the 14th Dalai Lama, in a speech at the meeting of the Society for Neuroscience, listed a "suspicion of absolutes" and a reliance on causality and empiricism as common philosophical principles shared between Buddhism and science.

Buddhism and the Scientific Method

More consistent with the scientific method than traditional, faith-based religion, the Kalama Sutta insists on a proper assessment of evidence, rather than a reliance on faith, hearsay or speculation:

"Yes, Kalamas, it is proper that you have doubt, that you have perplexity, for a doubt has arisen in a matter which is doubtful. Now, look you Kalamas, do not be led by reports, or tradition, or hearsay. Be not led by the authority of religious texts, not by mere logic or inference, nor by considering appearances, nor by the delight in speculative opinions, nor by seeming possibilities, nor by the idea: 'this is our teacher'. But, O Kalamas, when you know for yourselves that certain things are unwholesome (akusala), and wrong, and bad, then give them up...And when you know for yourselves that certain things are wholesome (kusala) and good, then accept them and follow them."

The general tenor of the sutta is also similar to "Nullius in verba" - often translated as "Take no-one's word for it", the motto of the Royal Society.

Buddhism and Psychology

During the 1970s, several experimental studies suggested that Buddhist meditation could produce insights into a wide range of psychological states. Interest in the use of meditation as a means of providing insight into mind-states has recently been revived, following the increased availability of such brain-scanning technologies as fMRI and SPECT.

Such studies are enthusiastically encouraged by the present Dalai Lama, Tenzin Gyatso who has long expressed an interest in exploring the connection between Buddhism and science, and regularly attends the Mind and Life Institute Conferences. However, some scientists are concerned by the popular coverage given to Buddhism's applications in neuroscience, believing that it will open up the field to mysticism.

In 1974 the Kagyu Buddhist teacher Chögyam Trungpa predicted that "Buddhism will come to the West as psychology". This view was apparently regarded with considerable scepticism at the time, but Buddhist concepts have indeed made most in-roads in the psychological sciences. Some modern scientific theories, such as Rogerian psychology, show strong parallels with Buddhist thought. Some of the most interesting work on the relationship between Buddhism and science is being done in the area of comparison between Yogacara theories regarding the store consciousness and modern evolutionary biology, especially DNA. This is because the Yogacara theory of karmic seeds works well in explaining the nature/nurture problem.

William James often drew on Buddhist cosmology when framing perceptual concepts, such as his term "stream of consciousness," which is the literal English translation of the Pali vinnana-sota. In his text, Varieties of Religious Experience, James also promoted for modern psychology the functional value of meditation. He wrote: "This is the psychology everybody will be studying twenty-five years from now."

Buddhism and Linguistics

The Buddhist ideas of emptiness, impermanence and dependent arising have much in common with ideas within the Cognitive Linguistics school of thought such as subjectivity, cognitive grammar ("meaning is conceptualization") and frame semantics.

Buddhism and Philosophy

Arthur Schopenhauer wrote of Buddhism in terms of western philosophy:

> We find the doctrine of metempsychosis, springing from the earliest and noblest ages of the human race, always spread abroad in the earth as the belief of the great majority of mankind, nay, really as the teachings of all religions with the exception of that of the Jews and the two which have preceded from it: in the most subtle form, however, and coming nearest to the truth, as has already been mentioned, in Buddhism.

It almost seems that, as the oldest languages are the most perfect so also are the oldest religions. If I were to take the results of my philosophy as a yardstick of the truth, I would concede to Buddhism the pre-eminence of all religions of the world.

Buddhism as "Science"

Buddhist teacher S.N. Goenka describes *Buddhadharma* as a 'pure science of mind and matter'. He claims Buddhism uses precise, analytical philosophical and psychological terminology and reasoning. Goenka's presentation describes Buddhism not so much belief in a body of unverifiable dogmas but an active, impartial, objective investigation of things as they are.

What is generally accepted in Buddhism is that effects arise from causation. From his very first discourse onwards, the Buddha explains the reality of things in terms of cause and effect. The existence of misery and suffering in any given individual is due to the presence of causes. One way to describe the Buddhist eightfold path — a personal path from misery to the bliss of nirvana -- is a turning towards the reality of things as they are right now and understanding reality directly. Though it is debated the degree to which these investigations are metaphysical or epistemological.

Notable Scientists on Buddhism

Einstein did comment that Buddhism "contains a much stronger element of [the cosmic religious feeling, by which] the religious geniuses of all ages have been distinguished."

Erwin Schroedinger (1887-1961), Austrian theoretical physicist, best known for his discovery of wave mechanics, which won him the Nobel Prize for Physics in 1933, wished to see: "Some blood transfusion from the East to the West" to save Western science from spiritual anemia."

David Bohm, who had a series of meetings with the Dalai Lama, was impressed with Eastern transcendental practices:

> editation would even bring us out of all [the difficulties] we've been talking about. . . omewhere we've got to leave thought behind, and come to this emptiness of manifest thought altogether. . . In other words, meditation actually transforms the mind. It transforms consciousness.

Niels Bohr, who developed the Bohr Model of the atom, said,

> For a parallel to the lesson of atomic theory...[we must turn] to those kinds of epistemological problems with which already thinkers like the Buddha and Lao Tzu have been confronted, when trying to harmonize our position as spectators and actors in the great drama of existence.

British mathematician, philosopher and Nobel Prize winner Alfred North Whitehead (co-author, with Bertrand

Russell, of Principia Mathematica, widely considered by specialists in the subject to be one of the most important and seminal works in mathematical logic and philosophy) declared, "Buddhism is the most colossal example in the history of applied metaphysics."

Bertrand Russell, another Nobel Prize winner, discovered a superior scientific method—one that reconciled the speculative and the rational while investigating the ultimate questions of life:

> Buddhism is a combination of both speculative and scientific philosophy. It advocates the scientific method and pursues that to a finality that may be called Rationalistic. In it are to be found answers to such questions of interest as: 'What is mind and matter? Of them, which is of greater importance? Is the universe moving towards a goal? What is man's position? Is there living that is noble?' It takes up where science cannot lead because of the limitations of the latter's instruments. Its conquests are those of the mind.

The American physicist J. Robert Oppenheimer made an analogy to Buddhism when describing the Heisenberg uncertainty principle thusly:

> If we ask, for instance, whether the position of the electron remains the same, we must say 'no;' if we ask whether the electron's position changes with time, we must say 'no;' if we ask whether the electron is at rest, we must say 'no;' if we ask whether it is in motion, we must say 'no.' The Buddha has given such answers when interrogated as to the conditions of man's self after his death; but they are not familiar answers for the tradition of seventeenth and eighteenth-century science.

●●

5
History of Buddhism

The History of Buddhism spans the 6th century BCE to the present, starting with the birth of Buddha Siddhartha Gautama in Lumbini, Nepal. This makes it one of the oldest religions practiced today. Starting in Nepal, the religion evolved as it spread through Central Asia, East Asia, and Southeast Asia. At one time or another it affected most of the Asian continent. The history of Buddhism is also characterized by the development of numerous movements and schisms among them the Theravâda, Mahâyâna and Vajrayâna traditions, with contrasting periods of expansion and retreat.

Life of the Buddha

According to the Buddhist tradition, the historical Buddha Siddhartha Gautama was born to the Shakya clan in Mithila Kingdom, at the beginning of the Magadha period (546–324 BCE). He is also known as the *Shakyamuni* (literally "The sage of the Shakya clan").

After an early life of luxury under the protection of his father, Œuddhodana, the ruler of Kapilavastu which later became incorporated into the state of Magadha, Siddhartha entered into contact with the realities of the world and concluded that life was inescapably bound up with suffering and sorrow. Siddhartha renounced his meaningless life of luxury to become an ascetic. He ultimately decided that asceticism couldn't end suffering, and instead chose a middle way, a path of moderation away from the extremes of self-indulgence and self-mortification.

Under a fig tree, now known as the Bodhi tree, he vowed never to leave the position until he found Truth. At the age of 35, he attained Enlightenment. He was then known as Gautama Buddha, or simply "The Buddha", which means "the enlightened one", or "the awakened one".

For the remaining 45 years of his life, he traveled the Gangetic Plain of central India (the region of the Ganges/ Ganga river and its tributaries), teaching his doctrine and discipline to a diverse range of people. By the time of his death, he had thousands of followers.

The Buddha's reluctance to name a successor or to formalise his doctrine led to the emergence of many movements during the next 400 years: first the schools of Nikaya Buddhism, of which only Theravada remains today, and then the formation of Mahayana and Vajrayana, pan-Buddhist sects based on the acceptance of new scriptures and the revision of older techniques.

Followers of Buddhism, called Buddhists in English, referred to themselves as *Sakyan*-s or *Sakyabhiksu* in ancient India. Buddhist scholar Donald S. Lopez asserts they also used the term *Bauddha,* although scholar Richard Cohen asserts that that term was used only by outsiders to describe Buddhists.

Early Buddhism

Early Buddhism remained centered around the Ganges valley, spreading gradually from its ancient heartland. The canonical sources record two Councils, where the monastic Sangha established the textual collections based on the Buddha's teachings, and settled certain disciplinary problems within the community.

1st Buddhist Council (5th c. BCE)

The first Buddhist council was held soon just after Buddha died, and presided by Venerable Mahakasyapa, one of the most senior disciples, at Rajagriha (today's Rajgir). The objective of the council was to record the Buddha's doctrinal teachings (sutra) and to codify the monastic rules (vinaya): Ananda, one of the Buddha's main disciples and his cousin, was called upon to recite the discourses of the Buddha, and Upali, another disciple, recited the rules of the vinaya. These became the basis of the Tripitaka, which is preserved in Pali, Chinese, and Tibetan, and has been the orthodox text of reference throughout the history of Buddhism.

2nd Buddhist Council (4th c. BCE)

The second Buddhist council was held at Vaisali following a dispute that had arisen in the Sangha over the relaxation by some monks of various points of discipline. Eventually it was decided to hold a second Council at which the original Vinaya texts that had been preserved at the first Council were cited to show that these relaxations went against the recorded teachings of the Buddha.

Ashokan Proselytism (c. 261 BCE)

The Mauryan Emperor Ashoka the Great (273–232 BCE) converted to Buddhism after his bloody conquest of the territory of Kalinga (modern Orissa) in eastern India during the Kalinga War. Regreting the horrors brought about by the conflict, the king decided to renounce violence, and propagate the faith by building stupas and pillars urging amongst other things respect of all animal life, and enjoining people to follow the Dharma. Perhaps the finest example of these is the Great Stupa in Sanchi, India (near Bhopal). It was constructed in the third century BCE and later enlarged. Its carved gates, called Tohans, are considered among the finest examples of Buddhist art in India. He also built roads, hospitals, resthouses, universities and irrigation systems around the country. He treated his subjects as equals regardless of their religion, politics or caste.

This period marks the first spread of Buddhism beyond India to other countries. According to the plates and pillars left by Ashoka (the Edicts of Ashoka), emissaries were sent to various countries in order to spread Buddhism, as far South as Sri Lanka, and as far West as the Greek kingdoms, in particular the neighboring Greco-Bactrian Kingdom, and possibly even farther to the Mediterranean.

3rd Buddhist Council (c.250 BCE)

King Ashoka convened the third Buddhist council around 250 BCE at Pataliputra (today's Patna). It was held by the monk Moggaliputtatissa. The objective of the council was to purify the Sangha, particularly from non-Buddhist ascetics who had been attracted by the royal patronage. Following the council, Buddhist missionaries were dispatched throughout the known world.

Hellenistic World

Some of the Edicts of Ashoka inscriptions describe the efforts made by Ashoka to propagate the Buddhist faith throughout the Hellenistic world, which at that time formed an uninterrupted continuum from the borders of India to Greece. The Edicts indicate a clear understanding of the political organization in Hellenistic territories: the names and location of the main Greek monarchs of the time are identified, and they are claimed as recipients of Buddhist proselytism: Antiochus II Theos of the Seleucid Kingdom (261–246 BCE), Ptolemy II Philadelphos of Egypt (285–247 BCE), Antigonus Gonatas of Macedonia (276–239 BCE), Magas of Cyrene (288–258 BCE) in Cyrenaica (modern Libya), and Alexander II of Epirus (272–255 BCE) in Epirus (modern Northwestern Greece).

> "The conquest by Dharma has been won here, on the borders, and even six hundred yojanas (5,400–9,600 km) away, where the Greek king Antiochos rules, beyond

> there where the four kings named Ptolemy, Antigonos, Magas and Alexander rule, likewise in the south among the Cholas, the Pandyas, and as far as Tamraparni (Sri Lanka)." (Edicts of Ashoka, 13th Rock Edict, S. Dhammika).

Furthermore, according to Pali sources, some of Ashoka's emissaries were Greek Buddhist monks, indicating close religious exchanges between the two cultures:

> "When the thera (elder) Moggaliputta, the illuminator of the religion of the Conqueror (Ashoka), had brought the (third) council to an end (...) he sent forth theras, one here and one there: (...) and to Aparantaka (the "Western countries" corresponding to Gujarat and Sindh) he sent the Greek (Yona) named Dhammarakkhita". (Mahavamsa XII).

The fact that some of Ashoka's emissaries were Greek agrees with Dr. Ranajit Pal's observation that Ashoka was the same as the Indo-Greek King Diodotus-I. Ashoka also issued Edicts in the Greek language as well as in Aramaic. One of them, found in Kandahar, advocates the adoption of "Piety" (using the Greek term Eusebeia for Dharma) to the Greek community:

> "Ten years (of reign) having been completed, King Piodasses (Ashoka) made known (the doctrine of) Piety to men; and from this moment he has made men more pious, and everything thrives throughout the whole world."
>
> (Trans. from the Greek original by G.P. Carratelli)

It is not clear how much these interactions may have been influential, but some authors have commented that some level of syncretism between Hellenist thought and Buddhism may have started in Hellenic lands at that time. They have pointed to the presence of Buddhist communities in the Hellenistic world around that period, in particular in Alexandria (mentioned by Clement of Alexandria), and to the pre-Christian monastic order of the Therapeutae (possibly a deformation of the Pali word "Theravada"), who may have "almost entirely drawn (its) inspiration from the teaching and practices of Buddhist asceticism"., and may even have been descendants of Ashoka's emissaries to the West. The philosopher Hegesias of Cyrene, from the city of Cyrene where Magas of Cyrene ruled, is sometimes thought to have been influenced by the teachings of Ashoka's Buddhist missionnaries.

Buddhist gravestones from the Ptolemaic period have also been found in Alexandria, decorated with depictions of the Dharma wheel (Tarn, "The Greeks in Bactria and India"). Commenting on the presence of Buddhists in Alexandria, some scholars have even pointed out that "It was later in this very place that some of the most active centers of Christianity were established" (Robert Linssen "Zen living").

In the 2nd century CE, the Christian dogmatist Clement of Alexandria recognized Bactrian Buddhists (Sramanas) and Indian Gymnosophists for their influence on Greek thought:

> "Thus philosophy, a thing of the highest utility, flourished in antiquity among the barbarians, shedding its light over the nations. And afterwards it came to Greece. First in its ranks were the prophets of the Egyptians; and the Chaldeans among the Assyrians; and the Druids among the Gauls; and the **Sramanas** among the Bactrians ("Óáñìáíáßïé ÂÜêôñùí"); and the philosophers of the Celts; and the Magi of the Persians, who foretold the Saviour's birth, and came into the land of Judaea guided by a star. The Indian gymnosophists are also in the number, and the other barbarian philosophers. And of these there are two classes, some of them called Sramanas, and others Brahmins." Clement

of Alexandria "The Stromata, or Miscellanies" Book I, Chapter XV

According to Donald A. Mackenzie, Saint Origen in the 2nd century CE mentioned Buddhists co-existing with Druids in pre-Christian Britain:

> "The island (Britain) has long been predisposed to it (Christianity) through the doctrines of the Druids and Buddhists, who had already inculcated the doctrine of the unity of the Godhead" - Origen, *Commentary on Ezekiel.*

Expansion to Sri Lanka and Burma

Sri Lanka was proselytized by Ashoka's son Mahinda and six companions during the 2nd century BCE. They converted the king Devanampiya Tissa and many of the nobility. This is when the Mahavihara monastery, a center of Sinhalese orthodoxy, was built. The Pali Canon was written down in Sri Lanka during the reign of king Vattagamani (29–17 BCE), and the Theravada tradition flourished there. Later some great commentators worked there, such as Buddhaghosa (4th–5th century) and Dhammapala (5th–6th century), and they systemised the traditional commentaries that had been handed down. Although Mahayana Buddhism gained some influence in Sri Lanka at that time, Theravada ultimately prevailed, and Sri Lanka turned out to be the last stronghold of Theravada Buddhism, from where it would expand again to South-East Asia from the 11th century.

In the areas east of the Indian subcontinent (modern Burma and Thailand), Indian culture strongly influenced the Mons. The Mons are said to have been converted to Buddhism from the 3rd century BCE under the proselytizing of the Indian Emperor Ashoka the Great, before the fission between Mahayana and Hinayana Buddhism. Early Mon Buddhist temples, such as Peikthano in central Burma, have been dated between the 1st and the 5th century CE.

The Buddhist art of the Mons was especially influenced by the Indian art of the Gupta and post-Gupta periods, and their mannerist style spread widely in South-East Asia following the expansion of the Mon kingdom between the 5th and 8th centuries. The Theravada faith expanded in the northern parts of Southeast Asia under Mon influence, until it was progressively displaced by Mahayana Buddhism from around the 6th century CE.

According to the *Ashokavadana* (2nd century CE), Ashoka sent a missionary to the north, through the Himalayas, to Khotan in the Tarim Basin, then the land of the Tocharians, speakers of an Indo-European language.

Rise of the Sunga (2nd–1st c. BCE)

The Sunga dynasty (185–73 BCE) was established in 185 BCE, about 50 years after Ashoka's death. After assassinating King Brhadrata (last of the Mauryan rulers), military commander-in-chief Pusyamitra Sunga took the throne. Buddhist religious scriptures such as the Ashokavadana allege that Pusyamitra (an orthodox Brahmin) was hostile towards Buddhists and persecuted the Buddhist faith. Buddhists wrote that he "destroyed monasteries and killed Monks" : 84,000 Buddhist stupas which had been built by Ashoka were "destroyed" (R. Thaper), and 100 gold coins were offered for the head of each Buddhist monk . In addition, Buddhist sources allege that a large number of Buddhist monasteries (viharas) were converted to Hindu temples, in such places as Nalanda, Bodhgaya, Sarnath, or Mathura.

Following Ashoka's sponsorship of Buddhism, it is possible that Buddhist institutions fell on harder times under the Sungas but no evidence of active persecution has been noted. Etienne Lamotte observes: *"To judge from the documents, Pushyamitra must be acquitted through lack of proof."* . Another eminent historian, Romila Thapar, points to archaeological evidence that "suggests the contrary [to the claim that

Pusyamitra was a fanatical anti-Buddhist]" and never actually destroyed 84000 stupas as claimed by Buddhist works. Thapar stresses that Buddhist accounts are probably hyperbolic renditions of Pusyamitra's attack of the Mauryas, and merely reflect the frustration of the Buddhist religious figures to the decline in the importance of their religion by the Sungas. .

During the period, Buddhist monks deserted the Ganges valley, following either the Northern road (Uttarapatha) or the Southern road (Daksinapatha). Conversely, Buddhist artistic creation stopped in the old Magadha area, to reposition itself either in Northwest area of Gandhara and Mathura, or in the Southeast around Amaravati. Some artistic activity also occurred in central India, as in Bharhut, to which the Sungas may or may not have contributed.

Greco-Buddhist Interaction (2nd c. BCE–1st c. CE)

In the areas west of the Indian subcontinent, neighboring Greek kingdoms had been in place in Bactria (today's northern Afghanistan) since the time of the conquests of Alexander the Great around 326 BCE: first the Seleucids from around 323 BCE, then the Greco-Bactrian kingdom from around 250 BCE.

The Greco-Bactrian king Demetrius I invaded India in 180 BCE as far as Pataliputra, establishing an Indo-Greek kingdom that was to last in various part of northern India until the end of the 1st century BCE. Buddhism flourished under the Indo-Greek kings, and it has been suggested that their invasion of India was intended to show their support for the Mauryan empire, and to protect the Buddhist faith from the alleged religious persecutions of the Sungas (185–73 BCE).

One of the most famous Indo-Greek kings is Menander (reigned c. 160–135 BCE). He apparently converted to Buddhism and is presented in the Mahayana tradition as one of the great benefactors of the faith, on a par with king Ashoka or the later Kushan king Kanishka. Menander's coins bear the mention "Saviour king" in Greek, and sometimes designs of the eight-spoked wheel. Direct cultural exchange is also suggested by the dialogue of the Milinda Panha between Menander and the monk Nagasena around 160 BCE. Upon his death, the honour of sharing his remains was claimed by the cities under his rule, and they were enshrined in stupas, in a parallel with the historic Buddha (Plutarch, Praec. reip. ger. 28, 6). Several of Menander's Indo-Greek successors inscribed the mention "Follower of the Dharma" in the Kharoshthi script on their coins, and depicted themselves or their divinities forming the *vitarka* mudra.

The interaction between Greek and Buddhist cultures may have had some influence on the evolution of Mahayana, as the faith developed its sophisticated philosophical approach and a man-god treatment of the Buddha somewhat reminiscent of Hellenic gods. It is also around that time that the first anthropomorphic representations of the Buddha are found, often in realistic Greco-Buddhist style: "One might regard the classical influence as including the general idea of representing a man-god in this purely human form, which was of course well familiar in the West, and it is very likely that the example of westerner's treatment of their gods was indeed an important factor in the innovation" (Boardman, "The Diffusion of Classical Art in Antiquity").

Central Asian Expansion

A Buddhist gold coin from India was found in northern Afghanistan at the archaeological site of Tillia Tepe, and dated to the 1st century CE. On the reverse, it depicts a lion with a nandipada, with the Kharoshthi legend "Sih vigatabhay" ("The lion who dispelled fear"). On the obverse, an almost naked man only wearing an Hellenistic chlamys and a petasus hat (an iconography similar to that of Hermes/ Mercury) rolls a Buddhist wheel. The legend in Kharoshthi reads "Dharmacakrapravata" ("The one who turned the Wheel of the Law"). It has been suggested that this may be an early representation of the Buddha.

Rise of Mahayana (1st c. BCE–2nd c. CE)

The rise of Mahayana Buddhism from the 1st century BCE was accompanied by complex political changes in northwestern India. The Indo-Greek kingdoms were gradually overwhelmed, and their culture assimilated by the Indo-Scythians, and then the Yuezhi, who founded the Kushan Empire from around 12 BCE.

The Kushans were supportive of Buddhism, and a fourth Buddhist council was convened by the Kushan emperor Kanishka, around 100 CE at Jalandhar or in Kashmir, and is usually associated with the formal rise of Mahayana Buddhism and its secession from Theravada Buddhism. Theravada Buddhism does not recognize the authenticity of this council, and it is sometimes called the "council of heretical monks".

The new form of Buddhism was characterized by an almost God-like treatment of the Buddha, by the idea that all beings have a Buddha-nature and should aspire to Buddhahood, and by a syncretism due to the various cultural influences within northwestern India and the Kushan Empire.

The Two Fourth Councils

The Fourth Council is said to have been convened in the reign of the Kushan emperor Kanishka, around 100 CE at Jalandhar or in Kashmir. Theravada Buddhism had its own Fourth Council in Sri Lanka about 200 years earlier in which the Pali Canon was written down *in toto* for the first time. Therefore there are two Fourth Councils: one in Sri Lanka (Theravada), and one in Kashmir (Sarvastivadin).

It is said that for the Fourth Council of Kashmir, Kanishka gathered 500 monks headed by Vasumitra, partly, it seems, to compile extensive commentaries on the Abhidharma, although it is possible that some editorial work was carried out upon the existing canon itself. Allegedly, during the council there were all together three hundred thousand verses and over nine million statements compiled, and it took twelve years to complete. The main fruit of this Council was the compilation of the vast commentary known as the Mahâ-Vibhâshâ ("Great Exegesis"), an extensive compendium and reference work on a portion of the Sarvâstivâdin Abhidharma.

Scholars believe that it was also around this time that a significant change was made in the language of the Sarvâstivâdin canon, by converting an earlier Prakrit version into Sanskrit. Although this change was probably effected without significant loss of integrity to the canon, this event was of particular significance since Sanskrit was the sacred language of Brahmanism in India, and was also being used by other thinkers (regardless of their specific religious or philosophical allegiance), thus enabling a far wider audience to gain access to Buddhist ideas and practices. For this reason, there was a growing tendency among Buddhist scholars in India thereafter to write their commentaries and treatises in Sanskrit. Many of the early schools, however, such as Theravada, never switched to Sanskrit, partly because Buddha explicitly forbade translation of his discourses into Sanskrit because it was an elitist religious language (like Latin was in Europe in earlier times). He wanted his monks to use a local language instead; a language which could be understood by all. Over time however, the language of the Theravadin scriptures (Pali) became a scholarly or elitist language as well.

Mahayana Expansion (1st c. CE–10th c. CE)

From that point on, and in the space of a few centuries, Mahayana was to flourish and spread in the East from India to South-East Asia, and towards the north to Central Asia, China, Korea, and finally to Japan in 538 CE.

India

After the end of the Kushans, Buddhism flourished in India during the dynasty of the Guptas (4th-6th century). Mahayana centers of learning were established, especially at Nalanda in north-eastern India, which was to become the largest and most influential Buddhist university for many centuries, with famous teachers such as Nagarjuna. The Gupta style of Buddhist art became very influential from South-East Asia to China as the faith was spreading there.

Indian Buddhism had weakened in the 6th century following the White Hun invasions and Mihirkulas persecution.

Xuanzang reports in his travels across India during the 7th century of Buddhism being popular in Andhra, Dhanyakataka, and Dravida which today roughly correspond to the modern day Indian states of Andhra Pradesh and Tamil Nadu. While reporting many deserted stupas in the area around modern day Nepal and the persecution of buddhists by Ssanka in the Kingdom of Gouda. (In modern day West Bengal.) Xuanzang compliments the patronage of Harshavardana during the same period. After Harshavardanas kingdom, the rise of many small kingdoms that lead to the rise of the Rajputs across the gangetic plains and marked the end of Buddhist ruling clans along with a sharp decline in royal patronage until a revival under the Pala Empire in the Bengal region. Here Mahayana Buddhism flourished and spread to Bhutan and Sikkim between the 8th and the 12th century before the Palas collapsed under the assault of the Hindu Sena dynasty. The Palas created many temples and a distinctive school of Buddhist art. Xuanzang noted in his travels that in various regions Buddhism was giving way to Jainism and Hinduism. By the 10th century Buddhism had experienced a sharp decline beyond the Pala realms in Bengal under a resurgent Hinduism and the incorporation in

Vaishnavite Hinduism of Buddha as the 9th incarnation of Vishnu.

A milestone in the decline of Indian Buddhism in the North occurred in 1193 when Turkic Islamic raiders under Muhammad Khilji burnt Nalanda. By the end of the 12th century, following the Islamic conquest of the Buddhist strongholds in Bihar, and the loss of political support coupled with social and caste pressures, the practice of Buddhism retreated to the Himalayan foothills in the North and Sri Lanka in the south. Additionally, the influence of Buddhism also waned due to Hinduism's revival movements such as Advaita, the rise of the bhakti movement and the missionary work of Sufis.

Central and Northern Asia

Central Asia

Central Asia had been influenced by Buddhism probably almost since the time of the Buddha. According to a legend preserved in Pali, the language of the Theravada canon, two merchant brothers from Bactria, named Tapassu and Bhallika, visited the Buddha and became his disciples. They then returned to Bactria and built temples to the Buddha (Foltz).

Central Asia long played the role of a meeting place between China, India and Persia. During the 2nd century BCE, the expansion of the Former Han to the west brought them into contact with the Hellenistic civilizations of Asia, especially the Greco-Bactrian Kingdoms. Thereafter, the expansion of Buddhism to the north led to the formation of Buddhist communities and even Buddhist kingdoms in the oases of Central Asia. Some Silk Road cities consisted almost entirely of Buddhist stupas and monasteries, and it seems that one of their main objectives was to welcome and service travelers between east and west.

The Theravada traditions first spread among the Turkic tribes before combining with the Mahayana forms during the

2nd and 3rd centuries BCE to cover modern-day Pakistan, Kashmir, Afghanistan, eastern and coastal Iran, Uzbekistan, Turkmenistan and Tajikistan. These were the ancient states of Gandhara, Bactria, Parthia and Sogdia from where it spread to China. Among the first of these Turkic tribes to adopt Buddhism was the Turki-Shahi who adopted Buddhism as early as the 3rd century BCE. It was not, however, the exclusive faith of this region. There were also Zoroastrians, Hindus, Nestorian Christians, Jews, Manichaeans, and followers of shamanism, Tengrism, and other indigenous, nonorganized systems of belief.

Various Nikaya schools persisted in Central Asia and China until around the 7th century CE. Mahayana started to become dominant during the period, but since the faith had not developed a Nikaya approach, Sarvastivadin and Dharmaguptakas remained the Vinayas of choice in Central Asian monasteries.

Various Buddhism kingdoms rose and prospered in both the Central Asian region and downwards into the Indian sub-continent such as Kushan Empire prior to the White Hun invasion in the 5th century where under the King Mihirkula they were heavily persecuted.

Buddhism in Central Asia started to decline with the expansion of Islam and the destruction of many stupas in war from the 7th century. The Muslims accorded them the status of dhimmis as "people of the Book", such as Christianity or Judaism and Al-Biruni wrote of Buddha as prophet "burxan".

Buddhism saw a surge during the reign of Mongols following the invasion of Genghis Khan and the establishment of the Il Khanate and the Chagatai Khanate who brought their Buddhist influence with them during the 13th century, however within a 100 years the Mongols who remained in that region would convert to Islam and spread Islam across all the regions across central Asia. Only the eastern Mongols and the Mongols of the Yuan dynasty would keep Vajrayana Buddhism.

Parthia

Buddhism expanded westward into Arsacid Parthia, at least to the area of Merv, in ancient Margiana, today's territory of Turkmenistan. Soviet archeological teams have excavated in Giaur Kala, near Merv, a Buddhist chapel, a gigantic Buddha statue, as well as a monastery.

Parthians were directly involved in the propagation of Buddhism: An Shigao (c. 148 CE), a Parthian prince, went to China, and is the first known translator of Buddhist scriptures into Chinese.

Tarim Basin

The eastern part of central Asia (Chinese Turkestan, Tarim Basin, Xinjiang) has revealed extremely rich Buddhist works of art (wall paintings and reliefs in numerous caves, portable paintings on canvas, sculpture, ritual objects), displaying multiple influences from Indian and Hellenistic cultures. Serindian art is highly reminiscent of the Gandharan style, and scriptures in the Gandhari script Kharosthi have been found.

Central Asians seem to have played a key role in the transmission of Buddhism to the East. The first translators of Buddhists scriptures into Chinese were either Parthian (Ch: Anxi) like An Shigao (c. 148 CE) or An Hsuan, Kushan of Yuezhi ethnicity like Lokaksema (c. 178 CE), Zhi Qian and Zhi Yao, or Sogdians (Ch: SuTe/Ÿ|yr) like Kang Sengkai. Thirty-seven early translators of Buddhist texts are known, and the majority of them have been identified as Central Asians.

Central Asian and East Asian Buddhist monks appear to have maintained strong exchanges until around the 10th century, as shown by frescoes from the Tarim Basin.

These influences were rapidly absorbed however by the vigorous Chinese culture, and a strongly Chinese particularism develops from that point.

China

Buddhism probably arrived in China around the 1st century CE from Central Asia, and through to the 8th century it became an extremely active center of Buddhism.

The year 67 CE saw Buddhism's official introduction to China with the coming of the two monks Moton and Chufarlan. In 68 CE, under imperial patronage, they established the White Horse Temple, which still exists today, close to the imperial capital at Luoyang. By the end of the second century, a prosperous community had been settled at Pengcheng (modern Xuzhou, Jiangsu).

The first known Mahayana scriptural texts are translations made into Chinese by the Kushan monk Lokaksema in Luoyang, between 178 and 189 CE. Some of the earliest known Buddhist artifacts found in China are small statues on "money trees", dated circa 200 CE, in typical Gandharan style (drawing): "That the imported images accompanying the newly arrived doctrine came from Gandhara is strongly suggested by such early Gandhara characteristics on this "money tree" Buddha as the high ushnisha, vertical arrangement of the hair, moustache, symmetrically looped robe and parallel incisions for the folds of the arms." ("Crossroads of Asia" p209)

Buddhism flourished during the beginning of the Tang Dynasty (618–907). The dynasty was initially characterized by a strong openness to foreign influences, and renewed exchanges with Indian culture due to the numerous travels of Chinese Buddhist monks to India from the 4th to the 11th century. The Tang capital of Chang'an (today's Xi'an) became an important center for Buddhist thought. From there

Buddhism spread to Korea, and Japanese embassies of Kentoshi helped gain footholds in Japan.

However foreign influences came to be negatively perceived towards the end of the Tang Dynasty. In the year 845, the Tang emperor Wuzong outlawed all "foreign" religions (including Christian Nestorianism, Zoroastrianism, and Buddhism) in order to support the indigenous Taoism. Throughout his territory, he confiscated Buddhist possessions, destroyed monasteries and temples, and executed Buddhist monks, ending Buddhism's cultural and intellectual dominance.

However, about a hundred years after the Great Anti-Buddhist Persecution, Buddhism revived during the Song Dynasty (1127–1279).

Pure Land and Chan Buddhism, however, continued to prosper for some centuries, the latter giving rise to Japanese Zen. In China, Chan flourished particularly under the Song dynasty (1127–1279), when its monasteries were great centers of culture and learning.

Today, China boasts one of the richest collections of Buddhist arts and heritages in the world. UNESCO World Heritage Sites such as the Mogao Caves near Dunhuang in Gansu province, the Longmen Grottoes near Luoyang in Henan province, the Yungang Grottoes near Datong in Shanxi province, and the Dazu Rock Carvings near Chongqing are among the most important and renowned Buddhist sculptural sites. The Leshan Giant Buddha, carved out of a hillside in the 8th century during Tang Dynasty and looking down on the confluence of three rivers, is still the largest stone Buddha statue in the world.

Korea

Buddhism was introduced around 372 CE, when Chinese ambassadors visited the Korean kingdom of Goguryeo, bringing scriptures and images. Buddhism prospered in Korea, and in particular Seon (Zen) Buddhism from the 7th century onward. However, with the beginning of the Confucean Yi Dynasty of the Joseon period in 1392, Buddhism was strongly discriminated against until it was almost completely eradicated, except for a remaining Seon movement.

Japan

The Buddhism of Japan was introduced from Three Kingdoms of Korea in the sixth century . The Chinese priest Ganjin offered the system of Vinaya to the Buddhism of Japan in 754. As a result, the Buddhism of Japan has developed rapidly. Saichô and Kûkai succeeded to a legitimate Buddhism from China in nine century.

Being geographically at the end of the Silk Road, Japan was able to preserve many aspects of Buddhism at the very time it was disappearing in India, and being suppressed in Central Asia and China.

From 710 CE numerous temples and monasteries were built in the capital city of Nara, such as the five-story pagoda and Golden Hall of the Hôryû-ji, or the Kôfuku-ji temple. Countless paintings and sculptures were made, often under governmental sponsorship. The creation of Japanese Buddhist art was especially rich between the 8th and 13th century during the periods of Nara, Heian, and Kamakura.

From the 12th and 13th, a further development was Zen art, following the introduction of the faith by Dogen and Eisai upon their return from China. Zen art is mainly characterized by original paintings (such as sumi-e and the Enso) and poetry (especially haikus), striving to express the true essence of the world through impressionistic and unadorned "non-dualistic" representations. The search for enlightenment "in the moment" also led to the development of other important derivative arts such as the Chanoyu tea ceremony or the Ikebana art of flower arrangement. This evolution went as far as considering almost any human activity as an art with a strong spiritual and aesthetic content, first and foremost in those activities related to combat techniques (martial arts).

Buddhism remains very active in Japan to this day. Around 80,000 Buddhist temples are preserved and regularly restored.

Southeast Asia

During the 1st century CE, the trade on the overland Silk Road tended to be restricted by the rise in the Middle-East of the Parthian empire, an unvanquished enemy of Rome, just as Romans were becoming extremely wealthy and their demand for Asian luxury was rising. This demand revived the sea connections between the Mediterranean and China, with India as the intermediary of choice. From that time, through trade connection, commercial settlements, and even political interventions, India started to strongly influence Southeast Asian countries. Trade routes linked India with southern Burma, central and southern Siam, lower Cambodia and southern Vietnam, and numerous urbanized coastal settlements were established there.

For more than a thousand years, Indian influence was therefore the major factor that brought a certain level of cultural unity to the various countries of the region. The Pali and Sanskrit languages and the Indian script, together with Theravada and Mahayana Buddhism, Brahmanism, and Hinduism, were transmitted from direct contact and through sacred texts and Indian literature such as the Ramayana and the Mahabharata.

From the 5th to the 13th century, South-East Asia had very powerful empires and became extremely active in Buddhist architectural and artistic creation. The main Buddhist influence now came directly by sea from the Indian subcontinent, so that these empires essentially followed the Mahayana faith. The Sri Vijaya Empire to the south and the Khmer Empire to the north competed for influence, and their art expressed the rich Mahayana pantheon of the Bodhisattvas.

Srivijayan Empire (7th–13th century)

Srivijaya, a maritime empire centered at Palembang on the island of Sumatra in Indonesia, adopted Mahayana and Vajrayana Buddhism under a line of rulers named the Sailendras. Yijing described Palembang as a great centre of Buddhist learning where the emperor supported over a thousand monks at his court. Atisha studied there before travelling to Tibet as a missionary.

Sriviijaya spread Buddhist art during its expansion in Southeast Asia. Numerous statues of Bodhisattvas from this period are characterized by a very strong refinement and technical sophistication, and are found throughout the region. Extremely rich architectural remains are visible at the temple of Borobudur (the largest Buddhist structure in the world, built from around 780 CE), in Java, which has 505 images of the seated Buddha. Srivijaya declined due to conflicts with the Chola rulers of India, before being destabilized by the Islamic expansion from the 13th century.

Khmer Empire (9th–13th century)

Later, from the 9th to the 13th century, the Mahayana Buddhist and Hindu Khmer Empire dominated much of the South-East Asian peninsula. Under the Khmer, more than 900 temples were built in Cambodia and in neighboring Thailand. Angkor was at the center of this development, with a temple complex and urban organization able to support around one million urban dwellers. One of the greatest Khmer kings, Jayavarman VII (1181–1219), built large Mahayana Buddhist structures at Bayon and Angkor Thom.

Vietnam

Following the destruction of Buddhism in mainland India during the 11th century, Mahayana Buddhism declined in Southeast Asia, to be replaced by the introduction of Theravada Buddhism from Sri Lanka.

Emergence of the Vajrayana (5th Century)

Vajrayâna Buddhism, also called Tantric Buddhism, first emerged in eastern India between the 5th and 7th centuries CE. It is sometimes considered a sub-school of Mahayana and sometimes a third major "vehicle" (*Yana*) of Buddhism in its own right. The Vajrayana is an extension of Mahayana Buddhism in that it does not offer new philosophical perspectives, but rather introduces additional techniques (upaya, or 'skilful means'), including the use of visualizations and other yogic practices. Many of the practices of Tantric Buddhism are common with Hindu tantricism (the usage of mantras, yoga, or the burning of sacrificial offerings).

Early Vajrayana practitioners were forest-dwelling mahasiddhas who lived on the margins of society, but by the 9th century Vajrayana had won acceptance at major Mahayana monastic universities such as Nalanda and Vikramashila. Along with much of the rest of Indian Buddhism, the Vajrayana was eclipsed in the wake of the late 12th century Muslim invasions. It has persisted in Tibet, where it was wholly transplanted from the 7th to 12th centuries and became the dominant form of Buddhism to the present day, and on a limited basis in Japan as well where it evolved into Shingon Buddhism.

Theravada Renaissance (11th Century CE—)

From the 11th century, the destruction of Buddhism in the Indian mainland by Islamic invasions led to the decline of the Mahayana faith in South-East Asia. Continental routes through the Indian subcontinent being compromised, direct sea routes between the Middle-East through Sri Lanka and to China developed, leading to the adoption of the Theravada Buddhism of the Pali canon, introduced to the region around the 11th century CE from Sri Lanka.

King Anawrahta (1044–1077); the historical founder of the Burmese empire, unified the country and adopted the Theravada Buddhist faith. This initiated the creation of thousands of Buddhist temples at Pagan, the capital, between the 11th and 13th century. Around 2,000 of them are still standing. The power of the Burmese waned with the rise of the Thai, and with the seizure of the capital Pagan by the Mongols in 1287, but Theravada Buddhism remained the main Burmese faith to this day.

The Theravada faith was also adopted by the newly founded ethnic Thai kingdom of Sukhothai around 1260. Theravada Buddhism was further reinforced during the Ayutthaya period (14th–18th century), becoming an integral part of the Thai society.

In the continental areas, Theravada Buddhism continued to expand into Laos and Cambodia in the 13th century. However, from the 14th century, on the coastal fringes and in the islands of South-East Asia, the influence of Islam proved stronger, expanding into Malaysia, Indonesia, and most of the islands as far as the southern Philippines.

However, since 1966 with Soeharto's rise of power in the aftermath of the bloody events after the so called "September 30th, 1965 murders", allegedly executed by the Communists Party, there has been a remarkable renaissance of Buddhism in Indonesia. This is partly due to the Soeharto's New Order's requirements for the people of Indonesia to adopt one of the five official religions: Islam, Protestantism, Catholicism, Hinduism or Buddhism. Today it is estimated there are some 10 millions Buddhists in Indonesia. A large part of them are people of Chinese ancestry.

Expansion of Buddhism to the West

After the Classical encounters between Buddhism and the West recorded in Greco-Buddhist art, information and legends about Buddhism seem to have reached the West sporadically. An account of Buddha's life was translated in to Greek by John of Damascus, and widely circulated to Christians as the story of Barlaam and Josaphat. By the 1300s this story of Josaphat had become so popular that he was made a Catholic saint.

The next direct encounter between Europeans and Buddhism happened in Medieval times when the Franciscan friar William of Rubruck was sent on an embassy to the Mongol court of Mongke by the French king Saint Louis in 1253. The contact happened in Cailac (today's Qayaliq in Kazakhstan), and William originally thought they were wayward Christians (Foltz, "Religions of the Silk Road").

In the period after Hulagu, the Mongol Ilkhans increasingly adopted Buddhism. Numerous Buddhist temples dotted the landscape of Persia and Iraq, none of which survived the 14th century. The Buddhist element of the Il-Khanate died with Arghun.

The Kalmyk Khanate was founded in the 17th century with Tibetan Buddhism as its main religion, following the earlier migration of the Oirats from Dzungaria through Central Asia to the steppe around the mouth of the Volga River. During the course of the 18th century, they were absorbed by the Russian Empire. At the end of the Napoleonic wars, Kalmyk cavalry units in Russian service entered Paris. Kalmykia is remarkable for being the only state in Europe where the dominant religion is Buddhism.

Interest in Buddhism increased during the colonial era, when Western powers were in a position to witness the faith and its artistic manifestations in detail. The opening of Japan in 1853 created a considerable interest in the arts and culture of Japan, and provided access to one of the most thriving Buddhist cultures in the world. Buddhism started to enjoy a strong interest from the general population in the West following the turbulence of the 20th century.

Buddhism has been displaying a strong power of attraction, due to its tolerance, its lack of deist authority and determinism, and its focus on understanding reality through self inquiry.

●●

6
Gautama Buddha

Siddhârtha Gautama (Pali: Siddhattha Gotama) was a spiritual teacher in the north eastern region of the Indian subcontinent who founded Buddhism. He is generally seen by Buddhists as the Supreme *Buddha* (Sammâsambuddha) of our age. The time of his birth and death are uncertain: most early 20th-century historians dated his lifetime as c. 563 BCE to 483 BCE; more recently, however, at a specialist symposium on this question, the majority of those scholars who presented definite opinions gave dates within 20 years either side of 400 BCE for the Buddha's death, with others supporting earlier or later dates.

Gautama, also known as *Úâkyamuni* or *Shakyamuni* ("sage of the Shakyas"), is the key figure in Buddhism, and accounts of his life, discourses, and monastic rules are believed by Buddhists to have been summarized after his death and memorized by his followers. Various collections of teachings attributed to Gautama were passed down by oral tradition, and first committed to writing about 400 years later. Early Western scholarship tended to accept the biography of the Buddha presented in the Buddhist scriptures as largely historical, but currently "scholars are increasingly reluctant to make unqualified claims about the historical facts of the Buddha's life and teachings."

Life

The primary sources of information regarding Siddhârtha Gautama's life are the Buddhist texts. The Buddha and his monks spent four months each year discussing and rehearsing his teachings, and after his death his monks set about preserving them. A council was held shortly after his death, and another was held a century later. At these councils the monks attempted to establish and authenticate the extant accounts of the life and teachings of the Buddha following systematic rules. They divided the teachings into distinct but overlapping bodies of material, and assigned specific monks to preserve each one. From then on, the teachings were transmitted orally. From internal evidence it seems clear that the oldest texts crystallized into their current form by the time of the second council or shortly after it. The scriptures were not written down until three or four hundred years after the Buddha's death. By this point, the monks had added or altered some material themselves, in particular magnifying the figure of the Buddha.

The ancient Indians were generally not concerned with chronologies, being far more focused on philosophy. The Buddhist texts reflect this tendency, providing a clearer picture of what Shakyamuni may have taught than of the dates of the events in his life. These texts contain descriptions of the culture and daily life of ancient India which can be corroborated from the Jain scriptures, and make the Buddha's time the earliest period in Indian history for which substantial accounts exist. According to Michael Carrithers, there are good reasons to doubt the traditional account, though the outline of "birth, maturity, renunciation, search, awakening and liberation, teaching, death" must be true.

Conception and Birth

Siddhartha was born in Lumbini and raised in the small kingdom or principality of Kapilvastu, both of which are in modern day Nepal. At the time of the Buddha's birth, the area was at or beyond the boundary of Vedic civilization, the dominant culture of northern India at the time; it is even possible that his mother tongue was not an Indo-Aryan language. At the time, a multitude of small city-states existed in ancient India, called janapadas. Republics and chiefdoms with diffused political power and limited social stratification, were not uncommon amongst them, and were referred to as gana-sanghas. The Buddha's community does not seem to have had a caste system, and their society was not structured according to Brahminical theory. It was not a monarchy, and seems to have been structured either as an oligarchy, or as a form of republic. The more egalitarian gana-sangha form of government, as a political alternative to the strongly hierarchical kingdoms, may have influenced the development of the Shramana type Jain and Buddhist sanghas, where monarchies tended toward Vedic Brahmanism.

According to the traditional biography, his father was King Suddhodana, the leader of Shakya clan, whose capital was Kapilavastu, and who were later annexed by the growing Kingdom of Kosala during the Buddha's lifetime; Gautama was the family name. His mother, Queen Maha Maya (Mâyâdevî) and Suddhodana's wife, was a Koliyan princess. On the night Siddhartha was conceived, Queen Maya dreamt that a white elephant with six white tusks entered her right side, and ten lunar months later Siddhartha was born. As was the Shakya tradition, when his mother Queen Maya became pregnant, she left Kapilvastu for her father's kingdom to give birth. However, she gave birth on the way, at Lumbini, in a garden beneath a sal tree.

The day of the Buddha's birth is widely celebrated in Theravada countries as Vesak. Various sources hold that the Buddha's mother died at his birth, a few days or seven days later. The infant was given the name Siddhartha (Pâli: Siddhatta), meaning "he who achieves his aim". During the birth celebrations, the hermit seer Asita journeyed from his mountain abode and announced that the child would either become a great king (chakravartin) or a great holy man. This occurred after Siddhartha placed his feet in Asita's hair and Asita examined the birthmarks. Suddhodana held a naming ceremony on the fifth day, and invited eight brahmin scholars to read the future. All gave a dual prediction that the baby would either become a great king or a great holy man. Kaundinya (Pali: Kondanna), the youngest, and later to be the first arahant, was the only one who unequivocally predicted that Siddhartha would become a Buddha.

While later tradition and legend characterized Suddhodana as a hereditary monarch, the descendant of the Solar Dynasty of Ikcvâku, many scholars believe that Úuddhodana was the elected chief of a tribal confederacy.

Early Life and Marriage

Siddhartha, destined to a luxurious life as a prince, had three palaces (for seasonal occupation) especially built for him. His father, King Suddhodana, wishing for Siddhartha to be a great king, shielded his son from religious teachings or knowledge of human suffering. Siddhartha was brought up by his mother's younger sister, Maha Pajapati.

As the boy reached the age of 16, his father arranged his marriage to Yaúodharâ (Pâli: Yasodharâ), a cousin of the same age. According to the traditional account, in time, she gave birth to a son, Rahula. Siddhartha spent 29 years as a Prince in Kapilavastu. Although his father ensured that Siddhartha was provided with everything he could want or need, Siddhartha felt that material wealth was not the ultimate goal of life.

Departure and Ascetic Life

At the age of 29, Siddhartha left his palace in order to meet his subjects. Despite his father's effort to remove the sick, aged and suffering from the public view, Siddhartha was said to have seen an old man. Disturbed by this, when told that all people would eventually grow old by his charioteer Channa, the prince went on further trips where he encountered, variously, a diseased man, a decaying corpse, and an ascetic. Deeply depressed by these sights, he sought to overcome old age, illness, and death by living the life of an ascetic.

Siddhartha escaped his palace, accompanied by Channa aboard his horse Kanthaka, leaving behind this royal life to become a mendicant. It is said that, "the horse's hooves were muffled by the gods" to prevent guards from knowing the Bodhisatta's departure. This event is traditionally called "The Great Departure". Siddhartha initially went to Rajagaha and began his ascetic life by begging for alms in the street. Having been recognised by the men of King Bimbisara, Bimbisara offered him the throne after hearing of Siddhartha's quest. Siddhartha rejected the offer, but promised to visit his kingdom of Magadha first, upon attaining enlightenment.

Siddhartha left Rajagaha and practised under two hermit teachers. After mastering the teachings of Alara Kalama, Siddhartha was asked by Kalama to succeed him, but moved on after being unsatisfied with his practices. He then became a student of Udaka Ramaputta (Skr. Udraka Râmaputra), but although he achieved high levels of meditative consciousness and was asked to succeed Ramaputta, he was still not satisfied with his path, and moved on.

Siddhartha and a group of five companions led by Kaundinya then set out to take their austerities even further. They tried to find enlightenment through near total deprivation of worldly goods, including food, practising self-mortification. After nearly starving himself to death by restricting his food intake to around a leaf or nut per day, he collapsed in a river while bathing and almost drowned. Siddhartha began to reconsider his path. Then, he remembered a moment in childhood in which he had been watching his father start the season's plowing, and he had fallen into a naturally concentrated and focused state that was blissful and refreshing, the jhana.

Enlightenment

After asceticism and concentrating on meditation and Anapana-sati (awareness of breathing in and out), Siddhartha is said to have discovered what Buddhists call the Middle Way—a path of moderation away from the extremes of self-indulgence and self-mortification. He accepted a little milk and rice pudding from a village girl named Sujata, who wrongly believed him to be the spirit that had granted her a wish, such was his emaciated appearance. Then, sitting under a pipal tree, now known as the Bodhi tree in Bodh Gaya, India, he vowed never to arise until he had found the Truth. Kaundinya and the other four companions, believing that he had abandoned his search and become undisciplined, left. After 49 days meditating, at the age of 35, he attained Enlightenment; according to some traditions, this occurred approximately in the fifth lunar month, and according to others in the twelfth. Gautama, from then on, was known as the *Buddha* or "Awakened One." Buddha is also sometimes translated as "The Enlightened One." Often, he is referred to in Buddhism as Shakyamuni Buddha or "The Awakened One of the Shakya Clan."

At this point, he is believed to have realized complete awakening and insight into the nature and cause of human suffering which was ignorance, along with steps necessary to eliminate it. This was then categorized into 'Four Noble Truths'; the state of supreme liberation—possible for any being—was called Nirvana. He then allegedly came to possess the Nine Characteristics, which are said to belong to every Buddha.

According to one of the stories in the *Âyâcana Sutta* (Samyutta Nikaya VI.1), a scripture found in the Pâli and other canons, immediately after his Enlightenment, the Buddha was wondering whether or not he should teach the *Dharma* to human beings. He was concerned that, as human beings were overpowered by greed, hatred and delusion, they would not be able to see the true *dharma*, which was subtle, deep and hard to understand. However, Brahmâ Sahampati, interceded and asked that he teach the *dharma* to the world, as "there will be those who will understand the *Dharma*". With his great compassion to all beings in the universe, the Buddha agreed to become a teacher.

Formation of the Sangha

After becoming enlightened, two merchants whom the Buddha met, named Tapussa and Bhallika became the first lay disciples. They are given some hairs from the Buddha's head, which are believed to now be enshrined in the Shwe Dagon Temple in Rangoon, Burma. The Buddha intended to visit Asita, and his former teachers, Alara Kalama and Uddaka Ramaputta to explain his findings, but they had already died.

The Buddha thus journeyed to Deer Park near VrGas+ (Benares) in northern India, he set in motion the Wheel of Dharma by delivering his first sermon to the group of five companions with whom he had previously sought enlightenment. They, together with the Buddha, formed the first saEgha, the company of Buddhist monks, and hence, the first formation of Triple Gem (Buddha, Dharma and Sangha) was completed, with Kaundinya becoming the first stream-enterer.

All five soon become arahants, and with the conversion of Yasa and fifty four of his friends, the number of arahants swelled to 60 within the first two months. The conversion of the three Kassapa brothers and their 200, 300 and 500 disciples swelled the sangha over 1000, and they were dispatched to explain the dharma to the populace.

It is unknown what language the Buddha spoke, and no conclusive documentation has been made at this point. However, some modern scholars, primarily philologists, believe it is most likely that the Buddha spoke a vulgate then current in eastern India, Mâgadhî Prakrit.

Travels and Teaching

For the remaining 45 years of his life, the Buddha is said to have traveled in the Gangetic Plain, in what is now Uttar Pradesh, Bihar and southern Nepal, teaching his doctrine and discipline to an extremely diverse range of people— from nobles to outcaste street sweepers, mass murderers such as Angulimala and cannibals such as Alavaka.

This extended to many adherents of rival philosophies and religions. The Buddha founded the community of Buddhist monks and nuns (the *Sangha*) to continue the dispensation after his *Parinirvâna* (Pâli: Parinibbâna) or "complete Nirvâna", and made thousands of converts.

His religion was open to all races and classes and had no caste structure. He was also subject to attack from opposition religious groups, including attempted murders and framings.

The sangha travelled from place to place in India, expounding the dharma. This occurred throughout the year, except during the four months of the vassana rainy season. Due to the heavy amount of flooding, travelling was difficult, and ascetics of all religions in that time did not travel, since it was more difficult to do so without stepping on submerged animal life, unwittingly killing them. During this period, the sangha would retreat to a monastery, public park or a forest and people would come to them.

The first vassana was spent at Varanasi when the sangha was first formed. After this, he travelled to Rajagaha, the capital of Magadha to visit King Bimbisara, in accordance with his promise after enlightenment. It was during this visit that Sariputta and Mahamoggallana were converted by Assaji, one of the first five disciples; they were to become the Buddha's two foremost disciples. The Buddha then spent the next three seasons at Veluvana Bamboo Grove monastery in Rajagaha, the capital of Magadha. The monastery, which was of a moderate distance from the city centre was donated by Bimbisara.

Upon hearing of the enlightenment, Suddhodana dispatched royal delegations to ask the Buddha to return to Kapilavastu. Nine delegations were sent in all, but the delegates joined the sangha and became arahants. Neglecting worldly matters, they did not convey their message. The tenth delegation, led by Kaludayi, a childhood friend, resulted in the message being successfully conveyed as well as becoming an arahant. Since it was not the vassana, the Buddha agreed, and two years after his enlightenment, took a two month journey to Kapilavastu by foot, preaching the dharma along the way. Upon his return, the royal palace had prepared the midday meal, but since no specific invitation had come, the sangha went for an alms round in Kapilavastu. Hearing this, Suddhodana hastened to approach the Buddha, stating "Ours is the warrior lineage of Mahamassata, and not a single warrior has gone seeking alms", to which the Buddha replied

That is not the custom of your royal lineage. But it is the custom of my Buddha lineage. Several thousands of Buddhas have gone by seeking alms.

Suddhodana invited the sangha back to the royal palace for the meal, followed by a dharma talk, after which he became a sotapanna. During the visit, many members of the royal family joined the sangha. His cousins Ananda and Anuruddha were to become two of his five chief disciples. His son Rahula also joined the sangha at the age of seven, and was one of the ten chief disciples. His half-brother Nanda also joined the sangha and became an arahant. Another cousin Devadatta also became a monk although he later became an enemy and tried to kill the Buddha on multiple occasions.

Of his disciples, Sariputta, Mahamoggallana, Mahakasyapa, Ananda and Anuruddha comprised the five chief disciples. His ten foremost disciples were completed by the quintet of Upali, Subhoti, Rahula, Mahakaccana and Punna.

In the fifth vassana, the Buddha was staying at Mahavana near Vesali. Hearing of the impending death of Suddhodana, the Buddha went to his father and preached the dharma, and Suddhodana became an arahant prior to death. The death and cremation led to the creation of the order of nuns. Buddhist texts record that he was reluctant to ordain women as nuns. His foster mother Maha Pajapati approached him asking to join the sangha, but the Buddha refused, and began the journey from Kapilavastu back to Rajagaha. Maha Pajapati was so intent on renouncing the world that she led a group of royal Sakyan and Koliyan ladies, following the sangha to Rajagaha. The Buddha eventually accepted them five years after the formation of the Sangha on the grounds that their capacity for enlightenment was equal to that of men, but he gave them certain additional rules (Vinaya) to follow. This occurred after Ananda interceded on their behalf. Yasodhara also became a nun, with both becoming arahants.

During his ministry, Devadatta (who was not an arahant) frequently tried to undermine the Buddha. At one point Devadatta asked the Buddha to stand aside to let him lead the sangha. The Buddha declined, and stated that

Devadatta's actions did not reflect on the Triple Gem, but on him alone. Devadatta conspired with Prince Ajatasattu, son of Bimbisara, so that they would kill and usurp the Buddha and Bimbisara respectively. Devadatta attempted three times to kill the Buddha. The first attempt involved the hiring of a group of archers, whom upon meeting the Buddha became disciples. A second attempt followed when Devadatta attempted to roll a large boulder down a hill. It hit another rock and splintered, only grazing the Buddha in the foot. A final attempt by plying an elephant with alcohol and setting it loose again failed. Failing this, Devadatta attempted to cause a schism in the sangha, by proposing extra restrictions on the vinaya. When the Buddha declined, Devadatta started a breakaway order, criticising the Buddha's laxity. At first, he managed to convert some of the bhikkhus, but Sariputta and Mahamoggallana expounded the dharma to them and succeeded in winning them back.

When the Buddha reached the age of 55, he made Ananda his chief attendant.

Death / Mahaparinirvana

According to the Mahaparinibbana Sutta of the Pali canon, at the age of 80, the Buddha announced that he would soon reach Parinirvana or the final deathless state abandoning the earthly body. After this, the Buddha ate his last meal, which he had received as an offering from a blacksmith named Cunda. Falling violently ill, Buddha instructed his attendant Ânanda to convince Cunda that the meal eaten at his place had nothing to do with his passing and that his meal would be a source of the greatest merit as it provided the last meal for a Buddha. Mettanando and von Hinüber argue that the Buddha died of mesenteric infarction, a symptom of old age, rather than food poisoning. The precise contents of the Buddha's final meal are not clear, due to variant scriptural traditions and ambiguity over the translation of certain significant terms; the Theravada tradition generally believes that the Buddha was offered some kind of pork, while the Mahayana tradition believes that the Buddha consumed some sort of truffle or other mushroom.

The Mahayana Vimalakirti Sutra claims, in Chapter 3, that the Buddha doesn't really become ill or old but purposely presents such an appearance only to teach those born into samsara about the impermanence and pain of defiled worlds and to encourage them to strive for Nirvana.

"Reverend Ánanda, the Tathágatas have the body of the Dharma—not a body that is sustained by material food. The Tathágatas have a transcendental body that has transcended all mundane qualities. There is no injury to the body of a Tathágata, as it is rid of all defilements. The body of a Tathágata is uncompounded and free of all formative activity. Reverend Ánanda, to believe there can be illness in such a body is irrational and unseemly!' Nevertheless, since the Buddha has appeared during the time of the five corruptions, he disciplines living beings by acting lowly and humble."

Ananda protested Buddha's decision to enter Parinirvana in the abandoned jungles of Kuúinâra (present-day Kushinagar, India) of the Malla kingdom. Buddha, however, reminded Ananda how Kushinara was a land once ruled by a righteous wheel-turning king that resounded with joy:

44. Kusavati, Ananda, resounded unceasingly day and night with ten sounds—the trumpeting of elephants, the neighing of horses, the rattling of chariots, the beating of drums and tabours, music and song, cheers, the clapping of hands, and cries of "Eat, drink, and be merry!"

Buddha then asked all the attendant Bhikshus to clarify any doubts or questions they had. They had none. He then finally entered Parinirvana. The Buddha's final words were, "All composite things pass away. Strive for your own liberation with diligence." The Buddha's body was cremated and the relics were placed in monuments or stupas, some of which are believed to have survived until the present. For example, The Temple of the Tooth or "Dalada Maligawa" in Sri Lanka is the place where the relic of the right tooth of Buddha is kept at present.

According to the Pâli historical chronicles of Sri Lanka, the D+pavaCsa and MahvaCsa, the coronation of Aúoka (Pâli: Asoka) is 218 years after the death of Buddha. According to one Mahayana record in Chinese, the coronation of Aúoka is 116 years after the death of Buddha. Therefore, the time of Buddha's passing is either 486 BCE according to Theravâda record or 383 BCE according to Mahayana record. However, the actual date traditionally accepted as the date of the Buddha's death in Theravâda countries is 544 or 543 BCE, because the reign of Aœoka was traditionally reckoned to be about 60 years earlier than current estimates.

At his death, the Buddha told his disciples to follow no leader, but to follow his teachings (dharma). However, at the First Buddhist Council, Mahakasyapa was held by the sangha as their leader, with the two chief disciples Mahamoggallana and Sariputta having died before the Buddha.

Physical Characteristics

Buddha is perhaps one of the few sages for whom we have mention of his rather impressive physical characteristics. A kshatriya by birth, he had military training in his upbringing, and by Shakyan tradition was required to pass tests to demonstrate his worthiness as a warrior in order to marry. He had a strong enough body to be noticed by one of the kings and was asked to join his army as a general. He is also believed by Buddhists to have "the 32 Signs of the Great Man".

The Brahmin Sonadanda described him as "handsome, good-looking, and pleasing to the eye, with a most beautiful complexion. He has a godlike form and countenance, he is by no means unattractive."(D,I:115).

> "It is wonderful, truly marvellous, how serene is the good Gotama's appearance, how clear and radiant his complexion, just as the golden jujube in autumn is clear and radiant, just as a palm-tree fruit just loosened from the stalk is clear and radiant, just as an adornment of red gold wrought in a crucible by a skilled goldsmith, deftly beaten and laid on a yellow-cloth shines, blazes and glitters, even so, the good Gotama's senses are calmed, his complexion is clear and radiant." (A,I:181)

A disciple named Vakkali, who later became an Arahant, was so obsessed by Buddha's physical presence that Buddha had to tell him to stop and reminded Vakkali to know Buddha through the Dhamma and not physical appearances.

Although the Buddha was not represented in human form until around the 1st century CE, the physical characteristics of fully-enlightened Buddhas are described by the Buddha in the Digha Nikaya's *LakkhaGa Sutta* (D,I:142). In addition, the Buddha's physical appearance is described by Yasodhara to their son Rahula upon the Buddha's first post-Enlightenment return to his former princely palace in the non-canonical Pali devotional hymn, *Narasîha Gâthâ* ("The Lion of Men").

Teachings

Some scholars believe that some portions of the Pali Canon and the Agamas could contain the actual substance of the historical teachings (and possibly even the words) of the

Buddha. This is **not** the case for the later Mahayana sutras. The scriptural works of Early Buddhism precede the Mahayana works chronologically, and are treated by many Western scholars as the main credible source for information regarding the actual historical teachings of Gautama Buddha.

Some of the fundamentals of the teachings of Gautama Buddha are:

- The Four Noble Truths: that suffering is an inherent part of existence; that the origin of suffering is ignorance and the main symptoms of that ignorance are attachment and craving; that attachment and craving can be ceased; and that following the Noble Eightfold Path will lead to the cessation of attachment and craving and therefore suffering.
- The Noble Eightfold Path: right understanding, right thought, right speech, right action, right livelihood, right effort, right mindfulness, and right concentration.
- Dependent origination: that any phenomenon 'exists' only because of the 'existence' of other phenomena in a complex web of cause and effect covering time past, present and future. Because all things are thus conditioned and transient (anicca), they have no real independent identity (anatta).
- Rejection of the infallibility of accepted scripture: Teachings should not be accepted unless they are borne out by our experience and are praised by the wise.
- *Anicca* (Sanskrit: *anitya*): That all things are impermanent.
- *Dukkha* (Sanskrit: *dukkha*): That all beings suffer from all situations due to unclear mind.

- *Anatta* (Sanskrit: *anâtman*): That the perception of a constant "self" is an illusion.

However, in some Mahayana schools, these points have come to be regarded as more or less subsidiary. There is some disagreement amongst various schools of Buddhism over more esoteric aspects of Buddha's teachings, and also over some of the disciplinary rules for monks.

According to tradition, the Buddha emphasized ethics and correct understanding. He questioned the average person's notions of divinity and salvation. He stated that there is no intermediary between mankind and the divine; distant gods are subjected to karma themselves in decaying heavens; and the Buddha is solely a guide and teacher for the sentient beings who must tread the path of NirvGa (Pâli: Nibbâna) themselves to attain the spiritual awakening called *bodhi* and see truth and reality as it is. The Buddhist system of insight and meditation practice is not believed to have been revealed divinely, but by the understanding of the true nature of the mind, which must be discovered by personally treading a spiritual path guided by the Buddha's teachings.

Iconography of Gautama Buddha in Laos and Thailand

The Iconography of Gautama Buddha in Laos and Thailand is referred to as *pang phraputtarup,* and a given pose as *pang* episode. These recall specific episodes during his travels and teachings that are familiar to Buddhists according to an iconography with specific rules; certain ones of these are considered particularly auspicious for those born on particular days of the week.

In other Buddhist countries, different but related iconography is used, for example the mudras in Indian art.

The Buddha is always represented with certain physical attributes, and in specified dress and specified poses. Each pose, and particularly the position and gestures of the Buddha's hands, has a defined meaning which is familiar to Buddhists.

For Buddhists, the correct depiction of the Buddha is not an anabolistic matter; Buddhists believe that a properly rendered Buddha image is a hypostasis: an actual spiritual emanation of the Buddha, which possesses supernatural qualities. Although the Buddha is not a god, Buddhists seek to communicate with the supernatural world through Buddha images, making offerings to them and praying before them.

Buddha images are not intended to be naturalistic representations of what Gautama Buddha looked like. There are no contemporary images of him, and the oldest Buddha images date from 500 to 600 years after his lifetime. But Buddhists believe that Buddha images represent an ideal reality of the Buddha, and that every Buddha image stands at the end of a succession of images reaching back to the Buddha himself.

When creating a Buddha image, the artist is expected to be in a spiritual and mental state (*samâdhi*) that will enable him to visualise this ideal reality. There is no requirement that every Buddha image be identical, and in fact there is a wide variety of artistic styles and national traditions in representing the Buddha. There are, however, certain rules of representation that must be adhered to.

The current range of postures in which the Buddha may be shown, and the gestures which may be depicted, evolved over the first millennium of the Buddhist era (roughly 500 BCE to 500 CE), mainly in India, the original homeland of Buddhism. In the early part of this period, the Buddha was usually shown giving a general gesture of benediction, with the right hand held at shoulder-height with the palm facing forward and the fingers together and slightly bent. By the end of the Gupta Empire (about 550 CE), the canon of representation had become more varied, with the seated meditative position becoming common, particularly in Sri Lanka. By the 7th century CE the canon was largely as it is seen today.

As Buddhism spread from India to other countries, variations in the depiction of the Buddha evolved. This article describes the canon of Buddha representation in Thailand and Laos. This canon was not formalised until the 19th century, as part of the general project of "modernisation" that followed the Buddhist world's encounter with Western civilisation. A key figure in this process was the Siamese royal prince and Buddhist monk Paramanuchit Chinorot, a son of King Rama I, who in 1814 was appointed administrator of the Wat Pho royal temple in Bangkok. At the request of King Rama III, Paramanuchit described and represented 40 different postures of the Buddha in an illustrated treatise called *Pathama Sambodhikatha*. Some of these, such as "Buddha threading a needle," were new, although justified through reference to the literary accounts of the Buddha's life. Paramanuchit's illustrations were later rendered as bronze miniatures, which can be seen today at Wat Phra Kaew in Bangkok and serve as templates for the creation of modern Buddhist imagery.

Attributes of the Buddha

The *Dîgha Nikâya,* a Pâli text of the 1st century BCE, gives a list of 32 physical attributes of the Buddha. Some of these are poetic or fanciful ("legs like an antelope's," "ankles like rounded shells"), while others are more specific: feet with level tread, projecting heels, long and slender fingers and toes, a tuft of hair between the eyebrows. Although it is not required that Buddha images reflect all of these attributes, many of them have acquired canonical status.

Most curiously, the Buddha is said to have had a protuberance on the top of his skull, the *usnîsa.* This is sometimes shown as a spire or spike, and sometimes only as a small bump. The Buddha always has a serene expression or a faint smile. The Buddha is also always depicted with very long ear-lobes. This may be because in his earlier life as a prince he had always worn heavy earrings, but has come to symbolize wisdom.

Posture and Dress

The Buddha may be depicted in one of four postures:

- Sitting: If seated, the Buddha may be shown in one of three different positions

  In the "heroic posture" (*vîrâsana*), with the legs folded over each other

  In the "adamantine posture" (*vajrâsana*), with the legs crossed so that the soles of both feet are turned up

  In the position of a person sitting in a chair (*pralambanâsana*)

- Standing: If standing, the Buddha may be shown either with his feet together, or with one foot forward

- Walking

- Reclining: The reclining posture may represent the Buddha resting or sleeping, but more usually represents the *mahâparinabbâna*: the Buddha's final state of enlightenment before his death

The Buddha is nearly always depicted wearing a monastic robe, of the type worn by Buddhist monks today. The robe may be shown as worn in the "covering mode" (draped over both shoulders) or in the "open mode" (leaving the right shoulder and breast uncovered). The robe is a representation of the Buddha's humility. (Gautama was originally a prince, who renounced the world to seek enlightenment, and his original robe was made from the shroud of a corpse.) The robe is sometimes shown as diaphanous, transparent or billowing mysteriously, suggesting the spiritual power emanating from the Buddha. Buddha images are often draped with real robes, which are renewed periodically, usually at major festivals. The Buddha may also be shown wearing royal attire, but this is uncommon.

Hand Gestures

The most important aspect of the iconography of the Buddha is gestures made with the hands, known as *mudrâ*. These gestures have meanings which are known throughout the Buddhist world, and when combined with the postures described above, give a complete representation, usually associated with a particular incident in the life of the Buddha.

The six *mudrâ* associated with the Buddha are:

- Touching the earth (*Bhûmisparsa mudrâ*) *pang maa-rá-wí-chai*: the right hand rests on the right thigh with the fingers pointing downwards and touching the earth (not always literally, as can be seen in the image at the top of this page). The left hand rests in the *dhyâna mudrâ* position in the Buddha's lap. This *mudrâ* is frequently called "calling the earth to witness," or by its more literal meaning, "Buddha subduing Mâra" (the demon who tempted the Buddha by trying to seduce him with the vision of beautiful women). The gesture thus symbolises the Buddha's renunciation of worldly desire, and since this is the central moral precept of Buddhism this is by far the most commonly depicted *mudrâ*.
- Meditation (*Dhyâna mudrâ*) *pang sà-mãa-tí*: the hands are shown lying flat in the Buddha's lap, palms upward.

This *mudrâ* is usually associated with a seated Buddha. It shows that the Buddha is disciplining his mind through mental concentration, a necessary step to achieving enlightenment.

- Charity (*Varana mudrâ*) *pang bprà-taan pon*: the right arm is shown pendent (extended downwards), with the open palm turned to the front and the fingers extended. This '*mudrâ* is usually associated with a standing Buddha. This position can signify either that the Buddha is granting or receiving charitable offerings.

- Absence of fear (*Abhâya mudrâ*) *pang bprà-taan à-pai*: either one or both arms are shown bent at the elbow and the wrist, with the palm facing outwards and the fingers pointing upwards. It shows the Buddha either displaying fearlessness in the face of adversity, or enjoining others to do so. Right hand raised is also called "calming animals" *pang pròht sàt*; both hands raised is also called "forbidding the relatives" *pang ham yat*. These '*mudrâ* are usually associated with a standing Buddha, but seated representations are not uncommon.

- Reasoning and exposition (*Vitarka mudrâ*): the arm and hand are positioned in the same manner as in the *abhâya mudrâ*, except that the thumb and forefinger are brought together. The gesture can be made with either the right or left hand (usually the right), but not both. This mudra signifies an appeal to reason, or the giving of instruction. Since the Buddha is appealing to reason, the gesture is often interpreted as an appeal for peace.

- Setting the wheel in motion (*Dharmachakrâ mudrâ*): the hands are held in front of the chest, with both hands in the *vitarka mudrâ* position, with the fingers of the left hand resting in the palm of the right hand. This is a less common *mudrâ* since it refers to a particular episode in the Buddha's life: his first sermon, when he "set the wheel (of his life's work) in motion." It can be used for both seated and standing images.

Over the centuries combinations and variations of these six *mudrâ* have evolved. For example the "double *abhâya mudrâ*", with both hands held up in the *abhâya mudrâ* position, became common in Thailand and Laos in the 16th century, and is now one of the most common representations of the Buddha in south-east Asian countries. It is sometimes interpreted as "Buddha teaching on reason." As artists wished to depict more of the specific incidents in the life of the Buddha, new, secondary *mudrâs* evolved, such as "Buddha holding an alms bowl", "Buddha receiving a mango" and Buddha performing various miracles. Many of these originated in Burma and then spread to other parts of the Buddhist world.

BUDDHA IMAGES IN THAILAND

A Buddha image in Thailand typically refers to three dimensional stone, wood, clay, or metal cast images of the Buddha. While there are such figures in all regions where Buddhism is commonly practiced, the appearance, composition and position of the images vary greatly from country to country.

Dvaravati Period

During the Dvaravati period (seventh through eleventh centuries), there were two factions of Buddhism practiced in the region that now encompasses present day Thailand, namely Mahayana and Theravada. The types of images constructed during this era reflects the distinction. Much of the basis for the Buddhist artwork of the Dvaravati period was influence from Buddhist art in India, including the Amaravati and Gupta styles, although there was also local and Khmer influence. Such images include the following classical archetypes:

- Buddha in the Tribhanga (leaning) position with somewhat Indian facial features and no aureole. The right hand is typically free, while the left is depicted grasping the Buddha's robe.
- Buddha in the Amaravati style with loosely folded legs and a lotus shaped aureole. Such statues have a continuous eye-brow, a flat nose and thick lips.
- Square faced cleft chin Buddha with some Khmer features. Legs are typically fully folded. The Buddha sits on a lotus base.

Sri Vijaya Images

Sri Vijaya images are found in southern Thailand. They were constructed between the eighth and thirteenth centuries. Typically, they reflect the teachings of the Mahayana school of Buddhism. Unlike other Thai Buddha images, Sri Vijaya images were generally made of clay, with less emphasis on durability, as their purpose was to benefit the deceased, rather than perpetuate the teachings of the Buddha.

Lopburi Images

Lopburi images date back to the eleventh century. They are typically found in Northeast Thailand, and their style is essentially similar to Cambodian Buddha images. Such images typically have a cone-shaped cranial protuberance in the form of tiers of lotus petals. The hair depicted in the images is considerably more realistic than the hair of the Dvaravati images, and may be either straight or curly. The face of the Buddha typically has a small smile, while the earlobes are in unusually large proportion relative to the rest of the face, often hanging down nearly to the image's shoulders. A second Lopburi style is the Naga Protected Buddha with the heads of Naga forming a protective taper around the Buddha's head.

Chiang Saen and Lanna Images

Chiang Saen and Lanna images were created in northern Thailand between the tenth and thirteenth centuries. Early images were similar to the Pala style Buddha images of India, with lotus bud or orb shaped hair curls, round faces, narrow lips and prominent chests. Such images were usually in the subduing Mara position, cross-legged, with the soles of the Buddha's feet visible. Many later Chiang Saen and Lanna images began to be constructed from crystals and gemstones.

Sukhothai Period

During the Sukhothai period (fourteenth century), the style of the Thai Buddha images radically changed due to the influx of new ideas from Sri Lankan Buddhism. Buddha images were cast with the intention of depicting superhuman traits of the Buddha, and were designed to express compassion and serenity in posture and facial expression.

The Sukhothai period witnessed the innovation of the four modern postures of the Thai Buddha, i.e. walking, standing, sitting and reclining. Images often had a flame-shaped aureole, finely curled hair, a slight smile, broad shoulders and an oval face.

A common pose was the subduing Mara, with the Buddha is seated on a plain base. Notable variations within the Sukhothai period include the Kamphaengpet, the Phra Buddha Chinnarat (such as the most famous Chinnarat at Wat Phra Sri Rattana Mahatat Woramahawihan), and the Wat Ta Kuan groups of images.

U Thong Images

There are three categories of U Thong images from the twelfth through fifteenth century in central Thailand. The first such style was a fusion of the Dvaravati and Khmer style images. They would typically adorn a lotus bud aureole and Khmer facial features. The second style was similar to the Lopburi images. The third and most recent U Thong style had considerable influence from the Sukhothai images, but often had hair bands unique to U Thong images.

Ayutthaya Period

Ayutthaya images were created between the tenth and eighteenth centuries. They had a unique hair frame and tell-tale narrow carvings above the lips and eyes. Early Ayutthaya images were carved in stone with heavy influence from the Lopburi images. Middle Ayutthaya images were similar to the Sukhothai images, and were in similar poses. During this period, the images were often cast in Bronze, and the size of the images were often large. In the late Ayutthaya period, the images typically depicted the Buddha in royal attire, and the bases of the images bore ornate design.

Modern Thai Buddha Images

In modern times, Buddha images are often replicas of images from the Sukhothai and other early periods, often more ornately and elaborately adorned. Faces in new innovative depictions are typically more realistic and human-like. An elongated flame aureole is popular. Robes depicted in modern images often depict floral designs. The Indian Gandhara style, as well as western art have also influenced many of the modern images.

Bunleua Sulilat's concrete sculpture gardens (Buddha Park and Sala Keoku) give an example of contemporary highly creative and unconventional artistic treatment of Buddhist subjects.

BUDDHIST ART

Buddhist art originated on the Indian subcontinent following the historical life of Siddhartha Gautama, 6th to 5th century BCE, and thereafter evolved by contact with other cultures as it spread throughout Asia and the world.

Early Buddhist art followed one Indian aniconic tradition, which avoids direct representation of the human figure. Around the 1st century CE an iconic period emerged lasting to this day which represents the Buddha in human form.

Buddhist art followed believers as the dharma spread, adapted, and evolved in each new host country. It developed to the north through Central Asia and into Eastern Asia to form the Northern branch of Buddhist art, and to the east as far as Southeast Asia to form the Southern branch of Buddhist art. In India, Buddhist art flourished and even influenced the development of Hindu art, until Buddhism nearly disappeared in India around the 10th century due in part to the vigorous expansion of Islam alongside Hinduism.

Aniconic Phase (5th Century - 1st Century BCE)

During the 2nd to 1st century BCE, sculptures became more explicit, representing episodes of the Buddha's life and teachings. These took the form of votive tablets or friezes, usually in relation to the decoration of stupas. Although India had a long sculptural tradition and a mastery of rich iconography, the Buddha was never represented in human form, but only through some of his symbols.

This reluctance towards anthropomorphic representations of the Buddha, and the sophisticated development of aniconic symbols to avoid it (even in narrative scene where other human figures would appear), seems to be connected to 70 of the Buddha's sayings, reported in the Dighanikaya, that disfavored representations of himself after the extinction of his body. This tendency remained as late as the 2nd century CE in the southern parts of India, in the art of the Amaravati school. It has been argued that earlier anthropomorphic representations of the Buddha may have been made of wood and may have perished since then. However, no related archaeological evidence has been found.

Iconic Phase (1st Century CE – Present)

Anthropomorphic representations of the Buddha started to emerge from the 1st century CE in northern India. The two main centers of creation have been identified as Gandhara in today's North West Frontier Province, in Pakistan, and the region of Mathura, in central northern India.

The art of Gandhara benefited from centuries of interaction with Greek culture since the conquests of Alexander the Great in 332 BCE and the subsequent establishment of the Greco-Bactrian and Indo-Greek Kingdoms, leading to the development of Greco-Buddhist art. Gandharan Buddhist sculpture displays Greek artistic influence, and it has been suggested that the concept of the "man-god" was essentially inspired by Greek mythological culture. Artistically, the Gandharan school of sculpture is said to have contributed wavy hair, drapery covering both shoulders, shoes and sandals, acanthus leaf decorations, etc.

The art of Mathura tends to be based on a strong Indian tradition, exemplified by the anthropomorphic representation of divinities such as the Yaksas, although in a style rather archaic compared to the later representations of the Buddha. The Mathuran school contributed clothes covering the left shoulder of thin muslin, the wheel on the palm, the lotus seat, etc.

Mathura and Gandhara also strongly influenced each other. During their artistic florescence, the two regions were even united politically under the Kushans, both being capitals of the empire. It is still a matter of debate whether the anthropomorphic representations of Buddha was essentially a result of a local evolution of Buddhist art at Mathura, or a consequence of Greek cultural influence in Gandhara through the Greco-Buddhist syncretism.

This iconic art was characterized from the start by a realistic idealism, combining realistic human features, proportions, attitudes and attributes, together with a sense of perfection and serenity reaching to the divine. This expression of the Buddha as both man and God became the iconographic canon for subsequent Buddhist art.

Buddhist art continued to develop in India for a few more centuries. The pink sandstone sculptures of Mathura evolved during the Gupta period (4th to 6th century) to reach a very high fineness of execution and delicacy in the modeling. The art of the Gupta school was extremely influential almost everywhere in the rest of Asia. By the 10th century, Buddhist art creation was dying out in India, as Hinduism and Islam ultimately prevailed.

As Buddhism expanded outside of India from the 1st century CE, its original artistic package blended with other artistic influences, leading to a progressive differentiation among the countries adopting the faith.

- A **Northern route** was established from the 1st century CE through Central Asia, Tibet, Bhutan, China, Korea, Japan and Vietnam, in which Mahayana Buddhism prevailed.
- A **Southern route**, where Theravada Buddhism dominated, went through Myanmar, Thailand, and Cambodia.

Northern Buddhist Art

The Silk Road transmission of Buddhism to Central Asia, China and ultimately Korea and Japan started in the 1st century CE with a semi-legendary account of an embassy sent to the West by the Chinese Emperor Ming (58-75 CE). However, extensive contacts started in the 2nd century CE, probably as a consequence of the expansion of the Kushan Empire into the Chinese territory of the Tarim Basin, with the missionary efforts of a great number of Central Asian Buddhist monks to Chinese lands. The first missionaries and translators of Buddhists scriptures into Chinese, such as Lokaksema, were either Parthian, Kushan, Sogdian or Kuchean.

Central Asian missionary efforts along the Silk Road were accompanied by a flux of artistic influences, visible in the development of Serindian art from the 2nd through the 11th century CE in the Tarim Basin, modern Xinjiang. Serindian art often derives from the Greco-Buddhist art of the Gandhara district of what is now Pakistan, combining Indian, Greek and Roman influences. Silk Road Greco-Buddhist artistic influences can be found as far as Japan to this day, in architectural motifs, Buddhist imagery, and a select few representations of Japanese gods.

The art of the northern route was also highly influenced by the development of Mahayana Buddhism, an inclusive faith characterized by the adoption of new texts, in addition to the traditional Pali canon, and a shift in the understanding of Buddhism. Mahayana goes beyond the traditional Theravada ideal of the release from suffering (dukkha) and personal enlightenment of the arhats, to elevate the Buddha to a god-like status, and to create a pantheon of quasi-divine Bodhisattvas devoting themselves to personal excellence, ultimate knowledge and the salvation of humanity. Northern Buddhist art thus tends to be characterized by a very rich and syncretic Buddhist pantheon, with a multitude of images of the various Buddhas, Bodhisattvas and lesser deities.

Afghanistan

Buddhist art in Afghanistan (old Bactria) persisted for several centuries until the spread of Islam in the 7th century. It is exemplified by the Buddhas of Bamyan. Other sculptures, in stucco, schist or clay, display very strong blending of Indian post-Gupta mannerism and Classical influence, Hellenistic or possibly even Greco-Roman.

Although Islamic rule was somewhat tolerant of other religions "of the Book", it showed little tolerance for Buddhism, which was perceived as a religion depending on "idolatry". Human figurative art forms also being prohibited under Islam, Buddhist art suffered numerous attacks, which culminated with the systematic destructions by the Taliban regime. The Buddhas of Bamyan, the sculptures of Hadda, and many of the remaining artifacts at the Afghanistan museum have been destroyed.

The multiple conflicts since the 1980s also have led to a systematic pillage of archaeological sites apparently in the hope of reselling in the international market what artifacts could be found.

Central Asia

Central Asia long played the role of a meeting place between China, India and Persia. During the 2nd century BCE, the expansion of the Former Han to the West led to increased contact with the Hellenistic civilizations of Asia, especially the Greco-Bactrian Kingdom.

Thereafter, the expansion of Buddhism to the North led to the formation of Buddhist communities and even Buddhist kingdoms in the oases of Central Asia. Some Silk Road cities consisted almost entirely of Buddhist stupas and monasteries, and it seems that one of their main objectives was to welcome and service travelers between East and West.

The eastern part of Central Asia (Chinese Turkestan (Tarim Basin, Xinjiang) in particular has revealed an extremely rich Serindian art (wall paintings and reliefs in numerous caves, portable paintings on canvas, sculpture, ritual objects), displaying multiple influences from Indian and Hellenistic cultures. Works of art reminiscent of the Gandharan style, as well as scriptures in the Gandhari script Kharoshti have been found. These influences were rapidly absorbed however by the vigorous Chinese culture, and a strongly Chinese particularism develops from that point.

China

Buddhism arrived in China around the 1st century CE, and introduced new types of art into China, particularly in the area of statuary. Receiving this distant religion, strong Chinese traits were incorporated into Buddhist art.

Northern Dynasties

In the 5th to 6th centuries, the Northern Dynasties, developed rather symbolic and abstract modes of representation, with schematic lines. Their style is also said to be solemn and majestic. The lack of corporeality of this art, and its distance from the original Buddhist objective of expressing the pure ideal of enlightenment in an accessible and realistic manner, progressively led to a change towards more naturalism and realism, leading to the expression of Tang Buddhist art.

Sites preserving Northern Wei Dynasty Buddhist sculpture:

- Longmen Grottoes, Henan
- Bingling Temple, Gansu

Tang Dynasty

Following a transition under the Sui Dynasty, Buddhist sculpture of the Tang evolved towards a markedly life-like expression. Because of the dynasty's openness to foreign influences, and renewed exchanges with Indian culture due to the numerous travels of Chinese Buddhist monks to India, Tang dynasty Buddhist sculpture assumed a rather classical form, inspired by the Indian art of the Gupta period. During that time, the Tang capital of Chang'an (today's Xi'an) became an important center for Buddhism. From there Buddhism spread to Korea, and Japanese embassies of Kentoshi helped it gain a foothold in Japan.

However, foreign influences came to be negatively perceived in China towards the end of the Tang dynasty. In the year 845, the Tang emperor Wuzong outlawed all "foreign" religions (including Christian Nestorianism, Zoroastrianism and Buddhism) in order to support the indigenous religion, Taoism. He confiscated Buddhist possessions, and forced the faith to go underground, therefore affecting the development of the religion and its arts in China.

Chán Buddhism however, as the origin of Japanese Zen, continued to prosper for some centuries, especially under the Song Dynasty (960-1279), when Chan monasteries were great centers of culture and learning.

The popularization of Buddhism in China has made the country home to one of the richest collections of Buddhist arts in the world. The Mogao Caves near Dunhuang and the Bingling Temple caves near Yongjing in Gansu province, the Longmen Grottoes near Luoyang in Henan province, the Yungang Grottoes near Datong in Shanxi province, and the Dazu Rock Carvings near Chongqing municipality are among the most important and renowned Buddhist sculptural sites.

The Leshan Giant Buddha, carved out of a hillside in the 8th century during the Tang Dynasty and looking down on the confluence of three rivers, is still the largest stone Buddha statue in the world.

Korea

Korean Buddhist art generally reflects an interaction between Chinese Buddhist influence and a strongly original Korean culture. Additionally, the art of the steppes, particularly Siberian and Scythian influences, are evident in early Korean Buddhist art based on the excavation of artifacts and burial goods such as Silla royal crowns, belt buckles, daggers, and comma-shaped gogok. The style of this indigenous art was geometric, abstract and richly adorned with a characteristic "barbarian" luxury. Although Chinese influence was strong, Korean Buddhist art "bespeaks a sobriety, taste for the right tone, a sense of abstraction but also of colours that curiously enough are in line with contemporary taste" (Pierre Cambon, *Arts asiatiques- Guimet'*).

Three Kingdoms of Korea

The first of the Three Kingdoms of Korea to officially receive Buddhism was Goguryeo in 372. However, Chinese records and the use of Buddhist motifs in Goguryeo murals indicate the introduction of Buddhism earlier than the official date. The Baekje Kingdom officially recognized Buddhism in 384. The Silla Kingdom, isolated and with no easy sea or land access to China, officially adopted Buddhism in 535 although the foreign religion was known in the kingdom due to the work of Goguryeo monks since the early fifth century. The introduction of Buddhism stimulated the need for artisans to create images for veneration, architects for temples, and the literate for the Buddhist sutras and transformed Korean civilization. Particularly important in the transmission of sophisticated art styles to the Korean kingdoms was the art of the "barbarian" Tuoba, a clan of non-Han Chinese Xianbei people who established the Northern Wei Dynasty in China in 386. The Northern Wei style was particularly influential in the art of the Goguryeo and Baekje. Baekje artisans later transmitted this style along with Southern Dynasty elements and distinct Korean elements to Japan. Korean artisans were highly selective of the styles they incorporated and combined different regional styles together to create a specific Korean Buddhist art style.

While Goguryeo Buddhist art exhibited vitality and mobility akin with Northern Wei prototypes, the Baekje Kingdom was also in close contact with the Southern Dynasties of China and this close diplomatic contact is exemplified in the gentle and proportional sculpture of the Baekje, epitomized by Baekje sculpture exhibiting the fathomless smile known to art historians as the Baekje smile. The Silla Kingdom also developed a distinctive Buddhist art tradition epitomized by the Bangasayusang, a half-seated contemplative maitreya whose Korean-made twin, the Miroku Bosatsu, was sent to Japan as a proselytizing gift and now resides in the Koryu-ji Temple in Japan. Buddhism in the Three Kingdoms period stimulated massive temple-building projects, such as the Mireuksa Temple in the Baekje Kingdom and the Hwangnyongsa Temple in Silla. Baekje architects were famed for their skill and were instrumental in building the massive nine-story pagoda at Hwangnyongsa and early Buddhist temples in Yamato Japan such as Hoko-ji (Asuka-dera) and Hôryû-ji. Sixth century Korean Buddhist art exhibited the cultural influences of China and India but began to show distinctive indigenous characteristics. These indigenous characteristics can be seen in early Buddhist art in Japan and some early Japanese Buddhist sculpture is now believed to have originated in Korea, particularly from Baekje, or Korean artisans who immigrated to Yamato Japan. Particularly, the semi-seated Maitreya form was adapted into a highly developed Korean style which was transmitted to Japan as evidenced by the Koryu-ji Miroku Bosatsu and the Chugu-ji Siddhartha statues. Although many historians portray Korea as a mere transmitter of Buddhism, the Three Kingdoms, and particularly Baekje, were instrumental as active agents in the introduction and formation of a Buddhist tradition in Japan in 538 or 552.

Unified Silla

During the Unified Silla period, East Asia was particularly stable with China and Korea both enjoying unified governments. Early Unified Silla art combined Silla styles and Baekje styles. Korean Buddhist art was also influenced by new Tang Dynasty styles as evidenced by a new popular Buddhist motif with full-faced Buddha sculptures. Tang China was the cross roads of East, Central, and South Asia and so the Buddhist art of this time period exhibit the so-called international style. State-sponsored Buddhist art flourished during this period, the epitome of which is the Seokguram Grotto.

Goryeo Dynasty

The fall of the Unified Silla Dynasty and the establishment of the Goryeo Dynasty in 918 indicates a new period of Korean Buddhist art. The Goryeo kings also lavishly sponsored Buddhism and Buddhist art flourished, especially Buddhist paintings and illuminated sutras written in gold and silver ink. . The crowning achievement of this period is the carving of approximately 80,000 woodblocks of the Tripitaka Koreana which was done twice.

Joseon Dynasty

The Joseon Dynasty actively suppressed Buddhism beginning in 1406 and Buddhist temples and art production subsequently decline in quality in quantity although beginning in 1549, Buddhist art does continue to be produced.

Japan

Before the introduction of Buddhism, Japan had already been the seat of various cultural (and artistic) influences, from the abstract linear decorative art of the indigenous Neolithic Jômon from around 10500 BCE to 300 BCE, to the art during the Yayoi and Kofun periods, with developments such as Haniwa art.

Japan, the largest Buddhist country today, discovered Buddhism in the 6th century when missionary monks travelled to the islands together with numerous scriptures and works of art. The Buddhist religion was adopted by the state in the following century. Being geographically at the end of the Silk Road, Japan was able to preserve many aspects of Buddhism at the very time it was disappearing in India, and being suppressed in Central Asia and China.

From 711, numerous temples and monasteries were built in the capital city of Nara, including a five-story pagoda, the Golden Hall of the Horyuji, and the Kôfuku-ji temple. Countless paintings and sculptures were made, often under governmental sponsorship. Indian, Hellenistic, Chinese and Korean artistic influences blended into an original style characterized by realism and gracefulness. The creation of Japanese Buddhist art was especially rich between the 8th and 13th centuries during the periods of Nara, Heian and Kamakura. Japan developed an extremely rich figurative art for the pantheon of Buddhist deities, sometimes combined with Hindu and Shinto influences. This art can be very varied, creative and bold.

From the 12th and 13th, a further development was Zen art, following the introduction of the faith by Dogen and

Eisai upon their return from China. Zen art is mainly characterized by original paintings (such as sumi-e) and poetry (especially haikus), striving to express the true essence of the world through impressionistic and unadorned "non-dualistic" representations. The search for enlightenment "in the moment" also led to the development of other important derivative arts such as the Chanoyu tea ceremony or the Ikebana art of flower arrangement. This evolution went as far as considering almost any human activity as an art with a strong spiritual and aesthetic content, first and foremost in those activities related to combat techniques (martial arts).

Buddhism remains very active in Japan to this day. Still around 80,000 Buddhist temples are preserved. Many of them are in wood and are regularly restored.

Tibet and Bhutan

Tantric Buddhism started as a movement in eastern India around the 5th or the 6th century. Many of the practices of Tantric Buddhism are derived from Brahmanism (the usage of mantras, yoga, or the burning of sacrificial offerings). Tantrism became the dominant form of Buddhism in Tibet from the 8th century. Due to its geographical centrality in Asia, Tibetan Buddhist art received influence from Indian, Nepali, Greco-Buddhist and Chinese art.

One of the most characteristic creations of Tibetan Buddhist art are the mandalas, diagrams of a "divine temple" made of a circle enclosing a square, the purpose of which is to help Buddhist devotees focus their attention through meditation and follow the path to the central image of the Buddha. Artistically, Buddhist Gupta art and Hindu art tend to be the two strongest inspirations of Tibetan art.

Vietnam

Chinese influence was predominant in the north of Vietnam (Tonkin) between the 1st and 9th centuries, and

Confucianism and Mahayana Buddhism were prevalent. Overall, the art of Vietnam has been strongly influenced by Chinese Buddhist art.

In the south thrived the former kingdom of Champa (before it was later overtaken by the Vietnamese from the north). Champa had a strongly Indianized art, just as neighboring Cambodia. Many of its statues were characterized by rich body adornments. The capital of the kingdom of Champa was annexed by Vietnam in 1471, and it totally collapsed in the 1720s, while Cham people remain an abundant minority across Southeast Asia.

SOUTHERN BUDDHIST ART

During the 1st century CE, the trade on the overland Silk Road tended to be restricted by the rise of the Parthian empire in the Middle East, an unvanquished enemy of Rome, just as Romans were becoming extremely wealthy and their demand for Asian luxury was rising. This demand revived the sea connections between the Mediterranean Sea and China, with India as the intermediary of choice. From that time, through trade connections, commercial settlements, and even political interventions, India started to strongly influence Southeast Asian countries. Trade routes linked India with southern Burma, central and southern Siam, lower Cambodia and southern Vietnam, and numerous urbanized coastal settlements were established there.

For more than a thousand years, Indian influence was therefore the major factor that brought a certain level of cultural unity to the various countries of the region. The Pali and Sanskrit languages and the Indian script, together with Mahayana and Theravada Buddhism, Brahmanism and Hinduism, were transmitted from direct contact and through sacred texts and Indian literature such as the Ramayana and the Mahabharata. This expansion provided the artistic context for the development of Buddhist art in these countries, which then developed characteristics of their own.

Between the 1st and 8th centuries, several kingdoms competed for influence in the region (particularly the Cambodian Funan then the Burmese Mon kingdoms) contributing various artistic characteristics, mainly derived from the Indian Gupta style. Combined with a pervading Hindu influence, Buddhist images, votive tablets and Sanskrit inscriptions are found throughout the area.

From the 9th to the 13th centuries, Southeast Asia had very powerful empires and became extremely active in Buddhist architectural and artistic creation. The Sri Vijaya Empire to the south and the Khmer Empire to the north competed for influence, but both were adherents of Mahayana Buddhism, and their art expressed the rich Mahayana pantheon of the Bodhisattvas. The Theravada Buddhism of the Pali canon was introduced to the region around the 13th century from Sri Lanka, and was adopted by the newly founded ethnic Thai kingdom of Sukhothai. Since in Theravada Buddhism only monks can reach Nirvana, the construction of **temple complexes** plays a particularly important role in the artistic expression of Southeast Asia from that time.

From the 14th century, the main factor was the spread of Islam to the maritime areas of Southeast Asia, overrunning Malaysia, Indonesia, and most of the islands as far as the Philippines. In the continental areas, Theravada Buddhism continued to expand into Burma, Laos and Cambodia.

Myanmar

A neighbor of India, Myanmar was naturally strongly influenced by the eastern part of Indian territory. The Mon of southern Burma are said to have been converted to Buddhism around 200 BCE under the proselytizing of the Indian king

Ashoka, before the schism between Mahayana and Hinayana Buddhism.

Early Buddhist temples are found, such as Beikthano in central Myanmar, with dates between the 1st and the 5th centuries. The Buddhist art of the Mons was especially influenced by the Indian art of the Gupta and post-Gupta periods, and their mannerist style spread widely in Southeast Asia following the expansion of the Mon Empire between the 5th and 8th centuries.

Later, thousands of Buddhist temples were built at Bagan, the capital, between the 11th and 13th centuries, and around 2,000 of them are still standing. Beautiful jeweled statues of the Buddha are remaining from that period. Creation managed to continue despite the seizure of the city by the Mongols in 1287.

Cambodia

Cambodia was the center of the Funan kingdom, which expanded into Burma and as far south as Malaysia between the 3rd and 6th centuries CE. Its influence seems to have been essentially political, most of the cultural influence coming directly from India.

Later, from the 9th to 13th centuries, the Mahayana Buddhist and Hindu Khmer Empire dominated vast parts of the Southeast Asian peninsula, and its influence was foremost in the development of Buddhist art in the region. Under the Khmer, more than 900 temples were built in Cambodia and in neighboring Thailand.

Angkor was at the center of this development, with a Buddhist temple complex and urban organization able to support around 1 million urban dwellers. A great deal of Cambodian Buddhist sculpture is preserved at Angkor;

however, organized looting has had a heavy impact on many sites around the country.

Often, Khmer art manages to express intense spirituality through divinely beaming expressions, in spite of spare features and slender lines.

Thailand

From the 1st to the 7th centuries, Buddhist art in Thailand was first influenced by direct contact with Indian traders and the expansion of the Mon kingdom, leading to the creation of Hindu and Buddhist art inspired from the Gupta tradition, with numerous monumental statues of great virtuosity.

From the 9th century, the various schools of Thai art then became strongly influenced by Cambodian Khmer art in the north and Sri Vijaya art in the south, both of Mahayana faith. Up to the end of that period, Buddhist art is characterized by a clear fluidness in the expression, and the subject matter is characteristic of the Mahayana pantheon with multiple creations of Bodhisattvas.

From the 13th century, Theravada Buddhism was introduced from Sri Lanka around the same time as the ethnic Thai kingdom of Sukhothai was established. The new faith inspired highly stylized images in Thai Buddhism, with sometimes very geometrical and almost abstract figures.

During the Ayutthaya period (14th-18th centuries), the Buddha came to be represented in a more stylistic manner with sumptuous garments and jeweled ornamentations. Many Thai sculptures or temples tended to be gilded, and on occasion enriched with inlays.

Indonesia

Like the rest of Southeast Asia, Indonesia seems to have been most strongly influenced by India from the 1st century

CE. The islands of Sumatra and Java in western Indonesia were the seat of the empire of Sri Vijaya (8th-13th century CE), which came to dominate most of the area around the Southeast Asian peninsula through maritime power. The Sri Vijayan Empire had adopted Mahayana and Vajrayana Buddhism, under a line of rulers named the Sailendra. Sri Vijaya spread Mahayana Buddhist art during its expansion into the Southeast Asian peninsula. Numerous statues of Mahayana Bodhisattvas from this period are characterized by a very strong refinement and technical sophistication, and are found throughout the region.

Extremely rich and refined architectural remains are found in Java and Sumatra. The most magnificent is the temple of Borobudur (the largest Buddhist structure in the world, built around 780-850 AD). This temple is modelled after the Buddhist concept of universe, the Mandala which counts 505 images of the seated Buddha and unique bell-shaped stupa that contains the statue of Buddha. Borobudur is adorned with long series of bas-reliefs narrated the holy Buddhist scriptures. The oldest Buddhist structure in Indonesia probably is the Batujaya stupas at Karawang, West Java, dated from around 4th century AD. This temple is some plastered brick stupas. However, Buddhist art in Indonesia reach the golden era during the Sailendra dynasty rule in Java. The bas-reliefs and statues of Boddhisatva, Tara, and Kinnara found in Kalasan, Sewu, Sari, and Plaosan temple is very graceful with serene expression, While Mendut temple near Borobudur, houses the giant statue of Vairocana, Avalokitesvara, and Vajrapani.

In Sumatra Sri Vijaya probably built the temple of Muara Takus, and Muaro Jambi. The the most beautiful example pf classical Javanese Buddhist art is the serene and delicate statue of Prajnaparamita (the collection of National Museum Jakarta) the goddess of transcendental wisdom from Singhasari kingdom. The Indonesian Buddhist Empire of Sri Vijaya declined due to conflicts with the Chola rulers of India, then followed by Majapahit empire, before being destabilized by the Islamic expansion from the 13th century.

●●

7

God in Buddhism

Since the time of the Buddha, the refutation of the existence of a creator has been seen as a key point in distinguishing Buddhist from non-Buddhist views. Buddhism is usually considered a religion, but is also commonly described as a "spiritual philosophy", because it generally lacks an Absolute creator god. The Buddhist approach is clinical and systematic. In the Four Noble Truths, the Buddha analyzed the problem of suffering, diagnosed its root cause and prescribed a method to dispel suffering. He taught that through insight into the nature of existence and the wisdom of "not-self" or "selflessness" (*anatta*) all sentient beings following the noble eightfold path can dispel ignorance and thereby suffering. Hence Buddhism does not hinge upon the concept of a Creator God but upon the personal practice of ethics, meditation, and wisdom. Buddhist philosophy can also be contrasted with Hindu ideas of an ultimate Self, the definition of which varies between sects.

However, in some Buddhist traditions, veneration of the Buddha as a teacher of Dharma is significant and an important part of spiritual development. While according to Pali Buddhism, the Buddha rejected being deified, in some streams of Mahayana Buddhism Gautama Buddha is worshipped as 'an omnipotent divinity endowed with numerous supernatural attributes and qualities'. and a number of Buddhist tantric scriptures promulgate the notion of Buddha as the omnipresent and primordial Lord, the eternal foundation of all that exists.

The Supernatural in Buddhism

While many Buddhist traditions do not deny the existence of supernatural beings (e.g., the *devas*, of which many are discussed in Buddhist scripture), it does not ascribe powers, in the typical Western sense, for creation, salvation or judgement, to the "gods". They are regarded as having the power to affect worldly events in much the same way as humans and animals have the power to do so. Just as humans can affect the world more than animals, *devas* can affect the world more than humans. While gods may be more powerful than humans, none of them are absolute (unsurpassed). Most importantly, gods, like humans, are also suffering in samsara, the ongoing cycle of death and subsequent rebirth. Gods have not attained nirvana, and are still subject to emotions, including jealousy, anger, delusion, sorrow, etc. Thus, since a Buddha shows the way to nirvana, a Buddha is called "the teacher of the gods and humans". According to the Pali Canon the gods have powers to affect only so far as their realm of influence or control allows them. In this sense therefore, they are no closer to nirvana than humans and no wiser in the ultimate sense.

The Pali Canon also attributes supernatural powers to enlightened beings (Buddhas), that even gods may not have. In a dialogue between king Ajatasattu and the Buddha, enlightened beings are ascribed supranormal powers (like human flight, walking on water etc.), clairaudience, mind reading, recollection of past lives of oneself and others. Yet, according to the Buddha, an enlightened person realizes the futility of these powers and instead unbinds himself completely from *samsara* through discernment.

Attitudes Towards Theories of Creation

Reflecting a common understanding of the Buddha's earliest teachings, Nyanaponika Thera asserts:

> From a study of the discourses of the Buddha preserved in the Pali canon, it will be seen that the idea of a

> personal deity, a creator god conceived to be eternal and omnipotent, is incompatible with the Buddha's teachings. On the other hand, conceptions of an impersonal godhead of any description, such as world-soul, etc., are excluded by the Buddha's teachings on Anatta, non-self or unsubstantiality. . . In Buddhist literature, the belief in a creator god (issara-nimmana-vada) is frequently mentioned and rejected, along with other causes wrongly adduced to explain the origin of the world.

In addition, nowhere in the Pali Canon, are Buddhas ascribed powers of creation, salvation and judgement. In fact, Buddhism is indifferent to all theories on the origin of the universe and holds the belief in creation as a fetter binding one to samsara. However, the Aggañña Sutta does contain a detailed account of the Buddha describing the origin of human life on earth. In this text, the Buddha provides an explanation of the caste system alternate to the one contained in the Vedas, and shows why one caste is not really any better than the other. According to scholar Richard Gombrich, the sutta gives strong evidence that it was conceived entirely as a satire of pre-existing beliefs, and he and scholar David Kalupahana have asserted that the primary intent of this text is to satirize and debunk the brahminical claims regarding the divine nature of the caste system, showing that it is nothing but a human convention. Strictly speaking, the sutta is not a cosmogony, as in Buddhism, an absolute beginning is inconceivable. Since the earliest times Buddhists have, however, taken it seriously as an account of the origins of society and kingship. Gombrich, however, finds it to be a parody of brahminical cosmogony as presented in the Rig Vedic "Hymn of creation" (RV X, 129) and BAU 1, 2. He states: "The Buddha never intended to propound a cosmogony. If we take a close look at the Aggañña Sutta, there are considerable incoherencies if it is taken seriously as an explanatory account - though once it is perceived to be a parody these inconsistencies are of no account." In particular, he finds that it violates the basic Buddhist theory of how the law of karma operates. However, scholar Rupert Gethin strongly disagrees, stating

While certain of the details of the Aggainia-sutta's account of the evolution of human society may be, as Gombrich has persuasively argued, satirical in intent, there is nothing in the Nikayas to suggest that these basic cosmological principles that I have identified should be so understood; there is nothing to suggest that the Aggafinia-sutta's introductory formula describing the expansion and contraction of the world is merely a joke. We should surely expect early Buddhism and indeed the Buddha to have some specific ideas about the nature of the round of rebirth, and essentially this is what the cosmological details presented in the Aggafifia-sutta and elsewhere in Nikayas constitute. . . far from being out of key with what we can understand of Buddhist thought from the rest of the Nikayas, the cosmogonic views offered by the Aggañña Sutta in fact harmonize very well with it . .I would go further and say that something along the lines of the Aggañña myth is actually required by it."

The Buddha did not expressly say that creation did not occur or that there is no creator. Instead, Buddhist focus is on the effect the belief in theories of creation and a creator have on the human mind. The Buddhist attitude towards every belief is one of critical examination from the perspective of what effect the belief has on the mind and whether the belief binds one to samsara or not.

The Buddha declared that "it is not possible to know or determine the first beginning of the cycle of existence of beings who wander therein deluded by ignorance and obsessed by craving." Speculation about the origin and extent of the universe is generally discouraged in early Buddhism.

Theravada

Huston Smith describes early Buddhism as psychological rather than metaphysical. Unlike theistic religions, which are founded on notions of God and related creation myths, Buddhism begins with the human condition as enumerated in the Four Noble Truths. Thus while most other religions attempt to pass a blanket judgement on the goodness of the world (eg. 'He then looked at the world and saw that it was good.' Book of Genesis, Old Testament, Christian Bible) and therefore derive the greatness of its Creator, Early Buddhism denies that the question is even worth asking to begin with . Instead it places emphasis on the human condition of clinging and the insubstantial nature of the world. This approach is often even in contrast with many of the Mahayana forms of Buddhism. No being, whether a god or an enlightened being (including the historical Buddha) is ascribed powers of creation, granting salvation and judgement. According to the Pali Canon, omnipotence cannot be ascribed to any being. Further, in Theravada Buddhism, there are no lands or heavens where a being is guaranteed nirvana, instead he can attain nirvana within a very short time, though nothing conclusive could be said about the effort required for that. In this sense therefore, there is no equivalent of the Mahayana "Pure Land" or magical abode of Buddhas where one is guaranteed to be enlightened, in Early Buddhist tradition.

However, Theravada Buddhism does mention the 'Pure Abodes' (pali: Sudhavasasa) in which Non-Returners (pali: Anagami) are born and there they attain Nibbana.

Mahayana

Mahayana Buddhism (like Theravada Buddhism) posits no Creator or ruler God. In the Avatamsaka Sutra it says, "If you want to understand all the Buddhas of the past, present, and future, then you should view the whole universe as being created by mind alone." In some major traditions of Mahayana Buddhism (the Tathagatagarbha and Pure Land streams of teaching) there is a notion of the Buddha as the omnipresent, omniscient, liberative essence of reality, and Buddhas are spoken of as generators of vast "pure lands", "Buddha lands", or "Buddha paradises", in which beings will unfailingly attain Nirvana.

Vajrayana

Tibetan schools of Buddhism all speak of two truths, absolute and relative. Relative truth is regarded as the chain of ongoing causes and conditions that define experience within samsara, and ultimate truth is synonymous with emptiness. There are many philosophical viewpoints, but unique to the Vajrayana perspective is the expression (by meditators) of emptiness in experiential language, as opposed to the language of negation used by scholars to undo any conceptual fixation that would stand in the way of a correct understanding of emptiness. For example, one teacher from the Tibetan Kagyu school of Buddhism, Kalu Rinpoche, elucidates: "...pure mind cannot be located, but it is omnipresent and all-penetrating; it embraces and pervades all things. Moreover, it is beyond change, and its open nature is indestructible and atemporal."

Veneration of the Buddha

Although an absolute creator god is absent in most forms of Buddhism, veneration or worship of the Buddha and other Buddhas does play a major role in all forms of Buddhism. While, in Buddhism all beings may strive for Buddhahood, striving to become a god or God in a monotheistic context (like in Abrahamic religions) would be futile or senseless, even heretical, due to a strict distinction between humanity and divinity. Throughout the schools of Buddhism, it is taught that being born in the human realm is best for realizing full enlightenment, whereas being born as a god presents one with too much pleasure and too many distractions to provide any motivation for serious insight meditation. Doctrines of theosis have played an important role in Christian thought, and there are a number of theistic variations of Hinduism where a practitioner can strive to become the godhead (for example Vedanta), but from a Buddhist perspective, such attainment would be disadvantageous to the attainment of nirvana.

In Buddhism, one venerates Buddhas and sages for their virtues, sacrifices, and struggles for perfect enlightenment, and as teachers who are embodiments of the Dhamma.

In Buddhism, this supreme victory of the human ability for perfect gnosis is celebrated in the concept of human saints known as Arahants which literally means "worthy of offerings" or "worthy of worship" because this sage overcomes all defilements and obtains perfect gnosis to obtain Nirvana.

Thought as Creator

In Buddhism, there is no Supreme creator. Yet thoughts (or mind, perceptions, etc.; Pali *manas, mano* in combined form) are the causes and conditions of the way we view the world.

The opening phrase of the Dhammapada expresses in a few words the most profound understanding in Buddhism of the role of thought in the creation of our perception of the things (*dhamma*) with which we construct our worldview. In modern parlance it expresses a psychology of phenomonologically ideal realism.

Manopubbangammâ dhammâ
Manosetthâ manomayâ
Manasâ ce padutthena

These words are of such integral importance to understanding the Buddhist view of the role of thinking in the construction of a worldview that no single English translation should be relied upon. For example, many English translations insert the pronoun "we" into the lines which does not appear in the original Pali. To demonstrate the variety of English translations:

> We are what we think.
> All that we are arises with our thoughts.
> With our thoughts we make the world.

> Preceded by perception are mental states.
> For them is perception supreme.
> From perception have they sprung.

> All mental phenomena are preceded by mind,
> Mind is their master,
> they are produced by mind.

In Buddhism there is no "designer" who is outside of the design. The recognition of a "design" (i.e., pattern recognition at all levels of mentation, perception, mental complexes, etc.) is the function of *manas* (thinking mind) and is otherwise known in Buddhist psychology as the Sixth Consciousness. It is this role of the Sixth Consciousness in creating the fundamental patterns for the building blocks of a worldview that makes thought the "creator" of the world. All the notions we have about ourselves and our world are fundamentally incorrect notions that become the root cause of ignorance. In Buddhism, the term *the world* does not refer to an objective empirical world accepted as real, but to the process of objectification of a world that we experience. In Buddhism the world arises moment by moment, and no thing exists beyond the thought-moment of its existence, but that thinking makes it seem to be so by stringing together thought-moments (for example, using memory and associations) into a tapestry of the illusion of a world. So in Buddhism, the words *the world* refers to *all this mass of stress* created by the delusions of our thought-designs interpreting, configuring, and constructing the world of experience (i.e., the first Five Consciousnesses).

It is noteworthy therefore that while creation in most other religions, as perceived by a person who objectifies themselves as a being, or separate entity, is the act of a divine being and viewed as a purely positive event, while in Buddhism, neither is creation divine nor is it only positive, but necessarily both positive and negative, plus and minus, in equal proportion. That is, when the undifferentiated mind (i.e., the Eighth Consciousnesses) discriminates itself (i.e., the functioning of the Seventh Consciousnesses), that discrimination is itself the activity of mind functioning in both plus and minus capacities. This discrimination function must necessarily include both poles of every "opposition" or "polarity" that is discriminated. When the thinking process (*manas*) then attempts to configure a design out of the multiplicity of oppositions, it naturally falls on or grasps at one side of the apparent opposition in distinction to the other side in order to create a sense of solidity or fixation to the world. By such "taking sides" or "one-sidedness", thinking makes itself appear supreme (*semmha*) in its own world, thus the designation *manosemmhâ* in line two of the *Dhammapada* above. In the Buddhist view, liberation occurs when our thinking mind (*manas*) comes down off its self-created throne and sees that the world it creates is illusory and that all things or patterns (i.e., *dhammas*) are not other than discrimination of Mind as the waves are the discrimination of the ocean. This Mind that is discriminated is designated in positive language as the Tathagata, Dharmakaya, Tathagatagarbha, Buddha Nature, Suchness, Thusness, etc. and in negative language as Sunyata, Emptiness, Non-dual, No-Mind, etc.

The statement "From consciousness as a requisite condition comes name-&-form" repeatedly occurs throughout the Pali canons, indicating that the Buddha had meant the world physically arises from consciousness.

GOD IN EARLY BUDDHISM

In early Buddhism, the Buddha clearly states that "reliance and belief" in creation by a supreme being leads to lack of effort and inaction: This is a significant hindrance in the path to liberation in the Buddha's view. It may be noted that the Buddha did not criticize veneration of the noble, veneration of the wise and learned, but only said that the belief in the existence of a creator God fetters the mind to samsara.

Having approached the priests & contemplatives who hold that...

> 'Whatever a person experiences... is all caused by a supreme being's act of creation,'

I said to them: 'Is it true that you hold that... "Whatever a person experiences... is all caused by a supreme being's act of creation?"'

> Thus asked by me, they admitted, 'Yes.'

> Then I said to them, 'Then in that case, a person is a killer of living beings because of a supreme being's act of creation. A person is a thief... unchaste... a liar... a divisive speaker... a harsh speaker... an idle chatterer... greedy... malicious... a holder of wrong views because of a supreme being's act of creation.'

When one falls back on creation by a supreme being as being essential, monks, there is no desire, no effort [at the thought], 'This should be done. This shouldn't be done.' When one can't pin down as a truth or reality what should and shouldn't be done, one dwells bewildered and unprotected. One cannot righteously refer to oneself as a contemplative. This was my second righteous refutation of those priests and contemplative who hold to such teachings, such views.

It is also noteworthy that gods in Buddhism have no role to play in liberation. Sir Charles Eliot describes god in early Buddhism as such:

> The attitude of early Buddhism to the spirit world — the hosts of deities and demons who people this and other spheres. Their existence is assumed, but the truths of religion are not dependent on them, and attempts to use their influence by sacrifices and oracles are deprecated as vulgar practices similar to juggling.

The systems of philosophy then in vogue were mostly not theistic, and, strange as the words may sound, religion had little to do with the gods. If this be thought to rest on a mistranslation, it is certainly true that the dhamma had very little to do with devas.

Often as the Devas figure in early Buddhist stories, the significance of their appearance nearly always lies in their relations with the Buddha or his disciples. Of mere mythology, such as the dealings of Brahma and Indra with other gods, there is little. In fact the gods, though freely invoked as accessories, are not taken seriously, and there are some extremely curious passages in which Gotama seems to laugh at them, much as the sceptics of the 18th century laughed at Jehovah. Thus in the [Pali Canon] Kevaddha Sutta he relates how a monk who was puzzled by a metaphysical problem applied to various gods and finally accosted Brahma himself in the presence of all his retinue. After hearing the question, which was "Where do the elements cease and leave no trace behind?" Brahma replies, "I am the Great Brahma, the Supreme, the Mighty, the All-seeing, the Ruler, the Lord of all, the Controller, the Creator, the Chief of all, appointing to each his place, the Ancient of days, the Father of all that are and are to be." "But," said the monk, "I did not ask you, friend, whether you were indeed all you now say, but I ask you where the four elements cease and leave no trace." Then the Great Brahma took him by the arm and led him aside and said, "These gods think I know and understand everything. Therefore I gave no answer in their presence. But I do not know the answer to your question and you had better go and ask the Buddha."

Even more curiously ironic is the account given of the origin of Brahma. There comes a time when this world system passes away and then certain beings are reborn in the "World of Radiance" and remain there a long time. Sooner or later, the world system begins to evolve again and the palace of Brahma appears, but it is empty. Then some being whose time is up falls from the "World of Radiance" and comes to life in the palace and remains there alone. At last he wishes for company, and it so happens that other beings whose time is up fall from the "World of Radiance" and join him. And the first being thinks that he is Great Brahma, the Creator, because when he felt lonely and wished for companions other beings appeared. And the other beings accept this view. And at last one of Brahma's retinue falls from that state and is born in the human world and, if he can remember his previous birth, he reflects that he is transitory but that Brahma still remains and from this he draws the erroneous conclusion that Brahma is eternal.

Brahmins and Communion with God

The Brahmins of the day apparently claimed that they were the link between humans and the devas. Often this would place the priestly class at an advantageous position. But the Pâli suttas dismiss the folly of those religious teachers who would lead others to what they themselves do not personally know, as "foolish talk", or "ridiculous, mere words, a vain and empty thing".

Brahma in the Pali Canon

Brahma is among the common gods found in the Pali Canon. Brahma (in common with all other devas) is subject to change, final decline and death, just as are all other sentient beings in samsara (the plane of continual reincarnation and suffering). In fact there are several different Brahma worlds and several kinds of Brahmas in Buddhism, all of which however are just beings stuck in samsara for a long while. Instead of belief in such a would-be Creator God as Brahma (a benign heavenly being who is in reality not yet free from self-delusion and the processes of rebirth), the wise are encouraged to practise the Dharma (spiritual truth) of the Buddha, in which the Noble Eightfold Path are paramount and are said to bring spiritual Liberation and Awakening.

Other Common Gods Referred to in the Canon

Many of the other gods in the Pali Canon find a common mythological role in Hindu literature. Some common gods and goddesses are Indra, Aapo (Varuna), Vayo (Vayu), Tejo (Agni), Surya, Pajapati (Prajapati), Soma, Yasa, Venhu (Visnu), Mahadeva (Siva), Vijja (Saraswati), Usha, Pathavi (Prithvi) Sri (Lakshmi) Kuvera (Kubera), several yakkhas (Yakshas), gandhabbas (Gandharvas), Nâgas, garula (Garuda), sons of Bali, Veroca, etc. While in Hindu texts some of these gods and goddesses are considered embodiments of the Supreme Being, to early Buddhists this is a ridiculous idea. In the Buddha's view all gods and goddesses were bound to samsara. The world of gods according to the Buddha presents a being with too many pleasures and distractions.

God as a Maintainer and the Force behind the World

One of the popular views emerging in the time of the Buddha and often seen even today was the view that even though the world was not created by a creator God, there is a driving force, a guiding principle behind the workings of the world. As an example, in ancient India, some Hindu sects considered God to be the dispenser of the results of action. According to the Buddha, this view was very dangerous in two ways.

One of the primary reasons is that this places a limitation in ones understanding of the mechanism of karma. Understanding the mechanism of karma is central to the understanding the Dharma leading to the cessation of stress and hence to complete unbinding (nirvana). In fact, when the Buddha attained enlightenment, he first used his insightful awareness to view his past lives and the past and future lives of all other beings and observed the law of karma in action. Belief that a Supreme God is the force behind this law of nature places a significant road-block in spiritual progress, thus disabling the person from understanding the mechanism of karma, in terms of paticcasamuppada (or dependent causality).

The second reason the Buddha considered this notion as egregious is that this belief makes God a dispenser of the results of our actions. Given this, we could try to bribe God or as was common in those days and even today, one would worship God (or confess) to ask for forgiveness. According to the Buddha, this only makes a person irresponsible. If he were solely responsible for the results of his own actions (as he truly is) he will have no one to ask for pardon. The tendency of the human mind to look for such a God is mainly due to its tendency to indulge and yet expect to be forgiven. However, only when we understand that we are entirely responsible for our own actions, and that results accrue as a law of nature and not due to some benign or judgmental being, will we understand the importance of skillful action and reflection that leads to happiness and escape from samsara.

Another view quite popular today which was also present at the time of the Buddha in India was that God is the principle of the law of nature that causes events to occur in a causal manner. In this belief he is not considered a being whose behaviour could be influenced by human endeavour, but nevertheless was a personified image that 'governs' the world. However this is essentially an egregious personification of the laws of causality that the Buddha ascribed to the workings of the world. According to the Buddha, the law of causality could be described briefly as:

> When this arises, that arises
> When this ceases, that ceases.

A detailed exposition of the dependent causality was needed to understand the more subtle function of the mind-body complex of the human world. The law of causality is not intended to explain the workings of every single phenomenon in the world, but to understand the nature of samsara, the round of birth and death and karma. Personifying this law of nature into a God is of no special benefit as seen from the Buddhist standpoint.

But more than that, the Buddha adopted here a radical viewpoint on the basic tendency of the human mind to posit a God or a governor. Humans tend to look for a governor or a God primarily because of his fundamental need for protection and self-preservation. This lack of security and human weakness was according to the Buddha, the root cause that inspires humans to posit a God. In Buddhism, it is precisely because of this clinging to self and the need for self-preservation that we conceive a self, a soul or a super-soul. It is the proximal cause of ignorance and the root cause of clinging, thus binding us to samsara.

Mahayana and Tantric Mystical Doctrines

Mahayana Buddhism, unlike Theravada, talks of Mind — using terms such as "the womb of the Thus-come One" — in a manner that is mistaken by some to indicate an "eternal entity". Such positive statements arose as a way to relate to the common misunderstanding of emptiness as nothingness, that is a nihilistic view of reality. The affirmation of emptiness by positive terminology appears quite radical when compared with early Buddhism's avoidance of "atman" and "god" terminology. Theravada, the oldest surviving school of Buddhism, generally does not subscribe to the idea of referring to the emptiness of mind with positive terminology. According to the Pali Canon, there is no eternal, all-pervading entity that is the source of all energy. Several Theravada scholars criticize the Mahayana scholars as having resorted to the same Vedantic ideas of eternal entities that the Buddha had rejected. From the Mahayana view, to the extent that any Mahayana practitioner actually asserts an "eternal entity" then this Theravada criticism is warranted. However, also from the Mahayana view, the Theravada criticism of Mahayana's use of postitive terminology as an assertion of "eternal entity" is itself a misperception of Mahayana and of Buddha's teaching.

Professor C.D. Sebastian writes in his study of tathagatagarbha doctrine that Mahayana Buddhism is not merely intellectual, but also encompasses the sphere of devotion. Buddha is taken as the Supreme Reality - a kind of God who assumed human form in order to benefit all humanity:

> 'Mahayana Buddhism is not only intellectual, but also it is devotional ... in Mahayana, Buddha was taken as God, as Supreme Reality itself that descended on the earth in human form for the good of mankind. The concept of Buddha (as equal to God in theistic systems) was never as a creator but as Divine Love that out of compassion (*karuna*) embodied itself in human form to uplift suffering humanity. He was worshipped with fervent devotion... He represents the Absolute (*paramartha satya*), devoid of all plurality (*sarva-prapancanta-vinirmukta*) and has no beginning, middle and end ... Buddha ... is eternal, immutable ... As such He represents Dharmakaya.'

Tathagata and Dharmakaya as God Equivalents

In some Mahayana traditions, the Buddha is indeed worshipped as a virtual divinity who is possessed of supernatural qualities and powers. Dr. Guang Xing writes: "The Buddha worshipped by Mahayanist followers is an omnipotent divinity endowed with numerous supernatural attributes and qualities ... is described almost as an omnipotent and almighty godhead.".

Buddhist scholar, Dr. B. Alan Wallace, has also indicated that saying that Buddhism as a whole is 'non-theistic' may be an over-simplification. Wallace discerns similarities between some forms of Vajrayana Buddhism and notions of a divine 'ground of being' and creation. He writes: 'a careful analysis of Vajrayana Buddhist cosmogony, specifically as presented in the Atiyoga tradition of Indo-Tibetan Buddhism, which presents itself as the culmination of all Buddhist teachings, reveals a theory of a transcendent ground of being and a process of creation that bear remarkable similarities with views presented in Vedanta and Neoplatonic Western Christian theories of creation.' In fact, Wallace sees these views as so similar that they seem almost to be different manifestations of the same theory. He comments: 'Vajrayana Buddhism, Vedanta, and Neoplatonic Christianity have so much in common that they could almost be regarded as varying interpretations of a single theory.'

Vedantic statements regarding an invariant substratum are, however, rejected by the Buddha of the earliest scriptures as "pernicious views." In fact, regarding attempts of Brahmins to merge with a professed eternal substratum (known as Brahman), the Buddha stated that such people were worrying about something that is "non-existent" (*asati*). Western analogues of aspects the thought of the Buddha as recorded in the earliest texts have only developed in modern times. In particular, early Buddhism has been compared to process philosophy (which existed in ancient Greece, but was eclipsed in Western thought by substance-attribute ontology until modern times), phenomenology, and deconstructionism.

According to the tathagatagarbha sutras, the Buddha also taught the existence of a spiritual essence called the tathagagatagarbha or Buddha-nature, which is present in all beings and phenomena. Dr. B. Alan Wallace writes of this doctrine:

> 'the essential nature of the whole of samsara and nirvana is the absolute space (*dhatu*) of the *tathagatagarbha,* but this space is not to be confused with a mere absence of matter. Rather, this absolute space is imbued with all the infinite knowledge, compassion, power, and enlightened activities of the Buddha. Moreover, this luminous space is that which causes the phenomenal world to appear, and it is none other than the nature of one's own mind, which by nature is clear light.'

Another scholar sees a Buddhist Absolute in Consciousness. Writing on the Yogacara school of Buddhism, Dr. A. K. Chatterjee remarks:

> 'The Absolute is a non-dual consciousness. The duality of the subject and object does not pertain to it. It is said to be void (*sunya*), devoid of duality; in itself it is perfectly real, in fact the only reality ...There is no consciousness *of* the Absolute; Consciousness *is* the Absolute.'

While this is a traditional Tibetan interpretation of Yogacara views, it has been rejected by modern Western scholarship, namely by Kochumuttom, Anacker, Kalupahana, Dunne, Lusthaus, Powers, and Wayman.. Scholar Dan Lusthaus writes: "They [Yogacarins] did not focus on consciousness to assert it as ultimately real (Yogâcâra claims consciousness is only conventionally real since it arises from moment to moment due to fluctuating causes and conditions), but rather because it is the cause of the karmic problem they are seeking to eliminate."

According to the earliest Buddhist scriptures, the Buddha placed the belief in an unchanging consciousness on par with denying the necessity of the practical foundation of monasticism, celibacy. The Buddha says of a monk holding the former view that this misunderstanding "both damages himself and generates much demerit." Gombrich writes: "A fundamental difference between the Buddha's view and the Upanishadic view is that the Buddha never confused epistemology with ontology ... The Buddha did not reify consciousness. Vinnana is one of the five khandha, and is a process, not a thing: consciousness is always consciousness *of*'. The clearest statement that consciousness is simply a process is the description of it as "dependently originated" (*paticca-samuppanna*).

A further name for the irreducible, time-and-space-transcending mysterious Truth or Essence of Buddhic Reality spoken of in some Mahayana and tantric texts is the Dharmakaya (Body of Truth). Of this the Zen master (Zen Buddhism is a Mahayana school), Sokei-An, says:

> ... *dharmakaya* the equivalent of God ... The Buddha also speaks of no time and no space, where if I make a sound there is in that single moment a million years. It is spaceless like radio waves, like electric space - intrinsic. The Buddha said that there is a mirror that reflects consciousness. In this electric space a million miles and a pinpoint - a million years and a moment - are exactly the same. It is pure essence ... We call it 'original consciousness' - 'original *akasha*' - perhaps God in the Christian sense. I am afraid of speaking about anything that is not familiar to me. No one can know what IT is ...

The same Zen adept, Sokei-An, further comments:

> The creative power of the universe is not a human being; it is Buddha. The one who sees, and the one who hears, is not this eye or ear, but the one who is *this* consciousness. *This One* is Buddha. *This One* appears in every mind. *This One* is common to all sentient beings, and is God.

The Rinzai Zen Buddhist master, Soyen Shaku, speaking to Americans at the beginning of the 20th century, discusses how in essence the idea of God is not absent from Buddhism, when understood as ultimate, true Reality:

> At the outset, let me state that Buddhism is not atheistic as the term is ordinarily understood. It has certainly a God, the highest reality and truth, through which and in which this universe exists. However, the followers of Buddhism usually avoid the term God, for it savors so much of Christianity, whose spirit is not always exactly in accord with the Buddhist interpretation of religious experience ... To define more exactly the Buddhist notion of the highest being, it may be convenient to borrow the term very happily coined by a modern German scholar, 'panentheism', according to which God is ... all and one and more than the totality of existence .... As I mentioned before, Buddhists do not make use of the term God, which characteristically belongs to Christian terminology. An equivalent most commonly used is Dharmakaya ... When the Dharmakaya is most concretely conceived it becomes the Buddha, or Tathagata ...

Primordial Buddhas

Theories regarding a self-existent "ground of being" were common in India prior to the Buddha, and were rejected by him: "The Buddha, however, refusing to admit any metaphysical principle as a common thread holding the moments of encountered phenomena together, rejects the Upanishadic notion of an immutable substance or principle underlying the world and the person and producing phenomena out of its inherent power, be it 'being', atman, brahman, or 'god.'"

In later Mahayana literature, however, the idea of an eternal, all-pervading, all-knowing, immaculate, uncreated and deathless Ground of Being (the *dharmadhatu,* inherently linked to the *sattvadhatu,* the realm of beings), which is the Awakened Mind (*bodhicitta*) or Dharmakaya ("body of Truth") of the Buddha himself, is attributed to the Buddha in a number of Mahayana sutras, and is found in various tantras as well. In some Mahayana texts, such a principle is occasionally presented as manifesting in a more personalised form as a primordial buddha, such as Samantabhadra, Vajradhara, Vairochana, and Adi-Buddha, among others.

In some Buddhist tantric and Dzogchen scriptures, too, this immanent and transcendent Dharmakaya (the ultimate essence of the Buddha's being) is portrayed as the primordial Buddha, Samantabhadra, worshipped as the primordial lord. In a study of Dzogchen, Dr. Sam van Schaik mentions how Samantabhadra Buddha is indeed seen as 'the heart essence of all buddhas, the Primordial Lord, the noble Victorious One, Samantabhadra'. Dr. Schaik indicates that Samantabhadra is not to be viewed as some kind of separate *mindstream,* apart from the mindstreams of sentient beings, but should be known as a universal nirvanic principle termed the Awakened Mind (*bodhi-citta*) and present in all. Dr. Schaik quotes from the tantric texts, *Experiencing the Enlightened Mind of Samantabhadra* and *The Subsequent Tantra of Great Perfection Instruction* to portray Samantabhadra as an uncreated, reflexive, radiant, pure and vital Knowing (gnosis) which is present in all things:

> 'The essence of all phenomena is the awakened mind; the mind of all buddhas is the awakened mind; and the life-

> force of all sentient beings is the awakened mind, too ... This unfabricated gnosis of the present moment is the reflexive luminosity, naked and stainless, the Primordial Lord himself.'

In the Mahavairocana Sutra, the essence of Vairocana, who is viewed in that scripture as the supreme Buddha, is said to be symbolised by the letter "A", which is claimed to reside in the hearts of all beings and of which Buddha Vairocana declares that "[the mystic letter 'A'] is placed in the heart location:

> it is Lord and Master of all,
> and it pervades entirely
> all the animate and inanimate.
> 'A' is the highest life-energy ...

The text refers to Vairocana Buddha as the "Bhagavat" ("Blessed One," a term traditionally linked in Indian discourse with "the Divine"), "Master of the Dharma, *the Sage who is completely perfect, who is all-pervasive, who encompasses all world systems, who is All-Knowing, the Lord Vairocana*".

The Tantric text, *The Sarva-Tathagata-Tattva-Samgraha,* characterizes Vairocana as follows:

> He is universal Goodness, beneficial, destroyer [of suffering], the great Lord of Happiness, sky womb, Great Luminosity ... the great All-perceiving Lord ... He is without beginning or end ... [He is] Vishnu ... Protector of the world, the sky, the earth ... The elements, the good benefactor of beings, All things ... the Blessed Rest, Eternal ... The Self of all the Buddhas ... Pre-eminent over all, and master of the world.

Similar God-like descriptions are encountered in the *All-Creating King Tantra* (Kunjed Gyalpo Tantra), where the universal Mind of Awakening (in its mode as "Samantabhadra Buddha") declares of itself:

> I am the core of all that exists. I am the seed of all that exists. I am the cause of all that exists. I am the trunk of all that exists. I am the foundation of all that exists. I am the root of existence. I am "the core" because I contain all phenomena. I am "the seed" because I give birth to everything. I am "the cause" because all comes from me. I am "the trunk" because the ramifications of every event sprout from me. I am "the foundation" because all abides in me. I am called "the root" because I am everything.

The Karandavyuha Sutra presents the great bodhisattva, Avalokitesvara, as a kind of supreme lord of the cosmos. A striking feature of Avalokitesvara in this sutra is his creative power, as he is said to be the progenitor of various heavenly bodies and divinities. Dr. Alexander Studholme, in his monograph on the sutra, writes:

> 'The sun and moon are said to be born from the bodhisattva's eyes, Mahesvara [Siva] from his brow, Brahma from his shoulders, Narayana [Vishnu] from his heart, Sarasvati from his teeth, the winds from his mouth, the earth from his feet and the sky from his stomach.'

Avalokitesvara himself is linked in the versified version of the sutra to the first Buddha, the Adi Buddha, who is 'svayambhu' (self-existent, not born from anything or anyone). Dr. Studholme comments:

> 'Avalokitesvara himself, the verse sutra adds, is an emanation of the *Adibuddha,* or 'primordial Buddha', a term that is explicitly said to be synoymous with *Svayambhu* and *Adinatha,* 'primordial lord'.'

That primordial Buddha, Âdibuddha (Adi-Buddha), figures prominently in the Kalachakra tantra. Âdibuddha is believed to be a primordial, self-existent, self-created Buddha who is the personification of Shunyata or emptiness [freedom from confining substance or conceptual graspability) enshrining the infinitely Knowing Mind of Great Compassion; all phenomena lack true separate existence yet still appear, and their basis is the undifferentiated and inconceivable Mind of Buddha (empty of all defects and ignorance). However, all these seemingly godlike figures (Samantabhadra, Vairochana, Vajradhara, etc.) are traditionally understood to be personifications of emptiness and compassion – the ungraspable, limitless, invisible, inconceivable, unimpeded benevolent Reality of Buddha-Mind and the true nature of all phenomena. Some Buddhists see the above quote from Samantabhadra Buddha as radically subjective psychology, while still others will insist that the words mean what they say and do communicate the sense of an actual sustaining force or spiritual essence behind and within all phenomena.

God as Manifestation of Mind

One of the Mahayana Sutras, the Lankavatara Sutra, states that the notions of a sovereign God, Atman are figments of the imagination or manifestations of the mind and can also be an impediment to perfection as this leads to attachment to the concept of God:

> All such notions as causation, succession, atoms, primary elements, that make up personality, personal soul, Supreme Spirit, Sovereign God, Creator, are all figments of the imagination and manifestations of mind.

No, Mahamati, the Tathágata's doctrine of the Womb of Tathágata-hood is not the same as the philosopher's Atman.

Instead of a personal creator God, the sutra speaks of creative Mind, and of Suchness (*tathata* - universal Truth-as-it-is), which is defined as: "... this Suchness may be characterised as Truth, Reality, exact knowledge, limit, source, self-substance, the Unattainable".

Moreover, the same sutra also sees the Buddha reveal that he is the unrecognised One who is actually being addressed when beings project from their unawakened minds notions of Divinity and address themselves to "God". The many names for such ultimate Being or Truth are in fact said by the Buddha to be unwitting appellations of the Buddha himself. He states:

> The same can be said of myself as I appear in this world of patience before ignorant people and where I am known by uncounted trillions of names.
>
> They address me by different names not realizing that they are all names of the one Tathagata.
>
> Some recognize me as Sun, as Moon; some as a reincarnation of the ancient sages; some as one of "ten powers"; some as Rama, some as Indra, and some as Varuna. Still there are others who speak of me as The Un-born, as Emptiness, as "Suchness," as Truth, as Reality, as Ultimate Principle; still there are others who see me as Dharmakaya, as Nirvana, as the Eternal; some speak of me as sameness, as non-duality, as un-dying, as formless; some think of me as the doctrine of Buddha-causation, or of Emancipation, or of the Noble Path; and some think of me as Divine Mind and Noble Wisdom.
>
> Thus in this world and in other worlds am I known by these uncounted names, but they all see me as the moon is seen in the water.
>
> Though they all honor, praise and esteem me, they do not fully understand the meaning and significance of the words they use; not having their own self-realization of Truth they cling to the words of their canonical books, or to what has been told to them, or to what they have imagined,

and fail to see that the name they are using is only one of the many names of the Tathagata.

In their studies they follow the mere words of the text vainly trying to gain the true meaning, instead of having confidence in the one "text" where self-confirming Truth is revealed, that is, having confidence in the self-realization of noble Wisdom.

In the "Sagathakam" section of the sutra (which contains some striking statements contradictory of earlier chapters of the sutra), one also reads of the reality of the pure Self (atman), which (while not identical to the atman of the Hindus) is equated with the Tathagatagarbha (Buddha-Essence):

> The *atma* [Self] characterised with purity is the state of self-realisation; this is the Tathagatagarbha, which does not belong to the realm of the theorisers.

This Tathagatagarbha is in the *Lankavatara Sutra* identified with the root or all-containing Consciousness of all beings, the Alaya-vijnana. This Tathagatagarbha-Alayavijnana is stated not to belong to the realm of speculation, but can be understood directly by

> those Bodhisatva-Mahasattvas [great Bodhisattvas] who like you [Mahamati] are endowed with subtle, fine, penetrative thought-power and whose understanding is in accordance with the meaning ...

Such an all-containing Buddhic Matrix (Tathagatagarbha) or basis of universal consciousness (Alayavijñana) has resonances with a conception of divinity which posits the latter as the underlying reality behind and within all things. This "Self" is in some Mahayana Buddhist scriptures and tantras equated with the original, primal, all-sustaining cosmic Buddha himself (viewed either as Samantabhadra or Mahavairochana).

Devas

Though not believing in a creator God, Buddhists inherited the Indian cosmology of the time which includes various types of 'god' realms such as the Heaven of the Thirty-Three, the Four Great Kings, and so on. Deva-realms are part of the various possible types of existence in the Buddhist cosmology. Rebirth as a deva is attributed to virtuous actions performed in previous lives. Beings that had meditated are thought to be reborn in more and more subtle realms with increasingly vast life spans, in accord with their meditative ability. In particular, the highest deva realms are pointed out as false paths in meditation that the meditator should be aware of. Like any existence within the cycle of rebirth (samsara), a life as a deva is only temporary. At the time of death, a large part of the former deva's good karma has been expended, leaving mostly negative karma and a likely rebirth in one of the three lower realms. Therefore, Buddhists make a special effort not to be reborn in deva realms.

●●

8

Buddhism and Hinduism

Buddhism and Hinduism are two closely related religions that are in some ways parallel and in other ways divergent in theory and practice.

The Vedic, Buddhist, and Jain religions share a common regional culture situated near and around north eastern India – modern day eastern Uttar Pradesh, Bihar and Nepal. Both the Buddha and Mahavira (the historical founder of Jainism), hailed from this region. Also the Brihadaranyaka Upanishad, considered to be among the very earliest Upanishads, was compiled in this region, under King Janaka of Mithila.

Ancient India had two philosophical streams of thought, the Shramana religions and the Vedic religion, parallel traditions that have existed side by side for thousands of years. Both Buddhism and Jainism are continuations of Shramana traditions, while modern Hinduism is a continuation of the Vedic tradition. These co-existing traditions have been mutually influential.

The Buddha rejected relying on Vedas for salvation, which included the earliest Upanishads. He redefined Indian cosmology, incorporating many existing terms in his doctrine, but redefining them for his purposes in explaining the Middle Path, also teaching that to achieve salvation one did not have to accept the authority of the scriptures or the existence of God. As regards Vedanta, though at the time of the early Buddhists there was no independent Vedanta school with a developed and organized philosophical system, the various philosophical theories of the Upanishads were quite widely disseminated. These intellectual trends are mentioned in the Buddhist texts, and rejected as "pernicious views".

Later Indian religious thought was in turn influenced by the new interpretations and novel ideas of the Buddhist tradition. Buddhism attained prominence on the Indian subcontinent, but was ultimately eclipsed (in the 11th century C.E.) at its point of origin by Hinduism and Islam. After this, Buddhism continued to flourish outside of India. Tibetan Buddhism predominates in the Himalayan region, as does Theravada Buddhism in Sri Lanka and Southeast Asia, and Mahayana Buddhism in East Asia.

Early History

Evidence from both Buddhist and Hindu scriptures show that the two traditions were in dialogue with one another from a very early date. The Buddha is mentioned in several of the Puranas that are believed to have been composed after his birth. Certain Buddhist teachings appear to have been formulated in response to ideas presented in the early Upanishads – in some cases concurring with them, and in other cases criticizing or re-interpreting them.

The Bhagavad Gita is a post-Buddhist text, and some scholars believe it was composed as part of the Hindu reaction to Buddhism. Prominent Indian scholars see the Bhagavad Gita as rather the product of intellectual currents then prevalent in India that pre-dated the emergence of Buddhism.

In later years, there is significant evidence that both Buddhism and Hinduism were supported by Indian rulers, regardless of the rulers own religious identity. Buddhist kings continued to revere Hindu deities and teachers, and many Buddhist temples were built under the patronage of Hindu rulers.

SIMILARITIES BETWEEN HINDUISM AND BUDDHISM

Technical Language

The Buddha adopted many of the terms already used in philosophical discussions of his era; however, many of these terms were then re-interpreted or redefined in the Buddhist tradition. For example, in the Samanna-phala Sutta, the Buddha is depicted presenting a notion of the 'three knowledges' (*tevijja*) – a term also used in the Vedic tradition to describe knowledge of the Vedas – as being not texts, but things that he had experienced. The true 'three knowledges' are said to be constituted by the process of achieving enlightenment, which is what the Buddha is said to have achieved in the three watches of the night of his enlightenment.

Ahimsa

Ahimsa is a religious concept which advocates non-violence and a respect for all life. *Ahimsa* is Sanskrit for avoidance of sacrificial *himsa,* or injury. The Buddha's dialogue in the *Culakammavibhanga Sutta* with the Brahmin Subha on killing is interesting considering the Vedic emphasis on sacrificial *himsa.* The focus on *ahimsa,* non-harm to all beings, in Buddhist ethics was a definitive move away from the killing inherent in the sacrifices of the Vedic ritual tradition. This move away from sacrificial *himsa* was also being made in other Sramana traditions. The Upanishadic literature, for example, is often critical of Vedic ritual and emphasises the internalization of the meaning and symbolism of sacrifice, rather than its literal enactment. Long life-span was much sought after by the composers of the Vedas. The Buddha's explanation of karma in the *Culakammavibhanga Sutta* challenges the Vedic idea that a life of sacrifice accrues benefits and excellence for oneself and one's family. The Buddha expounds his view that intentionally killing living beings leads not to the good, but to something that was problematic for the brahmins of his day, that is, shortness of life.

Karma

Karma is a word meaning *action* or *activity* and, often implies its subsequent results (also called karma-phala, "the fruits of action"). It is commonly understood as a term to denote the entire cycle of cause and effect as described in the philosophies of a number of cosmologies, including those of Buddhism and Hinduism.

Karma is a central part of Buddhist teachings. Buddhist teachings re-interpret certain aspects of the pre-Buddhist conception of karma, removing the idea of a perfect moral equilibrium present in some versions of those teachings.

Meanwhile, certain aspects of Buddhist teachings on karma, such as the 'transfer of merit' (Sanskrit: PariGâmanâ) or transfer of karma, seem to have been borrowed directly from earlier Hindu teachings, despite presenting apparent inconsistencies with the Buddhist doctrine of karma.

Dharma

Dharma means Natural Law or Reality, and with respect to its significance for spirituality and religion might be considered the Way of the Higher Truths. A Hindu appellation for Hinduism itself is *Sanatana Dharma* which translates to "the eternal dharma." Similarly, Buddhadharma in an appellation for Buddhism. The general concept of dharma forms a basis for philosophies, beliefs and practices originating in India. The four main ones are Hinduism, Buddhism, Jainism (Jaina Dharma), and Sikhism (Sikha Dharma), all of whom retain the centrality of dharma in their teachings. In these traditions, beings that live in harmony with dharma proceed more quickly toward, according to the tradition, Dharma Yukam, Moksha, or Nirvana (personal liberation). Dharma can refer generally to religious duty, and also mean social order, right conduct, or simply virtue.

Mantra

A mantra is a religious syllable or poem, typically from the Sanskrit language. Their use varies according to the school and philosophy associated with the mantra. They are primarily used as spiritual conduits, words or vibrations that instill one-pointed concentration in the devotee. Other purposes have included religious ceremonies to accumulate wealth, avoid danger, or eliminate enemies. Mantras existed in the Vedic religion and were later adopted by Buddhists, Sikhs and Jains, now popular in various modern forms of spiritual practice which are loosely based on practices of these Eastern religions.

Meditation

Meditation was an aspect of the practice of the yogis in the centuries preceding the Buddha. The Buddha built upon the yogis' concern with introspection and developed their meditative techniques, but rejected their theories of liberation. In Buddhism, sati and sampajanna (both translated into English as mindfulness) are to be developed at all times, in pre-Buddhist yogic practices there is no such injunction. A yogi in the Brahmanical tradition is not to practice while defecating, for example, while a Buddhist monastic should do so. This difference is due the different goals of the practice. The former practitioner is aiming for gnosis of an object outside of the world, while for the latter there is no such object; experience in the world is the object, which must be purified. Another new teaching of the Buddha was that meditative absorption should be combined with the practice of mindfulness.

Religious knowledge or 'vision' was indicated as a result of practice both within and outside of the Buddhist fold.

According to the *Samaññaphala Sutta* this sort of vision arose for the Buddhist adept as a result of the perfection of 'meditation' (Sanskrit: dhyâna) coupled with the perfection of 'ethics' (Sanskrit: úîla). Some of the Buddha's meditative techniques were shared with other traditions of his day, but the idea that ethics are causally related to the attainment of 'religious insight' (Sanskrit: prajñâ) was original.

The Buddhist texts are probably the earliest describing meditation techniques. They describe meditative practices and states which had existed before the Buddha as well as those which were first developed within Buddhism. Two Upanishads written after the rise of Buddhism do contain full-fledged descriptions of yoga as a means to liberation.

While there is no convincing evidence for meditation pre-Buddhist early Brahminic texts, Wynne argues that formless meditation originated in the Brahminic tradition, based on strong parallels between Upanishadic cosmological statements and the meditative goals of the two teachers of the Buddha as recorded in the early Buddhist texts. He mentions less likely possibilities as well. Having argued that the cosmological statements in the Upanishads also reflect a contemplative tradition, he argues that the Nasadiya Sukta contains evidence for a contemplative tradition, even as early as the late Rg Vedic period.

Reincarnation

In the Rig Veda, man is thought to be born and die only once. The Rig Veda mentions life after death in heaven in the company of ancestors. The ritual system of the Vedas was central to Vedic life and thought and depended 'on the notion of constant sacrifice, the reintegration of multiple elements into a moment of unity before a new dispersal into being'.

It is highly probable that in India the concept of reincarnation (along with karma, samsara, and moksha) was developed by non-Aryan people outside of the caste system whose spiritual ideas greatly influenced later Indian religious thought. Buddhism and Jainism are continuations of this tradition, and the early Upanishadic movement was influenced by it. Reincarnation was likely adopted from this religious culture by Brahmin orthodoxy, and Brahmins composed the earliest known scriptures containing these ideas in the early Upanishads. According to the Oxford Handbook of Eschatology, the Upanishadic treatments of samsara, karma, and reincarnation are "fundamental contributions of the Upanishads to Hindu—indeed, South Asian—eschatology."

According to Hinduism, the soul (*atman*) is immortal, while the body is subject to birth, decay, old age and death. The meme of reincarnation is intricately linked with the notion of karma, another concept first recorded in the Upanishads. Karma (literally: action) is the sum of one's actions, and the force that determines one's next reincarnation. The cycle of death and rebirth, governed by karma, is referred to as samsara.

The Shakyamuni Buddha rejected all theories according to which beings have an eternal, immutable self that transmigrated – the 'dweller within the body' or *atman* – he also criticized the statement "I have no self". Buddhism developed an understanding of a 'continuum or stream of skanda' through such disciplines as vipassanâ and shamata, which has become reified in later Buddhist discourse as the Mindstream doctrine, a reification that Shakyamuni Buddha would have challenged. Hence, it is to be understood as an upaya doctrine, as are all doctrines of the Buddhadharma. The mindstream was further developed by the Cittamatra and Yogacara schools and it impacted on the development of the 'store consciousness' (âlâyavijñâna) and the buddha nature conceptions and tathagatagarbha literature. In English Buddhist discourse the nomenclature 'reincarnation' is unfavoured due the insidious bias of an 'entity' that 'incarnates'. Buddhism challenges all such 'entities'. Instead of an 'entity', what is reborn is an 'evolving consciousness' (M.1.256) or 'stream of consciousness' (D.3.105), whose quality has been conditioned by karma.

Buddhist scriptures regularly discuss what is generally understood by the lay person as future and past lives, though these are more appropriately understood following Buddhavacana as the continuity of the mindstream of sentient beings. The phenomenon and institution of tulku within the Vajrayana tradition is an interesting qualification and analogue to the reification of the entity and the transmigration and reincarnation meme within many of the plethora of schools and sects of the Sanatana Dharma.

Yoga

The practice of Yoga is intimately connected to the religious beliefs and practices of both Buddhism and Hinduism. However there are distinct variations in the usage of yoga terminology in the two religions. In Hinduism, the term "Yoga" commonly refers to the eight limbs of yoga as defined in the Yoga Sutras of Patanjali, written some time after 100 BCE. Whereas in the Vajrāyana Buddhism of Tibet, the term "Yoga" is used to refer to any type of spiritual practice; from the various types of tantra (like Kriyayoga or Charyayoga) to 'Deity yoga' and 'guru yoga'. In the early translation phase of the Sutrayana and Tantrayana from India, China and other regions to Tibet, along with the practice lineages of sadhana, codified in the Nyingmapa canon, the most subtle 'conveyance' (Sanskrit: yana) is Adi Yoga (Sanskrit). A contemporary scholar with a focus on Tibetan Buddhism, Robert Thurman writes that Patanjali was influenced by the success of the Buddhist monastic system to formulate his own matrix for the version of thought he considered orthodox.

There is a range of common terminology and common descriptions of the meditative states that are seen as the foundation of meditation practice in both Hindu Yoga and Buddhism. Many scholars have noted that the concepts of dhyana and samâdhi - technical terms describing stages of meditative absorption - are common to meditative practices in both Hinduism and Buddhism. Most notable in this context is the relationship between the system of four Buddhist *dhyana* states (Pali: *jhana*) and the *samprajnata samadhi* states of Classical Yoga. Also, many (Tibetan) Vajrayana practices of the generation stage and completion stage work with the chakras, inner energy channels (nadis) and kundalini, called tummo in Tibetan.

Zen Buddhism

Zen is a form of Mahayana Buddhism. The Mahayana school of Buddhism is noted for its proximity with Yoga. In the west, Zen is often set alongside Yoga, the two schools of meditation display obvious family resemblances. Zen Buddhism traces some of its roots to yogic practices. Certain essential elements of Yoga are important both for Buddhism in general and for Zen in particular.

Tibetan Buddhism

Tibetan Buddhism is not a monolithic entity. What is known as Tibetan Buddhism, a particular tradition of Vajrayana, is a collection of practice lineages or traditions of sadhana transmission. These practice lineages are entwined and historically come from throughout the Asian region and include tantric elements from non-Buddhist schools. The modern nomenclature of western discourse that reifies a 'Buddhism' and a 'Hinduism' obscured the varigated and manifold entwined lineages of Tantra. It is important to remember that though Buddhism values scholarship, it is not a textual tradition (in the sense of the written word), but primarily one based on the practitioner's investigation and direct experience as demonstrated by the example of Shakyamuni, culminating in enlightenment under the Bodhi

Tree. Aspects of vipashyana and shamatha are entwined within tantric techniques. It is commonly held that Buddhism was introduced to Tibet from India, and though this is true, Buddhism from other areas such as China, Kashmir, Japan entered the Himalaya and is integrated with the practice lineages of the Nyingma, Kagyupa, Sakyapa and Gelukpa schools of Tibetan Buddhism, which in turn dialogued with the indigenous Bonpo traditions of the Himalaya.

Yoga is central to Tibetan Buddhism. In the Nyingma tradition, certain practitioners progress to increasingly profound levels of yoga, starting with Mahâ yoga, continuing to Anu yoga and ultimately undertaking the most subtle, Ati yoga. In qualification, the Nyingmapa do not equate a value judgment with the yana, one is not better than another, the yana most appropriate for a practitioner is determined by their karma, propensity and proclivity. The majority of practitioners stay within one yana for the duration of their lifetime. The Nyingmapa view all traditions, not just their own through the modal of the nine yana. The Bonpo have a comparable modal of nine. Elements of Adi Yoga for both the Bonpo and Nyingmapa are perceived in other traditions. Indeed, Nyingmapa and Bonpo are not the only source of Ati Yoga teachings as both traditions testify, as Adi Yoga is propagated in other worlds and dimensions. In the Sarma traditions, the Anuttara yoga class is equivalent to the three most subtle yana of the Nyingmapa. Other tantra yoga practices include a system of 108 bodily postures practiced with breath and heart rhythm timing in movement exercises is known as Trul khor or union of moon and sun (channel) prajna energies, and the body postures of Tibetan ancient yogis are depicted on the walls of the Dalai Lama's summer temple of Lukhang.

Tibetan Buddhist doctrines unite a seemingly diverse group of practices to offer a variety of ways to 'truth' (Sanskrit: satya; refer Two Truths) and 'enlightenment' (Sanskrit: bodhi) in accordance with the different qualities and capacities of sentient beings. These practices involve the use of tantra and yoga. Yoga used as a way to enhance concentration.

Nagarjuna's Madhyamika view and Yogacara's Mind-only view are used in Tibetan Buddhism as bases for Yoga practices. Focused meditation clears the mind of unenlightened concepts.

In the 13th and the 14th centuries, the Sarma traditions developed a fourfold classification system for Tantric texts based on the types of practices each contained, especially their relative emphasis on external ritual or internal yoga. The first two classes, the so-called lower tantras, are called the Kriya and the Chatya tantras; the two classes of higher tantras are the Yoga and the Anuttara Yoga (Highest Yoga).

Symbolism

- **Mudra**: This is a symbolic hand-gesture expressing an emotion. Depictions of the Buddha are almost always depicted performing a mudra.
- **Dharma Chakra**: The Dharma Chakra, which appears on the national flag of India and the flag of the Thai royal family, is a Buddhist symbol that is used by members of both religions.
- **Rudraraksh**: These are beads which devotees, usually monks use for praying.
- **Tilak**: Many Hindu devotees mark their heads with a tilak, which is interpreted as a third eye. A similar mark is one of the characteristic physical characteristics of the Buddha.
- **Swastika** and **Sauvastika**: both are sacred symbols. It can be either clockwise or counter-clockwise and both are seen in Hinduism and Buddhism. The Buddha is sometimes depicted with a swastika on his chest or the palms of his hands.

Cosmology and Worldview

Both Hinduism and Buddhism have the concept of Naraka and Svarga lokas, the mountain Sumeru, Jambudvipa, entities such as devas, asuras, nâga, preta, yaksha, gandharvas, kinnars, brahma, etc. Cosmological time is measured in kalpas.

DIFFERENCES BETWEEN THE TWO RELIGIONS

Despite the similarities there exist differences between the two religions. The major differences are mentioned below.

God

Gautama Buddha (as portrayed in the Pali scriptures, the agamas) set an important trend in nontheism in Buddhism in the sense of denying the notion of an omnipotent god. Nevertheless, in many passages in the Tripitaka gods (devas in Sanskrit) are mentioned and specific examples are given of individuals who were reborn as a god, or gods who were reborn as humans. Buddhist cosmology recognizes various levels and types of gods, but none of these gods is considered the creator of the world or of the human race.

Buddhist canonical views about God and the priests are mentioned below:

> 13. 'Well then, Vasettha, those ancient sages versed in ancient scriptures, the authors of the verses, the utterers of the verses, whose, ancient form of words so chanted, uttered, or composed, the priests of to-day chant over again or repeat; intoning or reciting exactly as has been intoned or recited-to wit, Atthaka, Vamaka, Vamadeva, Vessamitta, Yamataggi, Angirasa, Bharadvaja, Vasettha, Kassapa, and Bhagu — did even they speak thus, saying: " We know it, we have seen it", where the creator is whence the creator is, whither the creator is?

From the Buddhist perspective, man has created God out of the psychologically deep-rooted idea of self-protection.

Walpola Rahula writes that man depends on this creation "for his own protection, safety, and security, just as a child depends on his parent." He describes this as a product of "ignorance, weakness, fear, and desire," and writes that this "deeply and fanatically held belief" for man's consolation is "false and empty" from the perspective of Buddhism. He writes that man does not wish to hear or understand teachings against this belief, and that the Buddha described his teachings as "against the current" for this reason.

The Vedas

The Buddha is recorded in the Canki Sutta (Majjhima Nikaya 95) as saying to a group of Brahmins:

> O Vasettha, those priests who know the scriptures are just like a line of blind men tied together where the first sees nothing, the middle man nothing, and the last sees nothing.

In the same discourse, he says:

> It is not proper for a wise man who maintains truth to come to the conclusion: This alone is Truth, and everything else is false.

He is also recorded as saying:

> To be attached to one thing (to a certain view) and to look down upon other things (views) as inferior - this the wise men call a fetter.

> Walpola Rahula writes, "It is always a question of knowing and seeing, and not that of believing. The teaching of the Buddha is qualified as *ehi-passika,* inviting you to 'come and see,' but not to come and believe... It is always seeing through knowledge or wisdom, and not believing through faith."

In the Samanna-phala Sutta, the Buddha is depicted presenting a notion of the 'three knowledges' (*tevijja*)- a term also used in the Vedic tradition to describe knowledge of the Vedas- as being not of texts, but things that he had experienced. The true 'three knowledges' are said to be constituted by the process of achieving enlightenment, which is what the Buddha is said to have achieved in the three watches of the night of his enlightenment. These three are: memory of previous lives, seeing the rebirth of others according to their karma, and the four noble truths and the destruction of spiritual faults which fester in the mind and keep it unenlightened - the third is a composite. The third knowledge, according to the early Buddhist texts, was completed at dawn, and brought the perfect enlightenment he had been seeking. Gombrich notes that this definition of the true "three knowledges" occurs in multiple places in the Canon, and was likely intended to parallel and trump the "three knowledges" of the brahmins.

In Hinduism, philosophies are classified either as Astika or Nastika, that is, philosophies which either affirm or reject the authorities of the Vedas. According to this tradition, Buddhism is a Nastika school since it rejects the authority of the Vedas. Buddhists on the whole called those who did not believe in Buddhism the "outer path-farers" (*tiirthika*).

Conversion

Since the Hindu scriptures are essentially silent on the issue of religious conversion, the issue of whether Hindus evangelize is open to interpretations. Those who view Hinduism as an ethnicity more than as a religion tend to believe that to be a Hindu, one must be born a Hindu. However, those who see Hinduism primarily as a philosophy, a set of beliefs, or a way of life generally believe that one can convert to Hinduism by incorporating Hindu beliefs into one's life and by considering oneself a Hindu. The Supreme Court of India has taken the latter view, holding that the question of whether a person is a Hindu should be determined by the person's belief system, not by their ethnic or racial heritage.

Buddhism spread throughout Asia via evangelism and conversion. Buddhist scriptures depict such conversions in the form of lay followers declaring their support for the Buddha and his teachings, or via ordination as a Buddhist monk. Buddhist identity has been broadly defined as one who "takes refuge" in the Buddha, Dharma, and Sangha, echoing a formula seen in Buddhist texts. In some communities, formal conversion rituals are observed. No specific ethnicity has typically been associated with Buddhism, and as it spread beyond its origin in India immigrant monastics were replaced with newly ordained members of the local ethnic or tribal group.

Early Buddhism and Early Vedanta

Early Buddhist scriptures do not mention schools of learning directly connected with the Upanishads. Though the earliest Upanishads had been completed by the Buddha's time, they are not cited in the early Buddhist texts as Upanishads or Vedanta. For the early Buddhists they were likely not thought of as having any outstanding significance in and of themselves, and as simply one section of the Vedas.

The Buddhist texts do describe wandering, mendicant Brahmins who appear to have valued the early Upanishads' promotion of this lifestyle as opposed to living the life of the householder and accruing wealth from nobles in exchange for performing Vedic sacrifices. Furthermore, the early Buddhist texts mention ideas similar to those expounded in the early Upanishads, before controverting them.

Brahman

The old Upanishads largely consider Brahman (masculine gender, Brahmâ in the nominative case, henceforth "Brahmâ") to be a personal god, and Brahman (neuter gender, Brahma in the nominative case, henceforth "Brahman") to be the impersonal world principle. They do not strictly distinguish between the two, however. The old Upanishads ascribe these characteristics to Brahmâ: first, he has light and luster as his marks; second, he is invisible; third, he is unknowable, and it is impossible to know his nature; fourth, he is omniscient. The old Upanishads ascribe these characteristics to Brahman as well.

In the Buddhist texts, there are many Brahmâs. There they form a class of superhuman beings, and rebirth into the realm of Brahmâs is possible by pursuing Buddhist practices. In the early texts, the Buddha gives arguments to refute the existence of a creator.

In the Pâli scriptures, the neuter Brahman does not appear (though the word *brahma* is standardly used in compound words to mean "best", or "supreme"), however ideas are mentioned as held by various Brahmins in connection with Brahmâ that match exactly with the concept of Brahman in the Upanishads. Brahmins who appear in the Tevijja-suttanta of the Digha Nikaya regard "union with Brahmâ" as liberation, and earnestly seek it. In that text, Brahmins of the time are reported to assert: "Truly every Brahmin versed in the three Vedas has said thus: 'We shall expound the path for the sake of union with that which we do not know and do not see. This is the correct path. This path is the truth, and leads to liberation. If one practices it, he shall be able to enter into association with Brahmâ." The early Upanishads frequently expound "association with Brahmâ", and "that which we do not know and do not see" matches exactly with the early Upanishadic Brahman.

In the earliest Upanishad, the Brihadaranyaka Upanishad, the Absolute, which came to be referred to as Brahman, is referred to as "the imperishable". The Pâli scriptures present a "pernicious view" that is set up as an absolute principle corresponding to Brahman: "O Bhikkhus! At that time Baka, the Brahmâ, produced the following pernicious view: 'It is permanent. It is eternal. It is always existent. It is independent existence. It has the dharma of non-perishing. Truly it is not born, does not become old, does not die, does not disappear, and is not born again. Furthermore, no liberation superior to it exists elsewhere." The principle expounded here corresponds to the concept of Brahman laid out in the Upanishads. According to this text the Buddha criticized this notion: "Truly the Baka Brahmâ is covered with unwisdom."

The Buddha confined himself to what is empirically given. This empiricism is based broadly on both ordinary sense experience and extrasensory perception enabled by high degrees of mental concentration.

Atman

In Hinduism, the atman is considered the essential 'self' of a person.

The pre-Buddhist Upanishads link the Self to the feeling "I am." The Chandogya Upanishad for example does, and it sees Self as underlying the whole world, being "below," "above," and in the four directions. In contrast, the Buddhist Arahant says: "Above, below, everywhere set free, not considering 'this I am.'"

While the pre-Buddhist Upanishads link the Self to the attitude "I am," others like the post-Buddhist Maitri Upanishad hold that only the defiled individual self, rather than the universal self, thinks "this is I" or "this is mine". According to Peter Harvey,

This is very reminiscent of Buddhism, and may well have been influenced by it to divorce the universal Self from such egocentric associations.

The Upanishadic "Self" shares certain characteristics with nibbana; both are permanent, beyond suffering, and unconditioned. However, the Buddha shunned any attempt to see the spiritual goal in terms of "Self" because in his framework, the craving for a permanent self is the very thing which keeps a person in the round of uncontrollable rebirth, preventing him or her from attaining nibbana. Harvey continues:

> Both in the Upanishads and in common usage, self/Self is linked to the sense of "I am" ... If the later Upanishads came to see ultimate reality as beyond the sense of "I am", Buddhism would then say: why call it 'Self', then?

Buddhist mysticism is also of a different sort from that found in systems revolving around the concept of a "God" or "Self":

> If one would characterize the forms of mysticism found in the Pali discourses, it is none of the nature-, God-, or soul-mysticism of F.C. Happold. Though nearest to the latter, it goes beyond any ideas of 'soul' in the sense of immortal 'self' and is better styled 'consciousness-mysticism.'

Possibly the main philosophical difference between Hinduism and Buddhism is that the concept of atman was rejected by the Buddha. Terms like anatman (not-self) and shunyata (voidness) are at the core of all Buddhist traditions. The permanent transcendence of the belief in the separate existence of the self is integral to the enlightenment of an Arhat.

The Buddha criticized conceiving theories even of a unitary soul or identity immanent in all things as unskillful. In fact, according to the Buddha's statement in Khandha Samyutta 47, all thoughts about self are necessarily, whether the thinker is aware of it or not, thoughts about the five aggregates or one of them.

At the time of the Buddha some philosophers and meditators posited a "root": an abstract principle out of which all things emanated and which was immanent in all things. When asked about this, instead of following this pattern of thinking, the Buddha attacks it at its very root: the notion of a principle in the abstract, superimposed on experience. In contrast, a person in training should look for a different kind of "root" — the root of dukkha experienced in the present. According to one Buddhist scholar, theories of this sort have most often originated among meditators who label a particular meditative experience as the ultimate goal, and identify with it in a subtle way.

B. Alan Wallace writes that the transcendental notion of the self is an "idol" that cannot "withstand empirical investigation or rational analysis."

Rahula writes,

> Two ideas are psychologically deep-rooted in man: self-protection and self-preservation. For self-protection man has created God, on whom he depends for his own protection, safety, and security, just as a child depends on its parent. For self-preservation man has conceived the idea of an immortal Soul or Atman, which will live eternally. In his ignorance, fear, weakness, and desire, man needs these two things to console himself. Hence he clings to them deeply and fanatically. The Buddha's teaching does not support this ignorance, fear, weakness, and desire, but aims at making man enlightened by removing them and destroying them, striking at their very root. According to Buddhism, our ideas of God and Soul are false and empty. Though highly developed as theories, they are all the same extremely subtle mental projections, garbed in an intricate metaphysical and philosophical phraseology. These ideas are so deep-rooted in man, and so near and dear to him, that he does not wish to hear, nor does he want to understand, any teaching against them. The Buddha knew this quite

well. In fact, he said that his teaching was 'against the current,' against man's selfish desires.

Upanishadic Self Declared Non-Existent

The Buddha denies the existence of Self in the Alagaddupama Sutta (M I 135-136). Possibly the most famous Upanishadic dictum is *tat tvam asi,* "thou art that." Transposed into first person, the Pali version is *eso 'ham asmi,* "I am this." This is said in several suttas to be false. The full statement declared to be incorrect is "This is mine, I am this, this is my self/essence." This is often rejected as a wrong view. The Alagaduppama Sutta rejects this and other obvious echoes of surviving Upanishadic statements as well (these are not mentioned as such in the commentaries, and seem not to have been noticed until modern times). Moreover, the passage denies that one's self is the same as the world and that one will become the world self at death. The Buddha tells the monks that people worry about something that is non-existent externally (*bahiddhaa asati*) and non-existent internally (*ajjhattam asati*); he is referring respectively to the soul/essence of the world and of the individual. A similar rejection of "internal" Self and "external" Self occurs at AN II 212. Both are referring to the Upanishads. The most basic presupposition of early Brahminic cosmology is the identification of man and the cosmos (instances of this occur at TU II.1 and Mbh XII.195), and liberation for the yogin was thought to only occur at death, with the adept's union with brahman (as at Mbh XII.192.22). The Buddha's rejection of these theories is therefore one instance of the Buddha's attack on the whole enterprise of Upanishadic ontology.

Caste

The Buddha repudiated the caste distinctions of the Brahmanical religion, and was as a result described as a corrupter and opposed to true dharma in some of the Puranas.

Buddhism implicitly denied the validity of caste distinctions by offering ordination to all regardless of caste. The Buddhist writer Ashvaghosa directly opposed the caste system of Hinduism by drawing upon anomalous episodes in Hindu scriptures. While the caste system constitutes an assumed background to the stories told in Buddhist scriptures, the sutras do not attempt to justify or explain the system, and the caste system was not generally propagated along with the Buddhist teachings. The early texts state that caste is not determined by karma.

The notion of ritual purity also provided a conceptual foundation for the caste system, by identifying occupations and duties associated with impure or taboo objects as being themselves impure. Regulations imposing such a system of purity and taboos are absent from the Buddhist monastic code, and not generally regarded as being part of Buddhist teachings.

Soteriology

Upanishadic soteriology is focused on the static Self, while the Buddha's is focused on dynamic agency. In the former paradigm, change and movement are an illusion; to realize the Self as the only reality is to realize something that has always been the case. In the Buddha's system by contrast, one has to make things happen.

The fire metaphor used in the Aggi-Vacchagotta Sutta (which is also used elsewhere) is a radical way of making the point that the liberated sage is beyond phenomenal experience. It also makes the additional point that this indefinable, transcendent state is the sage's state even during life. This idea goes against the early Brahminic notion of liberation at death.

Liberation for the Brahminic yogin was thought to be the permanent realization at death of a nondual meditative state anticipated in life. In fact, old Brahminic metaphors for the liberation at death of the yogic adept ("becoming cool", "going out") were given a new meaning by the Buddha; their point of reference became the sage who is liberated in life. The Buddha taught that these meditative states alone do not offer a decisive and permanent end to suffering either during life or after death.

He stated that achieving a formless attainment with no further practice would only lead to temporary rebirth in a formless realm after death. Moreover, he gave a pragmatic refutation of early Brahminical theories according to which the meditator, the meditative state, and the proposed uncaused, unborn, unanalyzable Self, are identical. These theories are undergirded by the Upanishadic correspondence between macrocosm and microcosm, from which perspective it is not surprising that meditative states of consciousness were thought to be identical to the subtle strata of the cosmos. The Buddha, in contrast, argued that states of consciousness come about caused and conditioned by the yogi's training and techniques, and therefore no state of consciousness could be this eternal Self.

Nonduality

Both the Buddha's conception of the liberated person and the goal of early Brahminic yoga can be characterized as nondual, but in different ways. The nondual goal in early Brahminism was conceived in ontological terms; the goal was that into which one merges after death. According to Wynne, liberation for the Buddha "... is nondual in another, more radical, sense. This is made clear in the dialogue with Upasiva, where the liberated sage is defined as someone who has passed beyond conceptual dualities. Concepts that might have some meaning in ordinary discourse, such as consciousness or the lack of it, existence and non-existence, etc., do not apply to the sage. For the Buddha, propositions are not applicable to the liberated person, because language and concepts (Sn 1076: *vaadapathaa, dhammaa*), as well as any sort of intellectual reckoning (*sankhaa*) do not apply to the liberated sage."

The Term "Nirvana"

The word nirvana (Pali: Nibbana) was first used in its technical sense in Buddhism, and cannot be found in any of the pre-Buddhist Upanishads. The use of the term in the Bhagavad Gita may be a sign of the strong Buddhist influence upon Hindu thought. Although the word nirvana is absent from the Upanishads, the word itself existed prior to the Buddha. It must be kept in mind that nirvana is one of many terms for salvation that occur in the orthodox Buddhist scriptures. Other terms that appear are 'Vimokha', or 'Vimutti', implying 'salvation' and 'deliverance' respectively. Some more words synonymously used for nirvana in Buddhist scriptures are 'mokkha/moksha', meaning 'liberation' and 'kevala/ kaivalya', meaning 'wholeness'; these words were given a new Buddhist meaning.

The Buddha in Hindu Scriptures

In many Puranas, the Buddha is described as an incarnation of Vishnu who incarnated in order to delude either demons or mankind away from the Vedic dharma. The Bhavishya Purana posits:

At this time, reminded of the Kali Age, the god Vishnu became born as Gautama, the Shakyamuni, and taught the Buddhist dharma for ten years. Then Shuddodana ruled for twenty years, and Shakyasimha for twenty. At the first stage of the Kali Age, the path of the Vedas was destroyed and all men became Buddhists. Those who sought refuge with Vishnu were deluded.

It is believed by some scholars that the Buddha avatar, which occurs in different versions in various Puranas, may represent an attempt by Brahmin orthodoxy to slander the Buddhists by identifying them with the demons. Helmuth von Glasenapp attributed these developments to a Hindu desire to absorb Buddhism in a peaceful manner, both to win Buddhists to Vishnuism and also to account for the fact that such a significant heresy could exist in India.

Notable Views

Sarvepalli Radhakrishnan has claimed that the Buddha did not look upon himself as an innovator, but only a restorer of the way of the Upanishads, despite the fact that the Buddha did not accept the Upanishads, viewing them as comprising a pretentious tradition, foreign to his paradigm.

The Hindu philosopher, Vivekananda, wrote in glowing terms about Buddha, and visited Bodh Gaya several times.

Ananda Coomaraswamy, a proponent of the Perennial Philosophy, claimed:

> Hinduism is a religion both of Eternity and Time, while Gautama looks upon Eternity alone. it is not really fair to Gautama or to the Brahmans to contrast their Dharma; for they do not seek to cover the same ground. We must compare the Buddhist ethical ideal with the identical standard of Brahmanhood expected of the Brahman born; we must contrast the Buddhist monastic system with the Brahmanical orders; the doctrine of Anatta with the doctrine of Atman, and here we shall find identity. Buddhism stands for a restricted ideal, which contrasts with Brahmanism as a part contrasts with the whole.

He also maintained:

> The more superficially one studies Buddhism, the more it seems to differ from Brahmanism in which it originated; the more profound our study, the more difficult it

becomes to distinguish Buddhism from Brahmanism, or to say in what respects, if any, Buddhism is really unorthodox.

Some Hindu scholars have also accepted Buddhism as a fulfillment of Sanatana Dharma philosophy:

> The relation between Hinduism (by Hinduism, I mean the religion of the Vedas) and what is called Buddhism at the present day, is nearly the same as between Judaism and Christianity. Jesus Christ was a Jew, and Shakya Muni was a Hindu. The Jews rejected Jesus Christ, nay, crucified him, and the Hindus have accepted Shakya Muni as God and worship him. But the real difference that we Hindus want to show between modern Buddhism and what we should understand as the teachings of Lord Buddha, lies principally in this: Shakya Muni came to preach nothing new. He also, like Jesus, came to fulfill and not to destroy.

Steven Collins sees such Hindu claims regarding Buddhism as part of an effort - itself a reaction to Christian proselytizing efforts in India - to show that "all religions are one", and that Hinduism is uniquely valuable because it alone recognizes this fact.

Some scholars have written that Buddhism should be regarded as "reformed Brahmanism", and many Hindus consider Buddhism a sect of Hinduism.

Alan Watts wrote the following:

> Being a Hindu really involves living in India. Because of the differences of climate, or arts, crafts, and technology, you cannot be a Hindu in the full sense in Japan or in the United States. Buddhism is Hinduism stripped for export. The Buddha was a reformer in the highest sense: someone who wants to go to the original form, or to re-form it for the needs of a certain time... Buddha is the

> man who woke up, who discovered who he really was. The crucial issue wherein Buddhism differs from Hinduism is that it doesn't say who you are; it has no idea, no concept. I emphasize the words *idea* and *concept*. It has no idea and no concept of God because Buddhism is not interested in concepts, it is interested in direct experience only.

Buddhist scholar Rahula Walpole has written that the Buddha fundamentally denied all speculative views, such as the doctrinal Upanishadic belief in Atman.

B. R. Ambedkar, the founder of the Dalit Buddhist movement, believed that Buddhism offered an opportunity for low-caste and untouchable Hindus to achieve greater respect and dignity because of its non-caste doctrines. Among the 22 vows he prescribed to his followers is an injunction against having faith in Brahma, Vishnu and Mahesh. He also regarded the belief that the Buddha was an incarnation of Vishnu as "false propaganda".

●●

9

Buddhism and Christianity

There is speculation concerning a possible connection between both the Buddha and the Christ, and between Buddhism and Christianity. Buddhism originated in India about 500 years before the Apostolic Age and the origins of Christianity. Scholars have explored connections between Buddhism and Christianity. Elaine Pagels, professor of religion at Princeton University, analyzes similarities between some Early Christian texts and Buddhism. Describing teachings in the non-canonical Gnostic Gospel of Thomas, Pagels says, "Some of it looks like Buddhism, and may have in fact been influenced by a well-established Buddhist tradition at the time that these texts were first written." Albert Joseph Edmunds believed the Gospel of John to contain Buddhist concepts and others have compared the infancy account of Jesus in the Gospel of Luke to that of the Buddha in the later Lalitavistara Sutra. Godfrey Higgins claims in several of his books, that after Asoka's subtle mandate of Buddhist worship, Buddhist established themselves with the European outposts of Asoka's missionaries. During the life of Jesus Christ and the period in which texts like the Gospel of Thomas were composed, Buddhist missionaries lived in Alexandria, Egypt. Historians believe that in the fourth century, Christian monasticism developed in Egypt, and it emerged with a corresponding structure comparable to the Buddhist monasticism of its time and place.

In the thirteenth century, international travelers, such as Giovanni de Piano Carpini and William of Ruysbroeck, sent back reports of Buddhism as a religion whose scriptures, doctrine, saints, monastic life, meditation practices, and rituals were comparable to those of Christianity and of Nestorian Christian communities in close proximity to traditionally Buddhist communities. When European Christians made more direct contact with Buddhism in the early 16th century many Catholic missionaries (e.g. Francis Xavier) sent home idyllic accounts of Buddhism. At the same time, however, Portuguese colonizers of Sri Lanka confiscated Buddhist properties across the country, with the full cooperation of the Christian missionaries. This repression of Buddhism in Sri Lanka continued during the rule of subsequently the Dutch and the English. Portuguese historian Diego De Conto reminded the Vatican that their Christian Saint Josaephat was actually the Buddha.

With the arrival of Sanskrit studies in European universities in the late eighteenth century, and the subsequent availability of Buddhist texts, a discussion began of a proper encounter with Buddhism. The esteem for its teachings and practices grew, and at the end of the 19th century the first Westerners converted to Buddhism, and in the beginning of the 20th century the first westerners entered the Buddhist monastic life.

In the 20th century Christian monastics such as Thomas Merton, Wayne Teasdale, David Steindl-Rast and the former nun Karen Armstrong , and Buddhist monastics such as Ajahn Buddhadasa, Thich Nhat Hanh and the Dalai Lama have put energy into Buddhist/Christian dialogue. They each see in the otherwise disparate teachings of Jesus and the Buddha a basic commonality of insight and purpose which offers the possibility of profound remedy to an ailing world. The historian of world culture Arnold Toynbee has speculated that in centuries to come the encounter between Christianity and Buddhism may come to be seen as the momentous event of the 20th century.

Buddhist Culture and Pre-Christian Greece

By the time of Jesus, the teachings of the Buddha had already spread through much of India and penetrated into Sri Lanka, Central Asia and China. They display certain similarities to Christian moral precepts of more than five centuries later; the sanctity of life, compassion for others, rejection of violence, confession and emphasis on charity and the practice of virtue.

Will Durant, noting that the Emperor Ashoka sent missionaries, not only to elsewhere in India and to Sri Lanka, but to Syria, Egypt and Greece, speculated in the 1930s that they may have helped prepare the ground for Christian teaching.

Mauryan Proselytizing

Ashoka ascended the throne of India around 270 B.C.E.. After his conversion to Buddhism he dispatched missionaries to the four points of the compass. Archeological finds indicate these missions had been "favorably received" in lands to the West.

Ptolemy II Philadelphus, one of the monarchs Ashoka mentions in his edicts, is recorded by Pliny the Elder as having sent an ambassador named Dionysius to the Mauryan court at Pataliputra: "India has been treated of by several other Greek writers who resided at the courts of Indian kings, such, for instance, as Megasthenes, and by Dionysius, who was sent thither by Philadelphus, expressly for the purpose: all of whom have enlarged upon the power and vast resources of these nations."

Expansion of Buddhist Culture Westward

Meanwhile, the Buddha's teachings had spread north-west, into Parthian territory. Buddhist stupa remains have been identified as distant as the Silk Road city of Merv. Soviet archeological teams in Giaur Kala, near Merv, have uncovered a Buddhist monastery, complete with huge buddharupa.

Parthian nobles such as An Shih Kao are known to have adopted Buddhism and were among those responsible for its further spread towards China.

Archaeologist Donald Mackenzie believed that Buddhist missionaries had a good footing in pre-Christian Britain. He quotes the early Church father Saint Origen as saying, "The island (Britain) has long been predisposed to it (Christianity) through the doctrines of the Druids and Buddhists, who had already inculcated the doctrine of the unity of the Godhead" - Origen.

Christian Awareness of Buddhism

The Christian theologian Clement of Alexandria states in the 2nd century CE:

> "Thus philosophy, a thing of the highest utility, flourished in antiquity among the barbarians, shedding its light over the nations. And afterwards it came to Greece. First in its ranks were the prophets of the Egyptians; and the Chaldeans among the Assyrians; and the Druids among the Gauls; and the Sarmanas among the Bactrians; and the philosophers of the Celts; and the Magi of the Persians, who foretold the Saviour's birth, and came into the land of Judaea guided by a star. The Indian gymnosophists are also in the number, and the other barbarian philosophers. And of these there are two classes, some of them called Sramanas, and others Brahmins."
>
> —Clement of Alexandria "The Stromata, or Miscellanies" Book I, Chapter XV

> "Among the Indians are those philosophers also who follow the precepts of Boutta, whom they honour as a god on account of his extraordinary sanctity."
>
> — Clement of Alexandria, *Stromata* (*Miscellanies*), Book I, Chapter XV

Early 3rd-4th century Christian writers such as Hippolytus and Epiphanius write of one Scythianus who visited India around 50 CE, whence he brought the "doctrine of the Two Principles". Scythianus' pupil Terebinthus supposedly presented himself as a "Buddha" ("he called himself Buddas" Cyril of Jerusalem) and became well known in Judaea. The same author says his books and knowledge were taken over by Mani, and became the foundation of the Manichean doctrine.

> "Terebinthus, his disciple in this wicked error, inherited his money and books and heresy, and came to Palestine, and becoming known and condemned in Judaea he resolved to pass into Persia: but lest he should be recognised there also by his name he changed it and called himself Buddas."
>
> —Cyril of Jerusalem, Sixth Catechetical Lecture Chapter 22-24

Hippolytus, a Greek-speaking Christian in Rome, around 235 includes Indian ascetics among sources of heresy:

> There is ... among the Indians a heresy of those who philosophize among the Brahmins, who live a self-sufficient life, abstaining from (eating) living creatures and all cooked food . . . They say that God is light, not like the light one sees, nor like the sun nor fire, but to them God is discourse, not that which finds expression in articulate sounds, but that of knowledge (gnosis) through which the secret mysteries of nature are perceived by the wise.

The Syrian gnostic theologian Bar Daisan describes in the third century his exchanges with missions of holy men from India, passing through Syria on their way to Elagabalus or another Severan dynasty Roman Emperor. His accounts are quoted by Porphyry (De abstin., iv, 17) and Stobaeus (Eccles., iii, 56, 141).

Barlaam and Josaphat

The Greek legend of Barlaam and Ioasaph, sometimes mistakenly attributed to the seventh century John of Damascus but first recorded by the Georgian monk Euthymius of Athos in the eleventh century, was ultimately derived, via Arabic and Georgian versions, from the life story of the Buddha. The king-turned-monk Ioasaph (Georgian *Iodasaph*, Arabic *Yûdhasaf* or *Bûdhasaf*) also gets his name from the Sanskrit Bodhisattva, the term traditionally used to refer to Gautama before he becomes a buddha.

Barlaam and Ioasaph were placed in the Orthodox calendar of saints on 26 August, and in the Roman martyrology they were canonized (as "Barlaam and Josaphat") and assigned 27 November. The story was translated into Hebrew in the Middle Ages as "Ben-Hamelekh Vehanazir" ("The Prince and the Nazirite"). Thus the Buddhist story was turned into a Christian and Jewish legend.

Possible Buddhist Influence

In general there are two views regarding a possible connection betweeen Buddhism and Christianity; 1.Buddhism borrowed from Christianity. 2. Christianity borrowed from Buddhism. Those who believe the former point to the many Buddhist/Christian parallels appearing in Mahayana literature which was developed around the same time as the gospels were. Some of those who believe the latter point to the many Pali, or Theravadin Buddhist/Christian parallels, and claim that the Buddhist legends circulating before the said of time of Jesus shows that the Buddha legend had no need for a selfless servant, as the early Jesus was portrayed.

Some scholars have suggested that the apocryphal Gospel of Thomas and the Nag Hammadi texts display Buddhist influence. Elaine Pagels in her widely noted *The Gnostic Gospels* (1979), and in *Beyond Belief* (2003), makes mention of such theories

As far back as 1816 the historian George Faber in his book, The Origin of Pagan Idolatry Ascertained from Historical Testimony, stated, "There is so strong a resemblance between the characters of Jesus and of Buddha, that it cannot have been purely accidental."

In 1883, Max Müller, the pioneering scholar of comparative religion and orientalist, asserted in his *India: What it Can Teach Us*: "That there are startling coincidences between Buddhism and Christianity cannot be denied, and it must likewise be admitted that Buddhism existed at least 400 years before Christianity. I go even further, and should feel extremely grateful if anybody would point out to me the historical channels through which Buddhism had influenced early Christianity." It is interesting to note that Muller himself, before examining the Buddhist/Christian copycat claims, stated that he intended to prove the priority of the Jesus gospels over the Buddhist texts.

In *The Gospel of Jesus in relation to the Buddha Legend,* and again, in 1897, in *The Buddha Legend and the Life of Jesus,* Professor Rudolf Seydel of the University of Leipzig noted around fifty similarities between Buddhist and Christian parables and teachings.

In 1918, in his *History of Religions,* Professor E. Washburn Hopkins of Yale goes so far as to say, "Finally, the life, temptation, miracles, parables, and even the disciples of Jesus have been derived directly from Buddhism."

Much more recently, the historian Jerry H. Bentley notes "the possibility that Buddhism influenced the early development of Christianity" and that scholars "have drawn attention to many parallels concerning the births, lives, doctrines, and deaths of the Buddha and Jesus".

In his *Buddhism Omnibus* Iqbal Singh similarly acknowledges the possibility of early interaction and, thus, influence of Buddhist teachings upon the Christian tradition in its formative period.

In 1992 Zacharias P. Thundy, Professor of Literature, wrote a book titled, Buddha and Christ, Nativity stories from the Indian traditions in which Thundy concludes that there was a substantial amount of borrowing by Christianity from Buddhism. He prefers not to label Jesus either a Jew, Buddhist or a Buddhist-Jew, claiming that such distinctions are "fuzzy". Thundy further claims a long tradition of interchange between east and west and shows that western fables, such as those in Aesop's fables, and the story of Susans attached to the Book of Daniel, were originally Buddhist Jatakas. However, the Jataka tales did not take form until the 6th century AD and many were created up until the 19th Century AD, whereas the Book of Daniel is dated at the very latest to the 2nd Century BC.

In 2007 Doctor of Asian Studies Christian Lindtner published a book titled Geheimnisse um Jesus Christus. Dr. Lindtner compares the Pali and Sanskrit Buddhist texts with the Greek gospels and determines that the four gospels were reformulated from older Buddhist texts based on gematria values, puns, and syllabic equivalences. Those who have scrutinized his work claim that his gematria values and syllabic equivalences are coincidental and that his puns exist because the Greek and Sanskrit are from the same language family. Those in support of his work claim that is findings are unique and that similar finds could not be made in regard to any other seemingly non-connected literature.

Also, in 2007 the author Daniel Hopkins wrote a book named Father and Son, East is West, the Buddhist sources to Christianity and their influence on medieval myths, in which he claims that the Jesus gospels were highly allegorical and mysterious in order to hide the name of Jesus' father, which he claims was the Buddha's name.

Burkhard Scherer, Professor of Indo-Tibetan Studies at England's Canterbury Christ Church University has stated: "...it is very important to draw attention to the fact that there is [massive] Buddhist influence in the Gospels....Since more than a hundred years, Buddhist influence in the Gospels has been known and acknowledged by scholars from both sides." He adds: "Just recently, Duncan McDerret published his excellent *The Bible and the Buddhist* (Sardini, Bornato [Italy] 2001). With McDerret, I am convinced that there are many Buddhist narratives in the Gospels."

Thomas Tweed, Professor of Religious Studies at University of North Carolina at Chapel Hill, notes that between 1879 and 1907 there were a "number of impassioned discussions about parallels and possible historical influence between Buddhism and Christianity in ... a variety of periodicals". By 1906 interest waned somewhat. In the end, Albert Schweitzer's conclusion appears to have been favored: that, although some indirect influence through the wider culture was "not inherently impossible", the hypothesis that Jesus' novel ideas were borrowed directly from Buddhism was "unproved, unprovable and unthinkable."

Buddhism and Gnosticism

Edward Conze and Elaine Pagels have suggested that gnosticism blends teachings like those attributed to Jesus Christ with teachings found in Eastern traditions.

The word gnosis (knowledge) as used by the Gnostics is equivalent to the Buddhist word prajna. Both traditions of Buddhism and Gnosticism held that only direct knowledge was liberating. Some basic parallels held in common with the Buddhist and the Gnostic, and canonical gospels, is that the Buddhists believed that the Buddha was like a great father with sons of light (Bodhisattvas), while all Christians held that Jesus was the light and the son of a great father. While it is true that some Gnostics demonized the "Father", this concept could be the Buddhist concept of 'killing the Buddha', or leaving the raft (religion)behind. Scattered throughout the Gnostic gospels there can be found many exclusively Buddhist themes, such as within The Gospel of Mary can be found the stressing of matter as impermanent, within The Infancy of James those who chew, yet do not chew can be compared to the Bodhisattvas in the Surangama sutra who Taste, but do not taste, within the book Thomas the Contender, Jesus is recorded as saying, "woe to you , because the wheel that turns in your mind" which might reference the Buddhist wheel of dependent origination, within the Gospel of Thomas when Jesus is questioned about how disciples should prove that they were from God, Jesus says the proof of God in them was "motion, and rest" which again could reference the Buddhist belief that the easiest path to enlightenment was through contemplation on the ear organ and the understanding of its two defiling attributes of motion and stillness, the gospel of Phillip mentions that Jesus was martyred many times just as the Buddhist Jatakas and Pali texts mention of the Buddha in his former births.

Philip Jenkins writes that, since the mid-nineteenth century, new and fringe religious movements have often created images of Jesus, presenting him as a sage, philosopher and occult teacher, whose teachings are very similar to those of Asian religions. He asserts that the images generated by these religious movements share much in common with the images that increasingly dominate the mainstream critical scholarship of the New Testament, especially following the rediscovery of the Gnostic Gospels found at Nag Hammadi in Egypt in 1945. He alleges that, in modern scholarly writing, Jesus has become more of a Gnostic, Cynic or even a crypto-Buddhist than the traditional notion of the reformist Jewish rabbi.

Jenkins acknowledges that "the Jesus of the hidden gospels has many points of contact with the great spiritual traditions of Asia." Pagels has written that "one need only listen to the words of the Gospel of Thomas to hear how it resonates with the Buddhist tradition... these ancient gospels tend to point beyond faith toward a path of solitary searching to find understanding, or gnosis." She suggests that there is an explicitly Indian influence in the Gospel of Thomas, perhaps via the Christian communities in southern India, the so-called Thomas Christians.

It is believed by some that of all of the Nag Hammadi texts, the Gospel of Thomas has the most similarities with Pure Land Buddhism within it. Edward Conze has suggested that Hindu or Buddhist tradition may well have influenced Gnosticism. He points out that Buddhists were in contact with the Thomas Christians.

Elaine Pagels notes that the similarities between Gnosticism and Buddhism have prompted some scholars to question their interdependence and to wonder whether "...if the names were changed, the 'living Buddha' appropriately could say what the Gospel of Thomas attributes to the living Jesus. " However, she concludes that, although intriguing, the evidence is inconclusive, and she further concludes that these parallels might be coincidental since parallel traditions may emerge in different cultures without direct influence.

Therapeutae Influence

According to the Gospel of Matthew, Jesus spent his early childhood in Egypt which was at the end of the Silk Road. As a result of its role in trade with the East, Egypt was prosperous and enriched with religious diversity.

The Therapeutae (known only from Philo) were mystics and ascetics who lived especially in the area around Alexandria, Philo described the Therapeutae in the beginning of the 1st century CE in *De vita contemplativa* ("On the contemplative life"), written ca. 10 CE. By that time, the origins of the

Therapeutae were already lost in the past, and Philo was even unsure about the etymology of their name.

Philonian monachism has been seen as the forerunner of and the model for the Christian ascetic life. It has even been considered as the earliest description of Christian monasticism. This view was first espoused by Eusebius of Caesarea in his *Ecclesiastical History*.

According to the linguist Zacharias P. Thundy the name "Therapeutae" is simply an Hellenisation of the Pali term for the traditional Buddhist faith, "Theravada". The similarities between the monastic practices of the Therapeutae and Buddhist monastic practices have led to suggestions that the Therapeutae were in fact Buddhist monks who had reached Alexandria, descendants of Ashoka's emissaries to the West, and who influenced the early formation of Christianity. The evidence for this argument rests solely on the similarity of practices and the purported derivation of the name. There is no evidence from antiquity that supports this argument.

In their book *The Jesus Mysteries*, Timothy Freke and Peter Gandy argue that the Therapeutae are possible candidates for the origin of what they characterize as "the legend of Jesus Christ".

Elmar R. Gruber, a psychologist, and Holger Kersten, a specialist in religious history argue that Buddhism had a substantial influence on the life and teachings of Jesus. Gruber and Kersten claim that Jesus was brought up by the Therapeutae, teachers of the Buddhist Theravada school then living in the Bible lands. They assert that Jesus lived the life of a Buddhist and taught Buddhist ideals to his disciples; their work follows in the footsteps of the Oxford New Testament scholar Barnett Hillman Streeter, who established as early as the 1930s that the moral teaching of the Buddha has four remarkable resemblances to the Sermon on the Mount."

Asceticism can be seen as a common point between Buddhism and Christianity, and is in contrast to the absence of asceticism in Judaism:

> "Asceticism is indigenous to the religions which posit as fundamental the wickedness of this life and the corruption under sin of the flesh. Buddhism, therefore, as well as Christianity, leads to ascetic practices. Monasteries are institutions of Buddhism no less than of Catholic Christianity. The assumption, found in the views of the Montanists and others, that concessions made to the natural appetites may be pardoned in those that are of a lower degree of holiness, while the perfectly holy will refuse to yield in the least to carnal needs and desires, is easily detected also in some of the teachings of Gautama Buddha. The ideal of holiness of both the Buddhist and the Christian saint culminates in poverty and chastity; i.e., celibacy. Fasting and other disciplinary methods are resorted to to curb the flesh"
>
> —The Jewish Encyclopedia

The "Lost Years" of Jesus & New Age Theories

One tradition claims that Jesus traveled to India and Tibet during the "Lost years of Jesus" before the beginning of his public ministry. In 1887 a Russian war correspondent, Nicolas Notovitch, visited India and Tibet. He claimed that, at the lamasery or monastery of Hemis in Ladakh, he learned of the "Life of Saint Issa, Best of the Sons of Men." His story, with a translated text of the "Life of Saint Issa," was published in French in 1894 as *La vie inconnue de Jesus Christ*. It was subsequently translated into English, German, Spanish, and Italian.

The "Life of Saint Issa, Best of the Sons of Men" purportedly recounts the travels of one known in the East as Saint Issa, whom Notovitch identified as Jesus. After initially doubting Notovitch, a disciple of Sri Ramakrishna, Swami Abhedananda, journeyed to Tibet, investigated his claim, helped translate part of the document, and later championed his views..

Notovitch's writings were immediately controversial. The German orientalist Max Müller corresponded with the Hemis monastery that Notovitch claimed to have visited and Archibald Douglas visited Hemis Monastery. Neither found any evidence that Notovich (much less Jesus) had even been there himself, so they rejected his claims. The head of the Hemis community signed a document that denounced Notovitch as a liar.

Despite this contradictory evidence, a number of New Age or spiritualist authors have taken this information and have incorporated it into their own works. For example, in her book *The Lost Years of Jesus: Documentary Evidence of Jesus' 17-Year Journey to the East,* Elizabeth Clare Prophet asserts that Buddhist manuscripts provide evidence that Jesus traveled to India, Nepal, Ladakh and Tibet.

Parallels

According to Jerry Bentley, "Scholars have often considered the possibility that Buddhism influenced the early development of Christianity. They have drawn attention to many parallels concerning the births, lives, doctrines, and deaths of the Buddha and Jesus" .

Birthday of the Buddha and the Christ

Although the Buddha's birthday is celebrated in most traditions in May, which relates to the Buddha's mother Maya Devi, there is no early textual evidence to validate this birthday. Others, such as the author of The Angel-Messiah of the Buddhist, Essenes, and Christians, claim, that based on the ancient Indian calendar in use around 600 b.c. the new year of the Indians was November 17, and so he concludes that since the Buddha was said to be born on the eighth day of the second month that the Buddha's birthday was December 25. This belief held by Buddhists is validated by certain ancient birth accounts of the Buddha, such as in the Asvaghosha-Kirita the Buddha is described as a descendent of solar kings, who was born when the sun retired; "There the sun, even although he had retired, was unable to scorn the moon-like faces of its women which put the lotuses to shame, and as if from the access of passion, hurried towards the western ocean to enter the (cooling)water". This Buddhist text also compares the birth of the Buddha to the constellation of the seven Rishis, which some have compared to the early Christian art depicting "seven-rays" coming out of a white dove. Others have linked this to the Pali text titled Seven Suns.

Administrative Structures

The administrative structures formed by Buddhism share the following similarities with those formed by Christianity:

- initiation into a holy trinity.
- monasticism and communal living for spiritual adherents which adhered to principles of practicing poverty and chastity.
- early Christian Councils reminiscent in organization to the Buddhist councils.
- missionaries and missions which were first organized and established by Buddhists, all predate the early Christian organizations in the same areas where Christianity was first established (Antioch, etc.).

Buddha and Jesus

It is agreed that the Buddha legend was known in the general western world and it has been asserted by Orientalist Samuel Beal that the story of the birth of the Buddha was well known in the West, and possibly influenced the story of the birth of Jesus.

Saint Jerome (4th century CE) mentions the birth of the Buddha, who he says "was born from the side of a virgin" (the Buddha was, according to Buddhist tradition, born from the hip of his mother). The story of the birth of the Buddha was also known: a fragment of *Archelaos of Carrha* (278 CE) mentions the Buddha's virgin-birth.

In the 1893 book, *Influence of Buddhism on Primitive Christianity*, Arthur Lillie argues that the birth accounts of the Buddha were copied into the gospels listing the following infancy parallels:

1. The palm-tree bends down to Mary as the Asoka tree to Yashodara.
2. The story of Simeon, the accounts of the bright light being almost word for word the same.
3. The idol bending down to the infant Jesus.
4. The miracle of the sparrows restored to life.
5. Judas Iscariot in early life attacked Jesus, just as Devadetta, the Judas of Buddhism, attacked Buddha. A violent blow that Jesus received in the left side made a mark that was destined to be the exact spot that received the mortal spear-thrust at the Crucifixion.
6. The whole story of the disputation with the doctors seems copied servilely from the "Lalita Vistara." # Buddhism had invaded Persia, and Maitreya, the coming Buddha, was expected 500 years after Buddha's death. The Persian Buddhists called him Sosiosh. The Gospel of the Infancy explains the presence of the Magi, which in the Canonical Gospels is quite unintelligible. Why should Persians come with hysterical enthusiasm to greet a Messiah whose chief exploit was to be the slaughter of all Persians and all the other nations except Jews? The "Gospel of the Infancy" announces that

Zoroaster had sent them. The Persians mixed up Sakyamuni Buddha, Mithras and Zoroaster and were expecting Sosiosh at the time.

Since publication it has been discovered that both the Lalitavistara Sutra and the Archelaos of Carrha are of later composition than the canonical gospels, including the infancy narratives.

Queen Maya came to bear the Buddha after receiving a prophetic dream in which she saw the descent of the Bodhisattva (Buddha-to-be) from the Tucita heaven into her womb, in the shape of a small white elephant. This story has some parallels with the story of Jesus being conceived in connection with the visitation of the Holy Spirit to the Virgin Mary.

The classical scene of the Virgin Mary being supported by two attendants at her side, may have been influenced by earlier iconography, such as the rather similar Buddhist theme of Queen Maya giving birth.

The iconography of Mary breastfeeding the child Jesus, unknown in the West until the 5-6th century (probable date of a frieze excavated in Saqqara), has also been connected to the much more ancient iconography of the goddess Hariti, also breastfeeding her child, and wearing Hellenistic clothes in the Greco-Buddhist art of Gandhara.

Parallel Lives

Scholars see strong parallels in both the myth and life of Buddha and Jesus. Buddha and his disciples traveling preachers going into homes and preaching gospels to those who hear, is one obvious parallel of a literary motif not found in other traditions. Jesus too pursues this form of preaching and teaching. Jesus speaks of himself as the 'the light' and the son of a great father while the Buddha proclaims himself to be a great father with sons of light (Bodhisattva). Jesus proclaims to come to convert the wicked while the Buddha proclaims that his main goal is to save those of noble character or 'those with little dust in their eyes' although in the Lotus sutra the Buddha claims to create an illusionary 'half-way point' for those who are wicked.

Ernest De Bunsen states, "With the remarkable exception of the death of Jesus on the cross, and of the doctrine of atonement by vicarious suffering, which is absolutely excluded by Buddhism, the most ancient of the Buddhistic records known to us contain statements about the life and the doctrines of Gautama Buddha which correspond in a remarkable manner, *and impossibly by mere chance,* with the traditions recorded in the Gospels about the life and doctrines of Jesus Christ...." Although other scholars, like Zacharias P. Thundy and Dr. Christian Lindtner claim that the ancient Buddhist play Mrrcchakatika was the Buddhist source for the Christian passion narative because of the numerous parallels.

Religious Symbolism

T.W. Rhys Davids, British scholar of the Pâli language, was the earliest most energetic promoter of the Theravada tradition in the West. In 1878 he wrote of its northern counterpart: "Lamaism with its shaven priests, its bells and rosaries, its images and holy water, its popes and bishops, its abbots and monks of many grades, its processions and feast days, its confessional and purgatory, and its worship of the double Virgin, so strongly resembles Romanism that the first Catholic missionaries thought it must be an imitation by the devil of the religion of Christ."

The Buddhist symbol of the eight spoked wheel is also found in Saint Peter's Plaza in Vatican.

It is believed use of rosaries spread from India to Western Europe during the Crusades via its Muslim version, the tasbih. Some, however, suggest an alternative route. A form of prayer rope appears to have been used in Eastern Christendom much earlier; so, it is argued, the Muslim tasbih may in fact originate at a Christian source. Both, it is pointed out, have 33 beads, corresponding to the years of Christ's life.

Prayer with the palms touching one another, the Añjali Mudrâ, is a common form of greeting and prayer gesture in all Indian spiritual traditions, including the Buddhist. It is absent in Jewish traditions, whose scriptures specify raised or clasped hands. Prayer with the palms touching one another is, however, depicted in Christian art from the Middle Ages onwards.

In 1921 the Buddhist Scholar and diplomat Sir Charles Eliot, writing of apparent similarities between Christian practices and their counterparts in Buddhist tradition, expressed the view that: " When all allowance is made for similar causes and coincidences, it is hard to believe that a collection of such practices as clerical celibacy, confession, the veneration of relics, the use of the rosary and bells can have originated independently in both religions."

Criticism

Although Greek rulers as far as the Mediterranean are mentioned as having received Buddhist missionaries, only in Bactria and the Kabul valley did Buddhism really take root. Also, the statement in the late Buddhist chronicle of the Mahavamsa, that among the Buddhists who came to the dedication of a great Stupa in Sri Lanka in the second century BCE, "were over thirty thousand monks from the vicinity of Alassada, the capital of the Yona country" is sometimes taken to suggest that long before the time of Christ, Alexandria in Egypt was the centre of flourishing Buddhist communities. Although it is true that Alassada is the Pali for Alexandria; but it is usually thought that the city meant here is not the ancient capital of Egypt, but as the text indicates, the chief city of the Yona country, the Yavana country of the rock-inscriptions: Bactria and vicinity. And so, the city referred to is most likely Alexandria of the Caucasus.

Also, there are various views on the origins of the oldest Buddhist teachings of the Pali Canon. The origin of the later teachings of Mahayana Buddhism are especially obscure. It is believed that most of the Mahayana sutras only appeared after 100 BCE, and most did not reach their final form until much later, just as the Gospels would not reach a standard form until the Nicene version.

The earlier teachings of the Pali Canon and the Agamas however, are clearly up to four centuries older than Christianity. Although Buddhism is older than Christianity, and some Buddhist influence, such as Barlaam and Josaphat, is clearly evident.

Buddhist Views of Jesus

Buddhist views of Jesus differ, since Jesus is not mentioned in any Buddhist text. Some Buddhists, including Tenzin Gyatso, the 14th Dalai Lama regard Jesus as a bodhisattva who dedicated his life to the welfare of human beings. Both Jesus and Buddha advocated radical alterations in the common religious practices of the day. There are occasional similarities in language, such as the use of the common metaphor of a line of blind men to refer to religious authorities with whom they disagreed (DN 13.15, Matthew 15:14). Some believe there is a particularly close affinity between Buddhism (or Eastern spiritual thought generally) and the doctrine of Gnostic texts such as The Gospel of Thomas

The 14th century Zen master Gasan Joseki indicated that the Gospels were written by an enlightened being:

> "And why take ye thought for raiment? Consider the lilies of the field, how they grow. They toil not, neither do they spin, and yet I say unto you that even Solomon in all his glory was not arrayed like one of these...Take

therefore no thought for the morrow, for the morrow shall take thought for the things of itself."

Gasan said: "Whoever uttered those words I consider an enlightened man."

Guanyin and the Virgin Mary

The Sinologist Martin Palmer has commented on the similarity between the Blessed Virgin Mary and Guan Yin. The Tzu-Chi Foundation, a Taiwanese Buddhist organization, also noticing the similarity, commissioned a portrait of Guan Yin and a baby that resembles the typical Madonna and Child painting.

Some Chinese of the overwhelmingly Roman Catholic Philippines, in an act of syncretism, have identified Guan Yin with the Virgin Mary.

During the Edo Period in Japan, when Christianity was banned and punishable by death, some underground Christian groups venerated the Virgin Mary disguised as a statue of Kannon; such statues are known as *Maria Kannon*. Many had a cross hidden in an inconspicuous location.

Christian Attempts at Conversion of Buddhists

In several Asian countries, Christian missionaries over the centuries have converted in many traditionally Buddhist communities. Buddhism in Sri Lanka was for several centuries heavily affected by Christian efforts to convert the population under subsequent Portuguese, Dutch and English colonizers. In the late 19th century a national Buddhist movement started, inspired by the American Buddhist Henry Steel Olcott, and empowered by the results of the Panadura debate between a Christian priest and the Buddhist monk Migettuwatte Gunananda Thera.

Significant Christian populations exist in South Korea, Thailand and Japan. In countries like Thailand and Japan, Christianity is a small minority among other beliefs.

In Literature

H.G. Wells in his *Outline of History* draws parallels between what he sees as the essentially similar messages of the Buddha and of Jesus, and contends that in each case followers and priests distorted the original teachings. Will Durant in *The Story of Philosophy* suggests that *Jesus-Buddha* corresponds to a "feminine ideology," Nietzsche to a masculine, and that *Plato-Socrates* fall somewhere in between. Paul Carus's *The Gospel of Buddha*, published in 1894, was modeled on the New Testament and told the story of Buddha through parables.

Christopher Moore published in 2002 *Lamb: The Gospel According to Biff, Christ's Childhood Pal*, a novel which seeks to fill in the "lost" years of Jesus from the point of view of Jesus' childhood pal, "Levi bar Alphaeus who is called Biff". They journey to the east, where they study Hindu, Taoist and Buddhist teachings.

Other writers on the relationship between Buddhism and Christianity include the authors Arthur Lillie, Godfrey Higgins, Edward Washburn Hopkins, Zacharias P. Thundy, Christian Lindtner, Gene Matlock, Daniel Hopkins and Alexander Harris.

●●

10

Buddhism in Thailand

Buddhism in Thailand is largely of the Theravada school. Nearly 95% of Thailand's population is Buddhist of the Theravada school, though Buddhism in this country has become integrated with folk beliefs such as ancestor worship as well as Chinese religions from the large Thai-Chinese population. Buddhist temples in Thailand are characterized by tall golden stupas, and the Buddhist architecture of Thailand is similar to that in other Southeast Asian countries, particularly Cambodia and Laos, with which Thailand shares cultural and historical heritage.

Thai Buddhism was based on the religious movement founded in the sixth century B.C. by Siddhartha , later known as the Buddha, who urged the world to relinquish the extremes of sensuality and self-mortification and follow the enlightened Middle Way. The focus of this religion is on man, not gods; the assumption is that life is pain or suffering, which is a consequence of craving, and that suffering can end only if desire ceases. The end of suffering is the achievement of nirvana (in Theravada Buddhist scriptures, nibbana), often defined as the absence of craving and therefore of suffering, sometimes as enlightenment or bliss.

By the third century B.C., Buddhism had spread widely in Asia, and divergent interpretations of the Buddha's teachings had led to the establishment of several sects. The teachings that reached Ceylon (present-day Sri Lanka) were given in a final written form in Pali (an Indo-Aryan language closely related to Sanskrit) to religious centers there in the first century A.D. and provided the Tipitaka (the scriptures or "three baskets", in Sanskrit, Tripitaka) of Theravada Buddhism. This form of Buddhism reached what is now Thailand around the sixth century A.D. Theravāda Buddhism was made the state religion only with the establishment of the Thai kingdom of Sukhothai in the thirteenth century A.D..According to many historians around 228 BC Sohn Uttar Sthavira (one of the royal monks)to Ashoka the great came in Thailand (Suvarnabhumi or Suvannabhumi) with other monks and sacred books.

The details of the history of Buddhism in Thailand from the thirteenth to the nineteenth century are obscure, in part because few historical records or religious texts survived the Burmese destruction of Ayutthaya, the capital city of the kingdom, in 1767. The anthropologist-historian S.J. Tambiah, however, has suggested a general pattern for that era, at least with respect to the relations between Buddhism and the sangha on the one hand and the king on the other hand. In Thailand, as in other Theravada Buddhist kingdoms, the king was in principle thought of as patron and protector of the religion (sasana) and the sangha, while sasana and the sangha were considered in turn the treasures of the polity and the signs of its legitimacy. Religion and polity, however, remained separate domains, and in ordinary times the organizational links between the sangha and the king were not close.

Among the chief characteristics of Thai kingdoms and principalities in the centuries before 1800 were the tendency to expand and contract, problems of succession, and the changing scope of the king's authority. In effect, some Thai kings had greater power over larger territories, others less, and almost invariably a king who sought successfully to expand his power also exercised greater control over the sangha. That control was coupled with greater support and patronage of the ecclesiastical hierarchy. When a king was weak, however, protection and supervision of the sangha also weakened, and the sangha declined. This fluctuating pattern appears to have continued until the emergence of the Chakkri Dynasty in the last quarter of the eighteenth century.

By the nineteenth century, and especially with the coming to power in 1851 of King Mongkut, who had been a monk himself for twenty-seven years, the sangha, like the kingdom, became steadily more centralized and hierarchical in nature and its links to the state more institutionalized. As a monk, Mongkut was a distinguished scholar of Pali Buddhist scripture. Moreover, at that time the immigration of numbers of monks from Burma was introducing the more rigorous discipline characteristic of the Mon sangha. Influenced by the Mon and guided by his own understanding of the Tipitaka, Mongkut began a reform movement that later became the basis for the Dhammayuttika order of monks. Under the reform, all practices having no authority other than custom were to be abandoned, canonical regulations were to be followed not mechanically but in spirit, and acts intended to improve an individual's standing on the road to nirvana but having no social value were rejected. This more rigorous discipline was adopted in its entirety by only a small minority of monasteries and monks. The Mahanikaya order, perhaps somewhat influenced by Mongkut's reforms but with a less exacting discipline than the Dhammayuttika order, comprised about 95 percent of all monks in 1970 and probably about the same percentage in the late 1980s. In any case, Mongkut was in a position to regularize and tighten the relations between monarchy and sangha at a time when the monarchy was expanding its control over the country in general and developing the kind of bureaucracy necessary to such control. The administrative and sangha reforms that Mongkut started were continued by his successor. In 1902 King Chulalongkorn (Rama V, 1868-1910) made the new sangha hierarchy formal and permanent through the Sangha Law of 1902, which remained the foundation of sangha administration in modern Thailand.

Influences

Three major forces have influenced the development of Buddhism in Thailand. The most visible influence is that of the Theravada school of Buddhism, imported from Sri Lanka. While there are significant local and regional variations, the Theravada school provides most of the major themes of Thai Buddhism. By tradition, Pâli is the language of religion in Thailand. Scriptures are recorded in Pâli, using either the modern Thai script or the older Khom and Tham scripts. Pâli is also used in religious liturgy, despite the fact that most Thais understand very little of this ancient language. The Pâli Tipitaka is the primary religious text of Thailand, though many local texts have been composed in order to summarise the vast number of teachings found in the Tipitaka. The monastic code (Patimokkha) followed by Thai monks is taken from the Pâli Theravada—something that has provided a point of controversy during recent attempts to resurrect the bhikkhuni lineage in Thailand.

The second major influence on Thai Buddhism is Hindu beliefs received from Cambodia, particularly during the Sukhothai period. Vedic Hinduism played a strong role in the early Thai institution of kingship, just as it did in Cambodia, and exerted influence in the creation of laws and order for Thai society as well as Thai religion. Certain rituals practiced in modern Thailand, either by monks or by Hindu ritual specialists, are either explicitly identified as Hindu in origin, or are easily seen to be derived from Hindu practices. While the visibility of Hinduism in Thai society has been diminished substantially during the Chakri dynasty, Hindu influences, particularly shrines to the god Brahma, continue to be seen in and around Buddhist institutions and ceremonies.

Folk religion—attempts to propitiate and attract the favor of local spirits known as *phi*—forms the third major influence on Thai Buddhism. While Western observers (as well as urbane and Western-educated Thais) have often drawn a clear line between Thai Buddhism and folk religious practices, this distinction is rarely observed in more rural locales. Spiritual power derived from the observance of Buddhist precepts and rituals is employed in attempting to appease local nature spirits. Many restrictions observed by rural Buddhist monks are derived not from the orthodox Vinaya, but from taboos derived from the practice of folk magic. Astrology, numerology, and the creation of talismans and charms also play a prominent role in Buddhism as practiced by the average Thai—topics that are, if not proscribed, at least marginalized in Buddhist texts.

Additional, more minor influences can be observed stemming from contact with Mahayana Buddhism. Early Buddhism in Thailand is thought to have been derived from an unknown Mahayana tradition. While Mahayana Buddhism was gradually eclipsed in Thailand, certain features of Thai Buddhism—such as the appearance of the bodhisattva Lokesvara in some Thai religious architecture, and the belief that the king of Thailand is a bodhisattva himself—reveal the influence of Mahayana concepts.

The only other bodhisattva prominent in Thai religion is Maitreya, often depicted in Budai form, and often confused with. Images of one or both can be found in mant Thai Buddhist temples, and on amulets as well. Thai may pray to be reborn during the time of Maitreya, or dedicate merit from worship activities to that end.

In modern times, additional Mahayana influence has stemmed from the presence of Chinese immigrants in Thai society. While some Chinese have "converted" to Thai-style Theravada Buddhism, many others maintain their own separate temples in the East Asian Mahayana tradition. The growing popularity of the goddess Kuan Yin in Thailand (a form of Avalokitesvara) may be attributed to the Chinese Mahayanist presence in Thailand.

Government Ties

While Thailand is currently a constitutional monarchy, it inherited a strong Southeast Asian tradition of Buddhist kingship that tied the legitimacy of the state to its protection and support for Buddhist institutions. This connection has been maintained into the modern era, with Buddhist institutions and clergy being granted special benefits by the government, as well as being subjected to a certain amount of government oversight.

In addition to the ecclesiastic leadership of the *sangha,* a secular government ministry supervises Buddhist temples and monks. The legal status of Buddhist sects and reform movements has been an issue of contention in some cases, particularly in the case of Santi Asoke, which was legally forbidden from calling itself a Buddhist denomination, and in the case of the ordination of women- monks attempting to revive the Theravada bhikkhuni lineage have been prosecuted as though attempting to impersonate members of the clergy.

To obtain a passport for travel abroad, a monk must have an official letter from Sangha Supreme Council granting the applicant permission to travel abroad; Buddhist monk identification card; a copy of House/Temple Registration; and submit any previous Thai Passport or a certified copy thereof.

In addition to state support and recognition—-in the form of formal gifts to monasteries made by government officials and the royal family (for example, Kathin)—-a number of special rights are conferred upon Buddhist monks. They are granted free passage on public transportation, and most train stations and airports have special seating sections reserved for members of the clergy. Conversely, ordained monastics are forbidden from standing for office or voting in elections.

In 2007, calls were made by some Thais for Buddhism to be recognized in the new national constitution as a state religion. This suggestion was initially rejected by the committee charged with drafting the new constitution. This move prompted a number of protests from supporters of the initiative, including a number of marches on the capital and a hunger strike by twelve Buddhist monks. Some critics of the plan, including scholar and social critic Sulak Sivaraksa, have claimed that the movement to declare Buddhism a national religion is motivated by political gain, and may be being manipulated by supporters of ousted Prime Minister Thaksin Sinawatra.

The Constitution Drafting Committee later voted against the special status of Buddhism, provoking the religious groups. The groups condemned the Committee and the constitution draft. On August 11, Sirikit, the Queen of Thailand, expressed her concern over the issue. According to her birthday speech, Buddhism is beyond politics. Some Buddhist organizations announced the break of the campaigns a day after.

Ordination and Clergy

Like in most other Theravada nations, Buddhism in Thailand is represented primarily by the presence of Buddhist monks, who serve as officiants on ceremonial occasions, as well as being responsible for preserving and conveying the teachings of the Buddha.

Up until the latter half of the 20th century, most monks in Thailand began their careers by serving as *dek wat* (literally, 'child of the wat'). *Dek wat* are traditionally no younger than eight, and do minor housework around the temple. The primary reason for becoming a *dek wat* is to gain a basic education, particularly in basic reading and writing and the memorization of the scriptures chanted on ritual occasions. Prior to the creation of state-run primary schools in Thailand, village temples served as the primary form of education for most Thai boys. Service in a temple as a *dek wat* was a necessary prerequisite for attaining any higher education, and was the only learning available to most Thai peasants. Since the creation of a government-run educational apparatus in Thailand, the number of children living as *dek wat* has declined significantly. However, many government-run schools continue to operate on the premise of the local village temple.

After serving (typically for four years or more) as a *dek wat*, a future monk typically ordains as a novice (*samana* in Pâli, or *samanen*, but often shortened to *nen*. Novices live according to the Ten Precepts, as do monks, but are not formally required to follow the full range of monastic rules found in the Patimokkha (Buddhist monastic code). There are a few other significant differences between novices and monks. Novices often are in closer contact with their families, spending more time in the homes of their parents than monks. Novices do not participate in the recitation of the monastic code (and the confessions of violations) that take place on the uposatha days. Novices technically do not eat with the monks in their temple, but this typically only amounts to a gap in seating, rather than the separation observed between monks and the laity.

Young men typically do not live as a novice for longer than one or two years. At the age of 20, they become eligible to receive upasampada, the higher ordination that establishes them as a full bhikkhu. A novice is technically sponsored by his parents in his ordination, but in practice in rural villages the entire village participates by providing the robes, alms bowl, and other requisites that will be required by the monk in his monastic life.

Temporary ordination is the norm among Thai Buddhists. Most young men traditionally ordain for the term of a single rainy season (known in Pâli as *vassa,* and in Thai as *phansa*). Those who remain monks beyond their first *vassa* typically remain monks for between one and three years, officiating at religious ceremonies in surrounding villages and possibly receiving further education in reading and writing (possibly including the Kham or Tham scripts traditionally used in recording religious texts). After this period of one to three years, most young monks return to lay life, going on to marry and begin a family. Young men in Thailand who have undergone ordination are seen as being more suitable partners for marriage; unordained men are euphemistically called 'raw', while those who have been ordained are said to be 'cooked'. A period as a monk is a prerequisite for many positions of leadership within the village hierarchy. Most village elders or headmen were once monks, as were most traditional doctors, spirit priests, and some astrologists and fortune tellers.

Monks who do not return to lay life typically specialize in either scholarship or meditation. Those who specialize in scholarship typically travel to regional education centers to begin further instruction in the Pâli language and the scriptures, and may then continue on to the major monastic universities located in Bangkok. The route of scholarship is also taken by monks who desire to rise in the ecclesiastic hierarchy, as promotions within the government-run system is contingent on passing examinations in Pâli and Dhamma studies.

Monks who specialize in meditation typically seek out a known master in the meditation tradition, under whom they will study for a period of years. 'Meditation monks' are particularly revered in Thai society as possessing great virtue and as potential sources of supernatural powers. Ironically, monks of the Thai Forest Tradition often find themselves struggling to find time and privacy to meditate in the face of enthusiastic supporters seeking their blessings and attention.

Reform Movements

- Thammayut Nikaya (Pali) literally "Those adhering strictly to the monastic discipline", an order of Theravada Buddhist monks founded in the 19th century by King Mongkut, son of King Rama II as a reform movement that later became an independent denomination recognized by the Thai Sangha.
- Dhammakâya Movement founded in Thailand in the 1970s. It was criticized to be a cult of personality rather than a legit Buddhist movement, and was investigated by Thai government in the 1990s.
- Santi Asoke literally Peaceful Asoke established by Phra Bodhirak after he "declared independence from the Ecclesiastical Council (Sangha) in 1975"

Position of Women

Unlike in Myanmar (Burma) and Sri Lanka, the female Theravada bhikkhuni lineage was never established in Thailand. As a result, there is a wide-spread perception among Thais that women are not meant to play an active role in monastic life; instead, they are expected to live as lay followers, making merit in the hopes of being born in a different role in their next life. As a result, lay women primarily participate in religious life either as lay participants in collective merit-making rituals, or by doing domestic work around temples. A small number of women choose to become Mae Ji, non-ordained religious specialists who permanently observe either the eight or ten precepts. Mae Ji do not generally receive the level of support given to ordained monks, and their position in Thai society is the subject of some discussion.

Recently, there have been efforts to attempt to introduce a bhikkhuni lineage in Sri Lanka as a step towards improving the position of women in Thai Buddhism. Unlike similar efforts in Sri Lanka, these efforts have been extremely controversial in Thailand. Women attempting to ordain have been accused of attempting to impersonate monks (a civil offense in Thailand), and their actions have been denounced by many members of the ecclesiastic hierarchy. Most objections to the reintroduction of a female monastic role hinge on the fact that the monastic rules require that both five ordained monks and five ordained bhikkhunis be present for any new bhikkhuni ordination. Without such a quorum, critics say that it is not possible to ordain any new Theravada bhikkhuni. The Thai hierarchy refuses to recognize ordinations in the Taiwanese tradition (the only currently existing bhikkhuni ordination lineage) as valid Theravada ordinations, citing differences in philosophical teachings, and (more critically) monastic discipline.

LAO BUDDHIST SCULPTURE

Lao artisans have, throughout the past, used a variety of media in their sculptural creations. Of the metals, bronze is probably the most common, but gold and silver images also exist. Typically, the precious metals are used only for smaller objects, but some large images have been cast in gold, most notably the Phra Say of the sixteenth century, which the Siamese carried home as booty in the late eighteenth century. Today, it is in enshrined at Wat Po Chai in Nongkhai, Thailand, just across the Mekong River from Vientiane. The Phra Say's two companion images, the Phra Seum and Phra Souk, are also in Thailand. One is in Bangkok and the other is in Lopburi. Perhaps the most famous sculpture in Laos, the Phra Bang, is also cast in gold, but the craftsmanship is held to be of Sinhalese, rather than Lao, origin. Tradition maintains that relics of the Buddha are contained in the image.

Bronze is an alloy of copper, containing about two percent tin. Other materials are often added, however, and the balance of ingredients determines the characteristics of the bronze. In Laos, like Cambodia and Thailand, the bronze, which is called *samrit*, includes precious metals, and often has a relatively high percentage of tin, which gives the newly-cast images a lustrous dark gray color. Other images, such as the Buddha of Vat Chantabouri in Vientiane, have a higher copper and, probably, gold content that give them a muted gold color.

A number of colossal images in bronze exist. Most notable of these are the Phra Ong Teu (16th century) of Vientiane, the Phra Ong Teu of Sam Neua, the image at Vat Chantabouri (16th century) in Vientiane and the image at Vat Manorom (14th century) in Luang Phrabang, which seems to be the oldest of the colossal sculptures. The Manorom Buddha, of which only the head and torso remain, shows that colossal bronzes were cast in parts and assembled in place.

Brick-and-mortar also seems to be a favorite medium for colossal images. Perhaps the most famous of these is the image of Phya Vat (16th century) in Vientiane, though apparently an unfortunate renovation completely altered the appearance of the sculpture, and it no longer resembles a Lao Buddha.

Wood is popular for small, votive Buddhist images that are often left in caves. Wood is also very common for large, life-size standing images of the Buddha.

The most famous two sculptures carved in semi-precious stone are the Phra Keo (The Emerald Buddha) and the Phra Phuttha Butsavarat. The Phra Keo, which is probably of Xieng Sen (Chiang Saen) origin, is carved from a solid block of jade. It rested in Vientiane for two hundred years before the Siamese carried it away as booty in the late eighteenth century. Today it serves as the palladium of the Kingdom of Thailand, and resides at the Grand Palace in Bangkok. The Phra Phuttha

Butsavarat, like the Phra Keo, is also enshrined in its own chapel at the Grand Palace in Bangkok. Before the Siamese seized it in the early nineteenth century, this crystal image was the palladium of the Lao kingdom of Champassack.

Many mostly wooden Lao Buddhist sculptures have been assembled inside the Pak Ou caves.

Modern Developments

The religious art tradition of the region has received an original contemporary twist in the monumental fantastic sculpture gardens of Luang Pu Bunleua Sulilat: Buddha Park near Vientiane, and Sala Keoku near Nong Khai, Thailand.

●●

11
Indian Religions

Indian religions are the related religious traditions that originated in the Indian subcontinent, namely Hinduism, Jainism, Buddhism, Sikhism and Ayyavazhi, inclusive of their sub-schools and various related traditions. They form a subgroup of the larger class of "Eastern religions". Indian religions have similarities in core beliefs, modes of worship, and associated practices, mainly due to their common history of origin and mutual influence.

The documented history of Indian religions begins with historical Vedic religion, the religious practices of the early Indo-Aryans, which were collected and later redacted into the *Samhitas,* four canonical collections of hymns or mantras composed in archaic Sanskrit. These texts are the central *shruti* (revealed) texts of Hinduism. The period of the composition, redaction and commentary of these texts is known as the Vedic period, which lasted from roughly 1500 to 500 BCE.

The late Vedic period (9th to 6th centuries BCE) marks the beginning of the Upanisadic or Vedantic period. This period heralded the beginning of much of what became classical Hinduism, with the composition of the Upanishads, later the Sanskrit epics, still later followed by the Puranas.

Jainism and Buddhism arose from the sramana culture. Buddhism was historically founded by Siddhartha Gautama, a Kshatriya prince-turned-ascetic, and was spread beyond India through missionaries. It later experienced a decline in India, but survived in Nepal and Sri Lanka, and remains more widespread in Southeast and East Asia. Jainism was established by a lineage of 24 enlightened beings culminating with Parsva (9th century BCE) and Mahavira (6th century BCE).

Certain scholarship holds that the practices, emblems and architecture now commonly associated with the Hindu pantheon and Jainism may go back as far as Late Harappan times to the period 2000-1500 BCE.

Hinduism is divided into numerous denominations, primarily Shaivism, Shaktism, Vaishnavism, Smarta and much smaller groups like the conservative Shrauta. Hindu reform movements and Ayyavazhi are more recent. About 90% of Hindus reside in the Republic of India, accounting for 83% of its population.

Sikhism was founded in the 15th century on the teachings of Guru Nanak and the nine successive Sikh Gurus in Northern India. The vast majority of its adherents originate in the Punjab region.

Common Traits

Sometimes summarised as "Dharmic" religions or dharmic traditions, (though the 'subtler' meaning of *Dharma* or *dhamma* differs per religion); Hinduism, Buddhism, Jainism and Sikhism share certain key concepts, which are interpreted differently by different groups and individuals. Common traits can also be observed in both the ritual and the literary sphere. For example, the head-anointing ritual of *abhiseka* is of importance in three of these distinct traditions, excluding Sikhism. Other noteworthy rituals are the cremation of the dead, the wearing of vermilion on the head by married women, and various marital rituals. In literature, many classical narratives and purana have Hindu, Buddhist or Jain versions. All four traditions have notions of *karma, dharma, samsara, moksha* and various *yogas*. Of course, these terms may be perceived differently by different religions. For instance, for a Hindu, *dharma* is his duty. For a Jain, *dharma* is righteousness, his conduct. For a Buddhist, *dharma* is usually taken to be the Buddha's teachings. Similarly, for a Hindu, yoga is the cessation of all thoughts/activities of the mind. For Jains yoga is sum total all physical, verbal and mental activities.

Rama is a heroic figure in all of these religions. In Hinduism he is the God-incarnate in the form of a princely king; in Buddhism, he is a Bodhisattva-incarnate; in Jainism, he is the perfect human being. Among the Buddhist Ramayanas are: *Vessantarajataka*, Reamker, Ramakien, Phra Lak Phra Lam, Hikayat Seri Rama etc. There also exists the *Khamti Ramayana* among the Khamti tribe of Asom wherein Rama is an avatar of a Bodhisattva who incarnates to punish the demon king Ravana (B.Datta 1993). The *Tai Ramayana* is another book retelling the divine story in Asom.

Prehistory

Evidence attesting to prehistoric religion in the Indian subcontinent derives from scattered Mesolithic rock paintings such as at Bhimbetka, depicting dances and rituals. Neolithic agriculturalists inhabiting the Indus River Valley buried their dead in a manner suggestive of spiritual practices that incorporated notions of an afterlife and belief in magic. Other South Asian Stone Age sites, such as the Bhimbetka rock shelters in central Madhya Pradesh and the Kupgal petroglyphs of eastern Karnataka, contain rock art portraying religious rites and evidence of possible ritualised music. The Harappan people of the Indus Valley Civilization, which lasted from 3300–1300 BCE (mature period, 2600-1900 BCE) and was centered around the Indus and Ghaggar-Hakra river valleys, may have worshiped an important mother goddess symbolising fertility, a concept that has recently been challenged. Excavations of Indus Valley Civilization sites show small tablets with animals and altars, indicating rituals associated with animal sacrifice.

Vedic Tradition

Vedic Period

The Vedic Period is most significant for the composition of the four Vedas, Brahmanas and the older Upanishads (both presented as discussions on the rituals, mantras and concepts found in the four Vedas), which today are some of the most important canonical texts of Hinduism, and are the codification of much of what developed into the core beliefs of Hinduism.

The Vedas reflect the liturgy and ritual of Late Bronze Age to Early Iron Age Indo-Aryan speaking peoples in India. Religious practices were dominated by the Vedic priesthood administering domestic rituals/rites and solemn sacrifices. The Brahmanas, Aranyakas and some of the older Upanishads (such as BAU, ChU, JUB) are also placed in this period. Many elements of Vedic religion reach back to early Bronze Age Proto-Indo-Iranian times. The Vedic period is held to have ended around 500 BCE.

Specific rituals and sacrifices of the Vedic religion include:

- The *Soma* cult described in the Rigveda, descended from a common Indo-Iranian practice.
- Fire rituals, also a common Indo-Iranian practice (See Zoroastrianism):
  - o The *Agnihotra* or oblation to Agni.
  - o The *Agnistoma* or Soma sacrifice (including animal sacrifice) .
  - o The *Agnicayana*, the sophisticated ritual of piling the Uttara fire altar.
- The Darsapaurnamasa, the fortnightly New and Full Moon sacrifice
- The Caturmasya or seasonal sacrifices (every four months)

- a large number of sacrifices for special wishes (Kâmyecmi)
- The *Ashvamedha* or horse sacrifice.
- The *Purushamedha,* or sacrifice of a man, imitating that of the cosmic Purusha and Ashvamedha
- The rites referred to in the Atharvaveda are concerned with medicine and healing practices, as well as some charms and sorcery (white and black magic).
- The domestic (grihya) rituals deal with the rites of passage from conception to death and beyond.

Vedanta

The period of *Vedanta* (Sanskrit : end of Vedas), typically thought to have begun around 600 BCE, marked the end of the evolution of the main Vedic texts; it also accompanied the transformation of the semi-nomadic nature of the Indo-Aryan tribes to agriculture-based polities, as they increasingly formed permanent settlements in the Indo-Gangetic plain and other parts of Northern India. This period was foreshadowed by the Brahmanas that interpreted the four canonical Vedas in various fashions, which finally led to the Upanishads. While the ritualistic status of the four Vedas remained undiminished, the early Upanishads mainly relate to spiritual insights. At this time, the concepts of reincarnation, samsara, karma, and moksha began to be accepted in ancient India outside the sphere of the priestly establishment i.e. the Brahmana class. Some scholars think that these new concepts developed by aborigines outside the caste system, others detect Sramana or even Ksatriya influence. These concepts were eventually accepted by Brahmin orthodoxy, and were to form much of the core philosophies of the later epics and Hinduism, as well as, against a different philosophical and religious background, in Buddhism and Jainism.

Astika and Nastika Categorization

Astika and *nastika* are sometimes used to categorise Indian religions. Those religions that believe that God is the central actor in this world are termed as *astika*. Those religions that do not believe that God is the prime mover and actor are classified as *nastika* religions. From this point of view the Vedic religion (and Hinduism) is an *astika* religion, whereas Buddhism and Jainism are *nastika* religions.

Another definition of the terms *astika* and *nastika*, followed by Adi Shankara, classifies religions and persons as *astika* and *nastika* according to whether they accept the authority of the main Hindu texts, the Vedas, as supreme revealed scriptures, or not. By this definition, Nyaya, Vaisheshika, Samkhya, Yoga, Purva Mimamsa and Vedanta are classified as *astika* schools, while Charvaka is classified as a *nastika* school. By this definition, both Buddhism and Jainism are classified as *nastika* religions since they do not accept the authority of the Vedas.

Shramana Tradition

Vedic Brahmanism of Iron Age India co-existed and closely interacted with the parallel non-Vedic shramana traditions. These were not direct outgrowths of Vedism, but separate movements that influenced it and were influenced by it. The shramanas were wandering ascetics. Buddhism and Jainism are a continuation of the Shramana tradition, and the early Upanishadic movement was influenced by it. The 24th Jain Tirthankar, Mahavira (599–527 BCE), stressed five vows, including *ahimsa* (non-violence), *satya* (truthfulness), *asteya* (non-stealing) and *aparigraha* (non-attachment).

The historical Gautama Buddha, who was a Buddha, was born into the Shakya clan of Angirasa and Gautama Rishi lineage, just before the kingdom of Magadha (which lasted from 546–324 BCE) rose to power. His family was native to Kapilavastu and Lumbini, in what is now southern Nepal.

The Ajivikas and Samkhyas, both of which did not survive, also belonged to the sramana tradition.

Rise and Spread of Jainism and Buddhism

Both Jainism and Buddhism spread throughout India during the period of the Magadha empire. Scholars Jeffrey Brodd and Gregory Sobolewski write that *"Jainism shares many of the basic doctrines of Hinduism and Buddhism."* Jainism has declined since the 12th century in many regions, but continues to be an influential religion in Gujarat, Rajasthan, Madhya Pradesh, Maharashtra and Karnataka.

Buddhism in India spread during the reign of Asoka the Great of the Mauryan Empire, who patronised Buddhist teachings and unified the Indian subcontinent in the 3rd century BCE. He sent missionaries abroad, allowing Buddhism to spread across Asia. Indian Buddhism started declining following the rise of Puranic Hinduism during the Gupta dynasty, but continued to have a significant presence in some regions of India until the 12th century. Scholar James Bird writes, *"But when primitive Buddhism originated from Hindu schools of philosophy, it differed as widely from that of later times, as did the Brahmanism of the Vedas from that of the Puranas and Tantras."*

Period after 200 BCE

After 200 CE several schools of thought were formally codified in Indian philosophy, including Samkhya, Yoga, Nyaya, Vaisheshika, Purva-Mimamsa and Vedanta. Hinduism, otherwise a highly polytheistic, pantheistic or monotheistic religion, also tolerated atheistic schools. The thoroughly materialistic and anti-religious philosophical Cârvâka school that originated around the 6th century BCE is the most explicitly atheistic school of Indian philosophy. Cârvâka is classified as a *nastika* ("heterodox") system; it is not included among the six schools of Hinduism generally regarded as orthodox. It is noteworthy as evidence of a materialistic movement within Hinduism. Our understanding of Cârvâka philosophy is fragmentary, based largely on criticism of the ideas by other schools, and it is no longer a living tradition. Other Indian philosophies generally regarded as atheistic include Classical Samkhya and Purva Mimamsa.

Between 400 CE and 1000 CE Hinduism expanded as the decline of Buddhism in India continued. Buddhism subsequently became effectively extinct in India but survived in Nepal and Sri Lanka.

There were several Buddhistic kings who worshiped Vishnu, such as the Gupta, Pala, Malla, Somavanshi, and Sattvahana. Buddhism survived followed by Hindus. *National Geographic* edition reads, "*The flow between faiths was such that for hundreds of years, almost all Buddhist temples, including the ones at Ajanta, were built under the rule and patronage of Hindu kings.*"

Post-Vedic Development of Hinduism

The end of the Vedantic period around the 2nd century AD spawned a number of branches that furthered Vedantic philosophy, and which ended up being seminaries in their own right. The output generated by these specialized tributaries was automatically considered a part of the Hindu or even Indian philosophy. Prominent amongst these developers were Yoga, Dvaita, Advaita and the medieval Bhakti movement. The modern day popular movements were the ones founded by Swami Vivekananda, Sri Aurobindo, Raja Ram Mohan Roy among others.

In the latter Vedantic period, several texts were also composed as summaries/attachments to the Upanishads. These texts collectively called as Puranas allowed for a divine and mythical interpretation of the world, not unlike the ancient Hellenic or Roman religions. Legends and epics with a multitude of gods and goddesses with human-like characteristics were composed. Two of Hinduism's most revered *epics,* the Mahabharata and Ramayana were compositions of this period. Devotion to particular deities was reflected from the composition of texts composed to their worship. For example the *Ganapati Purana* was written for devotion to Ganapati (or Ganesh). Popular deities of this era were Shiva, Vishnu, Durga, Surya, Skanda, and Ganesh (including the forms/incarnations of these deities.)

Bhakti Movement

The Bhakti Movement began with the emphasis on the worship of God, regardless of one's status - whether priestly or laypeople, men or women, higher social status or lower social status.

The movements were mainly centered around the forms of Vishnu (Rama and Krishna) and Shiva. There were however popular devotees of this era of Durga.

Vaishnavism

The most well-known devotees are the Alwars from southern India. The most popular Vaishnava teacher of the south was Ramanuja, while of the north it was Ramananda.

Several important icons were women. For example, within the Mahanubhava sect, the women outnumbered the men, and administration was many times composed mainly of women. Mirabai is the most popular female saint in India.

Sri Vallabha Acharya (1479 - 1531) is a very important figure from this era. He founded the Shuddha Advaita (*Pure Non-dualism*) school of Vedanta thought.

Shaivism

The most well-known devotees are the Nayanars from southern India. The most popular Shaiva teacher of the south was Basava, while of the north it was Gorakhnath.

Recent Groups

The modern era has given rise to dozens of Hindu saints with international influence. For example, Brahma Baba established the Brahma Kumaris, one of the largest new Hindu religious movements teaches the discipline of Raja Yoga to millions. Representing traditional Gaudiya Vaishnavism, Prabhupada founded the Hare Krishna movement, also international with many followers. In late 18th century India, Swaminarayan founded the Swaminarayan Sampraday. Anandamurti, founder of the Ananda Marga, has influenced many worldwide. Through all these new Hindu denominations traveling international, many Hindu practices such as yoga, meditation, mantra, divination, vegetarianism have become absorbed by new coverts and others influenced.

Sikhism

Sikhism originated in fifteenth century Northern India with the teachings of Nanak and nine successive gurus. The principal belief in Sikhism is faith in *Vâhigurû*— represented by the sacred symbol of *ek Mankâr* [meaning one god]. Sikhism's traditions and teachings are distinctly associated with the history, society and culture of the Punjab. Adherents of Sikhism are known as Sikhs (*students* or *disciples*) and number over 23 million across the world.

Although it began as a relatively neutral faith system that proposed to include the best practices of Hinduism and Islam, over time its Gurus led followers in various rebellions and battles against the Islamic Mughal rulers of the time, most notably against Aurangzeb.

Status in the Republic of India

In a judicial reminder, the Indian Supreme Court observed Sikhism and Jainism to be sub-sects or *special* faiths within the larger Hindu fold, and that Jainism is a denomination within the Hindu fold. Although the government of British India counted Jains in India as a major religious community right from the first Census conducted in 1873, after independence in 1947 Sikhs and Jains were not treated as national minorities. In 2005 the Supreme Court of India declined to issue a writ of Mandamus granting Jains the status of a religious minority throughout India. The Court however left it to the respective states to decide on the minority status of Jain religion.

However, some individual states have over the past few decades differed on whether Jains, Buddhists and Sikhs are religious minorities or not, by either pronouncing judgments or passing legislation. One example is the judgment passed by the Supreme Court in 2006, in a case pertaining to the state of Uttar Pradesh, which declared Jainism to be undisputably distinct from Hinduism, but mentioned that, "The question as to whether the Jains are part of the Hindu religion is open to debate. However, the Supreme Court also noted various court cases that have held Jainism to be a distinct religion.

Another example is the Gujarat Freedom of Religion Bill, that is an amendment to a legislation that sought to define Jains and Buddhists as denominations within Hinduism. Ultimately on July 31, 2007, finding it not in conformity with the concept of freedom of religion as embodied in Article 25 (1) of the Constitution, Governor Naval Kishore Sharma returned back the Gujarat Freedom of Religion (Amendment) Bill, 2006 citing the widespread protests by the Jains as well as Supreme Court's extrajudicial observation that Jainism is a "special religion formed on the basis of quintessence of Hindu religion by the Supreme Court"

●●

12
Buddhist Architecture and Symbolism

Buddhist religious architecture developed in South Asia in the third century BC.

Three types of structures are associated with the religious architecture of early Buddhism: monasteries (viharas), stupas, and temples (chaitya grihas).

Viharas initially were only temporary shelters used by wandering monks during the rainy season, but later were developed to accommodate the growing and increasingly formalised Buddhist monasticism. An existing example is at Nalanda (Bihar). A distinctive type of fortress architecture found in the former and present Buddhist kingdoms of the Himalayas are dzongs.

The initial function of a stupa was the veneration and safe-guarding of the relics of the Buddha. The earliest surviving example of a stupa is in Sanchi (Madhya Pradesh).

In accordance with changes in religious practice, stupas were gradually incorporated into chaitya-grihas (temple halls). These reached their high point in the first century BC, exemplified by the cave complexes of Ajanta and Ellora (Maharashtra). The Mahabodhi Temple at Bodh Gaya in Bihar is another well known example.

The Pagoda is an evolution of the Indian stupa.

Early Development

Buddhist architecture emerged slowly in the period following the Buddha's life, building on Brahmanical Vedic models, but incorporating a specifically Buddhist symbols.

Brahmanical temples at this time followed a simple plan – a square inner space, the sacrificial arena, often with a surrounding ambulatory route separated by lines of columns, with a conical or rectangular sloping roof, behind a porch or entrance area, generally framed by freestanding columns or a colonnade. The external profile represents Mount Meru, the abode of the gods and centre of the universe. The dimensions and proportions were dictated by sacred mathematical formulae. This simple plan was adopted by early Buddhists, sometimes adapted with additional cells for monks at the periphery (especially in the early cave temples such as at Ajanta, India).

In essence the basic plan survives to this day in Buddhist temples throughout the world. The profile became elaborated and the characteristic mountain shape seen today in many Hindu temples was used in early Buddhist sites and continued in similar fashion in some cultures (such as the Khmer). In others, such as Japan and Thailand, local influences and differing religious practices led to different architecture.

Early temples were often timber, and little trace remains, although stone was increasingly used. Cave temples such as those at Ajanta have survived better and preserve the plan form, porch and interior arrangements from this early period. As the functions of the monastery-temple expanded, the plan form started to diverge from the Brahmanical tradition and became more elaborate, providing sleeping, eating and study accommodation.

A characteristic new development at religious sites was the stupa. Stupas were originally more sculpture than building, essentially markers of some holy site or commemorating a holy man who lived there. Later forms are more elaborate and also in many cases refer back to the Mount Meru model.

One of the earliest Buddhist sites still in existence is at Sanchi, India, and this is centred on a stupa said to have been built by Ashoka the Great (273-236 BCE). The original simple structure is encased in a later, more decorative one, and over two centuries the whole site was elaborated upon. The four cardinal points are marked by elaborate stone gateways.

As with Buddhist art, architecture followed the spread of Buddhism throughout south and east Asia and it was the early Indian models that served as a first reference point, even though Buddhism virtually disappeared from India itself in the 10th century.

Decoration of Buddhist sites became steadily more elaborate through the last two centuries BCE, with the introduction of tablets and friezes, including human figures, particularly on stupas. However, the Buddha was not represented in human form until the first century CE. Instead, aniconic symbols were used. This is treated in more detail in Buddhist art, Aniconic phase. It influenced the development of temples, which eventually became a backdrop for Buddha images in most cases.

As Buddhism spread, Buddhist architecture diverged in style, reflecting the similar trends in Buddhist art. Building form was also influenced to some extent by the different forms of Buddhism in the northern countries, practising Mahayana Buddhism in the main and in the south where Theravada Buddhism prevailed.

Buddhist Architecture

Buddhist religious architecture developed in South Asia in the third century BC.

Three types of structures are associated with the religious architecture of early Buddhism: monasteries (viharas), stupas, and temples (chaitya grihas).

Viharas initially were only temporary shelters used by wandering monks during the rainy season, but later were developed to accommodate the growing and increasingly formalised Buddhist monasticism. An existing example is at Nalanda (Bihar). A distinctive type of fortress architecture found in the former and present Buddhist kingdoms of the Himalayas are dzongs.

The initial function of a stupa was the veneration and safe-guarding of the relics of the Buddha. The earliest surviving example of a stupa is in Sanchi (Madhya Pradesh).

In accordance with changes in religious practice, stupas were gradually incorporated into chaitya-grihas (temple halls). These reached their high point in the first century BC, exemplified by the cave complexes of Ajanta and Ellora (Maharashtra). The Mahabodhi Temple at Bodh Gaya in Bihar is another well known example.

The Pagoda is an evolution of the Indian stupa.

Early Development

Buddhist architecture emerged slowly in the period following the Buddha's life, building on Brahmanical Vedic models, but incorporating a specifically Buddhist symbols.

Brahmanical temples at this time followed a simple plan – a square inner space, the sacrificial arena, often with a surrounding ambulatory route separated by lines of columns, with a conical or rectangular sloping roof, behind a porch or entrance area, generally framed by freestanding columns or a colonnade. The external profile represents Mount Meru, the abode of the gods and centre of the universe. The dimensions and proportions were dictated by sacred mathematical formulae. This simple plan was adopted by early Buddhists, sometimes adapted with additional cells for monks at the periphery (especially in the early cave temples such as at Ajanta, India).

In essence the basic plan survives to this day in Buddhist temples throughout the world. The profile became elaborated and the characteristic mountain shape seen today in many Hindu temples was used in early Buddhist sites and continued in similar fashion in some cultures (such as the Khmer). In others, such as Japan and Thailand, local influences and differing religious practices led to different architecture.

Early temples were often timber, and little trace remains, although stone was increasingly used. Cave temples such as those at Ajanta have survived better and preserve the plan form, porch and interior arrangements from this early period. As the functions of the monastery-temple expanded, the plan form started to diverge from the Brahmanical tradition and became more elaborate, providing sleeping, eating and study accommodation.

A characteristic new development at religious sites was the stupa. Stupas were originally more sculpture than building, essentially markers of some holy site or commemorating a holy man who lived there. Later forms are more elaborate and also in many cases refer back to the Mount Meru model.

One of the earliest Buddhist sites still in existence is at Sanchi, India, and this is centred on a stupa said to have been built by Ashoka the Great (273-236 BCE). The original simple structure is encased in a later, more decorative one, and over two centuries the whole site was elaborated upon. The four cardinal points are marked by elaborate stone gateways.

As with Buddhist art, architecture followed the spread of Buddhism throughout south and east Asia and it was the early Indian models that served as a first reference point, even though Buddhism virtually disappeared from India itself in the 10th century.

Decoration of Buddhist sites became steadily more elaborate through the last two centuries BCE, with the introduction of tablets and friezes, including human figures, particularly on stupas. However, the Buddha was not represented in human form until the first century CE. Instead, aniconic symbols were used. This is treated in more detail in Buddhist art, Aniconic phase. It influenced the development of temples, which eventually became a backdrop for Buddha images in most cases.

As Buddhism spread, Buddhist architecture diverged in style, reflecting the similar trends in Buddhist art. Building form was also influenced to some extent by the different forms of Buddhism in the northern countries, practising Mahayana Buddhism in the main and in the south where Theravada Buddhism prevailed.

BUDDHIST SYMBOLISM

Buddhist symbolism appeared from around the 2100 BC, and started with aniconic symbolism, avoiding direct representations of the Buddha. Anthropomorphic symbolism appeared from around the 1st century CE with the arts of Mathura and the Greco-Buddhist art of Gandhara, and were combined with the previous symbols. Various symbolic innovations were later introduced, especially through Tibetan Buddhism.

Early Aniconic Symbols

Among the earliest and most common symbols of Buddhism are the stupa, Dharma wheel, and the lotus flower. The dharma wheel, traditionally represented with eight spokes, can have a variety of meanings. It initially only meant royalty (concept of the "Monarch of the Wheel, or *Chakravatin*), but started to be used in a Buddhist context on the Pillars of

Ashoka during the 3rd century BCE. The Dharma wheel is generally seen as referring to the historical process of teaching the buddhadharma; the eight spokes refer to the Noble Eightfold Path. The lotus, as well, can have several meanings, often referring to the inherently pure potential of the mind.

The swastika was traditionally used in India by Buddhists and Hindus as a good luck sign. In East Asia, the swastika is often used as a general symbol of Buddhism. Swastikas used in this context can either be left or right-facing.

Other early aniconic symbols include the trisula, a symbol use since around the 2nd century BCE that combine the lotus, the vajra diamond rod and a symbolization of the three jewels (The Buddha, the dharma, the sangha).

The first hint of a human representation in Buddhist symbolism appear with the Buddha footprint.

Physical Characteristics of the Buddha

Although the Buddha was not represented in human form until around the 1st century CE, the Physical characteristics of the Buddha are described in one of the central texts of the traditional Pali canon, the Digha Nikaya, in the discourse titled "Sutra of the Marks" (Pali: *Lakkhana Sutta*) (D.iii.142ff.).

These characteristics comprise 32 signs, "The 32 signs of a Great Man" (Pali: *Lakkhana Mahapurisa 32*), and were supplemented by another 80 Secondary Characteristics (Pali:*Anubyanjana*). These traits are said to have defined the appearance of the historical Buddha, Siddhartha Gautama and have been used symbolically in many of his representations.

Mudras

The Mudras are a series of symbolic hand gestures describing the actions of the characters represented in only the most interesting Buddhist art.

Eight Auspicious Symbols

Mahayana and Vajrayana Buddhist art frequently makes use of a particular set of eight auspicious symbols, *ashtamangala*, in household and public art. These symbols have spread with Buddhism to many cultures' arts, including Indian, Tibetan, Nepalese, and Chinese art.

These symbols include:

1. Lotus flower. Representing purity and enlightenment.
2. Endless knot, or, the Mandala. Representing harmony.
3. Golden Fish pair. Representing conjugal happiness and freedom.
4. Victory Banner. Representing a victorious battle.
5. Wheel of Dharma or Chamaru in Nepali Buddhism. Representing knowledge.
6. Treasure Vase. Representing inexhaustible treasure and wealth.
7. Parasol. Representing the crown, and protection from the elements.
8. Conch shell. Representing the thoughts of the Buddha.

International Symbols of the World Fellowship of Buddhists

At its founding in 1952, the World Fellowship of Buddhists adopted two symbols. These were a traditional eight-spoked Dharma wheel and the five-colored flag which had been designed in Sri Lanka in the 1880s with the assistance of Henry Steele Olcott .

BOROBUDUR

Borobudur is a ninth-century Mahayana Buddhist Monument in Magelang, Central Java, Indonesia. The monument comprises six square platforms topped by three circular platforms, and is decorated with 2,672 relief panels and 504 Buddha statues. A main dome, located at the center of the top platform, is surrounded by 72 Buddha statues seated inside perforated stupa.

The monument is both a shrine to the Lord Buddha and a place for Buddhist pilgrimage. The journey for pilgrims begins at the base of the monument and follows a path circumambulating the monument while ascending to the top through the three levels of Buddhist cosmology, namely *Kâmadhâtu* (the world of desire), *Rupadhatu* (the world of forms) and *Arupadhatu* (the world of formlessness). During the journey the monument guides the pilgrims through a system of stairways and corridors with 1,460 narrative relief panels on the wall and the balustrades.

Evidence suggests Borobudur was abandoned following the fourteenth century decline of Buddhist and Hindu kingdoms in Java, and the Javanese conversion to Islam. Worldwide knowledge of its existence was sparked in 1814 by Sir Thomas Stamford Raffles, the then British ruler of Java, who was advised of its location by native Indonesians. Borobudur has since been preserved through several restorations. The largest restoration project was undertaken between 1975 and 1982 by the Indonesian government and UNESCO, following which the monument was listed as a UNESCO World Heritage Site. Borobudur is still used for pilgrimage; once a year Buddhists in Indonesia celebrate Vesak at the monument, and Borobudur is Indonesia's single most visited tourist attraction.

Etymology

In Indonesian, ancient temples are known as *candi*; thus "Borobudur Temple" is locally known as *Candi Borobudur*. The term *candi* is also used more loosely to describe any ancient structure, for example gates and bathing structures. The origins of the name *Borobudur* however are unclear, although the original names of most ancient Indonesian temples are no longer known. The name Borobudur was first written in Sir Thomas Raffles' book on Javan history. Raffles wrote about a monument called *borobudur*, but there are no older documents suggesting the same name. The only old Javanese manuscript that hints at the monument as a holy Buddhist sanctuary is Nagarakretagama, written by Mpu Prapanca in 1365.

The name 'Bore-Budur', and thus 'BoroBudur', is thought to have been written by Raffles in English grammar to mean the nearby village of Bore; most *candi* are named after a nearby village. If it followed Javanese language, the monument should have been named 'BudurBoro'. Raffles also suggested that 'Budur' might correspond to the modern Javanese word *Buda* ('ancient') – i.e., 'ancient Boro'. However, another archaeologist suggests the second component of the name ('Budur') comes from Javanese term *bhudhara* (or mountain).

Location

Approximately 40 kilometers (25 mi) northwest of Yogyakarta, Borobudur is located in an elevated area between two twin volcanoes, Sundoro-Sumbing and Merbabu-Merapi, and two rivers, the Progo and the Elo. According to local myth, the area known as Kedu Plain is a Javanese 'sacred' place and has been dubbed 'the garden of Java' due to its high agricultural fertility. Besides Borobudur, there are other Buddhist and Hindu temples in the area, including the Prambanan temples compound. During the restoration in the early 1900s, it was discovered that three Buddhist temples in the region, Borobudur, Pawon and Mendut, are lined in one straight line position. It might be accidental, but the temples' alignment is in conjunction with a native folk tale that a long time ago, there was a brick-paved road from Borobudur to Mendut with walls on both sides. The three temples (Borobudur–Pawon–Mendut) have similar architecture and ornamentation derived from the same time period, which suggests that ritual relationship between the three temples, in order to have formed a sacred unity, must have existed, although exact ritual process is yet unknown.

Unlike other temples, which were built on a flat surface, Borobudur was built on a bedrock hill, 265 m (869 ft) above sea level and 15 m (49 ft) above the floor of the dried-out paleolake. The lake's existence was the subject of intense discussion among archaeologists in the twentieth century; Borobudur was thought to have been built on a lake shore or even floated on a lake. In 1931, a Dutch artist and a scholar of Hindu and Buddhist architecture, W.O.J. Nieuwenkamp, developed a theory that Kedu Plain was once a lake and Borobudur initially represented a lotus flower floating on the lake. Lotus flowers are found in almost every Buddhist work of art, often serving as a throne for buddhas and base for stupas. The architecture of Borobudur itself suggests a lotus depiction, in which Buddha postures in Borobudur symbolize the Lotus Sutra, mostly found in many Mahayana Buddhism (a school of Buddhism widely spread in the east Asia region) texts. Three circular platforms on the top are also thought to represent a lotus leaf. Nieuwenkamp's theory, however, was contested by many archaeologists because the natural environment surrounding the monument is a dry land.

Geologists, on the other hand, support Nieuwenkamp's view, pointing out clay sediments found near the site. A study of stratigraphy, sediment and pollen samples conducted in 2000 supports the existence of a paleolake environment near Borobudur, which tends to confirm Nieuwenkamp's theory. The lake area fluctuated with time and the study also proves that Borobudur was near the lake shore circa thirteenth and fourteenth century. River flows and volcanic activities shape the surrounding landscape, including the lake. One of the most active volcanoes in Indonesia, Mount Merapi, is in the direct vicinity of Borobudur and has been very active since the Pleistocene.

History

Construction

There is no written record of who built Borobudur or of its intended purpose. The construction time has been estimated by comparison between carved reliefs on the temple's hidden foot and the inscriptions commonly used in royal charters during the eight and ninth centuries. Borobudur was likely founded around 800 AD. This corresponds to the period between 760–830 AD, the peak of the Sailendra dynasty in central Java, when it was under the influence of the Srivijayan Empire. The construction has been estimated to have taken 75 years and been completed during the reign of Samaratungga in 825.

There is confusion between Hindu and Buddhist rulers in Java around that time. The Sailendras were known as ardent followers of Lord Buddha, though stone inscriptions found at Sojomerto suggest they may have been Hindus. It was during this time that many Hindu and Buddhist monuments were built on the plains and mountain around the Kedu Plain. The Buddhist monuments, including Borobudur, were erected around the same time as the Hindu Shiva Prambanan temple compound. In 732 AD, the Shivaite King Sanjaya commissioned a Shivalinga sanctuary to be built on the Ukir hill, only 10 km (6.2 miles) east of Borobudur.

Construction of Buddhist temples, including Borobudur, at that time was possible because Sanjaya's immediate successor, Rakai Panangkaran, granted his permission to the Buddhist followers to build such temples. In fact, to show his respect, Panangkaran gave the village of Kalasan to the Buddhist community, as is written in the Kalasan Charter dated 778 AD. This has led some archaeologists to believe that there was never serious conflict concerning religion in Java as it was possible for a Hindu king to patronize the establishment of a Buddhist monument; or for a Buddhist king to act likewise. However, it is likely that there were two rival royal dynasties in Java at the time—the Buddhist Sailendra and the Saivite Sanjaya—in which the latter triumphed over their rival in the 856 battle on the Ratubaka plateau. This confusion also exists regarding the Lara Jonggrang temple at the Prambanan complex, which was believed that it was erected by the victor Rakai Pikatan as the Sanjaya dynasty's reply to Borobudur, but others suggest that there was a climate of peaceful coexistence where Sailendra involvement exists in Lara Jonggrang.

Abandonment

Borobudur lay hidden for centuries under layers of volcanic ash and jungle growth. The facts behind its abandonment remain a mystery. It is not known when active use of the monument and Buddhist pilgrimage to it ceased. Somewhere between 928 and 1006, the center of power moved to East Java region and a series of volcanic eruptions took place; it is not certain whether the latter influenced the former but several sources mention this as the most likely period of abandonment. Soekmono (1976) also mentions the popular belief that the temples were disbanded when the population converted to Islam in the fifteenth century.

The monument was not forgotten completely, though folk stories gradually shifted from its past glory into more superstitious beliefs associated with bad luck and misery. Two old Javanese chronicles (*babad*) from the eighteenth century mention cases of bad luck associated with the monument. According to the *Babad Tanah Jawi* (or the History of Java), the monument was a fatal factor for a rebel who revolted against the king of Mataram in 1709. The hill was besieged and the insurgents were defeated and sentenced to death by the king. In the *Babad Mataram* (or the History of the Mataram Kingdom), the monument was associated with the misfortune of the crown prince of the Yogyakarta Sultanate in 1757. In spite of a taboo against visiting the monument, "he took what is written as *the knight who was captured in a cage* (a statue in one of the perforated stupas)". Upon returning to his palace, he fell ill and died one day later.

Rediscovery

Following the Anglo-Dutch Java War, Java was under British administration from 1811 to 1816. The appointed governor was Lieutenant Governor-General Thomas Stamford Raffles, who took great interest in the history of Java. He collected Javanese antiques and made notes through contacts with local inhabitants during his tour throughout the island. On an inspection tour to Semarang in 1814, he was informed about a big monument deep in a jungle near the village of Bumisegoro. He was not able to make the discovery himself and sent H.C. Cornelius, a Dutch engineer, to investigate.

In two months, Cornelius and his 200 men cut down trees, burned down vegetation and dug away the earth to reveal the monument. Due to the danger of collapse, he could not unearth all galleries. He reported his findings to Raffles including various drawings. Although the discovery is only mentioned by a few sentences, Raffles has been credited with the monument's recovery, as one who had brought it to the world's attention.

Hartmann, a Dutch administrator of the Kedu region, continued Cornelius' work and in 1835 the whole complex was finally unearthed. His interest in Borobudur was more personal than official. Hartmann did not write any reports of his activities; in particular, the alleged story that he discovered the large statue of Buddha in the main stupa. In 1842, Hartmann investigated the main dome although what he discovered remains unknown as the main stupa remains empty.

The Dutch East Indies government then commissioned F.C. Wilsen, a Dutch engineering official, who studied the monument and drew hundreds of relief sketches. J.F.G. Brumund was also appointed to make a detailed study of the monument, which was completed in 1859. The government intended to publish an article based on Brumund study supplemented by Wilsen's drawings, but Brumund refused to cooperate. The government then commissioned another scholar, C. Leemans, who compiled a monograph based on Brumund's and Wilsen's sources. In 1873, the first monograph of the detailed study of Borobudur was published, followed by its French translation a year later. The first photograph of the monument was taken in 1873 by a Dutch-Flemish engraver, Isidore van Kinsbergen.

Appreciation of the site developed slowly, and it served for some time largely as a source of souvenirs and income for "souvenir hunters" and thieves. In 1882, the chief inspector of cultural artifacts recommended that Borobudur be entirely disassembled with the relocation of reliefs into museums due to the unstable condition of the monument. As a result, the government appointed Groenveldt, an archeologist, to undertake a thorough investigation of the site and to assess the actual condition of the complex; his report found that these fears were unjustified and recommended it be left intact.

Contemporary Events

Following the major 1973 renovation funded by UNESCO, Borobudur is once again used as a place of worship and pilgrimage. Once a year, during the full moon in May or June, Buddhists in Indonesia observe Vesak (Indonesian: *Waisak*) day commemorating the birth, death, and the time when Siddhârtha Gautama attained the highest wisdom to become the Buddha Shakyamuni. Vesak is an official national holiday in Indonesia and the ceremony is centered at the three Buddhist temples by walking from Mendut to Pawon and ending at Borobudur.

The monument is the single most visited tourist attraction in Indonesia. In 1974, 260,000 tourists of whom 36,000 were foreigners visited the monument. The figure hiked into 2.5 million visitors annually (80% were domestic tourists) in the mid 1990s, before the country's economy crisis. Tourism development, however, has been criticized for not including the local community on which occasional local conflict has arisen. In 2003, residents and small businesses around Borobudur organized several meetings and poetry protests, objecting to a provincial government plan to build a three-story mall complex, dubbed the 'Java World'.

On 21 January 1985, nine stupas were badly damaged by nine bombs. In 1991, a blind Muslim evangelist, Husein Ali Al Habsyie, was sentenced to life imprisonment for masterminding a series of bombings in the mid 1980s including the temple attack. Two other members of a right-wing extremist group that carried out the bombings were each sentenced to 20 years in 1986 and another man received a 13-year prison term. On 27 May 2006, an earthquake of 6.2 magnitude on the Richter scale struck the south coast of Central Java. The event had caused severe damage around the region and casualties to the nearby city of Yogyakarta, but Borobudur remained intact.

On 28 August 2006 the Trail of Civilizations symposium was held in Borobudur under the auspices of the governor of Central Java and the Indonesian Ministry of Culture and Tourism, also present the representatives from UNESCO and predominantly Buddhist nations of Southeast Asia, such as Thailand, Myanmar, Laos, Vietnam and Cambodia. Climax of the event was the "Mahakarya Borobudur" ballet performance in front of the temple of Borobudur. It was choreographed to feature traditional Javanese dancing, music and costumes, and tell the history about the construction of the Borobudur. After the symposium, the Mahakarya Borobudur ballet is performed several times, especially during annual national Waisak commemoration at Borobudur attended by Indonesian President.

Reliefs

Borobudur contains approximately 2,670 individual bas reliefs (1,460 narrative and 1,212 decorative panels), which cover the façades and balustrades. The total relief surface is 2,500 square meters (26,909.8 sq ft) and they are distributed at the hidden foot (*Kâmadhâtu*) and the five square platforms (*Rupadhatu*).

The narrative panels, which tell the story of Sudhana and Manohara, are grouped into 11 series encircled the monument with the total length of 3,000 meters (9,843 ft). The hidden foot contains the first series with 160 narrative panels and the remaining 10 series are distributed throughout walls and balustrades in four galleries starting from the eastern entrance stairway to the left. Narrative panels on the wall read from right to left, while on the balustrade read from left to right. This conforms with *pradaksina*, the ritual of circumambulation performed by pilgrims who move in a clockwise direction while keeping the sanctuary to their right.

The hidden foot depicts the workings of karmic law. The walls of the first gallery have two superimposed series of reliefs; each consists of 120 panels. The upper part depicts the biography of the Buddha, while the lower part of the wall and also balustrades in the first and the second galleries tell the story of the Buddha's former lives. The remaining panels are devoted to Sudhana's further wandering about his search, terminated by his attainment of the Perfect Wisdom.

The Law of Karma (Karmavibhangga)

The 160 hidden panels do not form a continuous story, but each panel provides one complete illustration of cause and effect. There are depictions of blameworthy activities, from gossip to murder, with their corresponding punishments. There are also praiseworthy activities, that include charity and pilgrimage to sanctuaries, and their subsequent rewards.

The pains of hell and the pleasure of heaven are also illustrated. There are scenes of daily life, complete with the full panorama of *samsara* (the endless cycle of birth and death).

The Birth of Buddha (Lalitavistara)

The story starts from the glorious descent of the Lord Buddha from the Tushita heaven, and ends with his first sermon in the Deer Park near Benares. The relief shows the birth of the Buddha as Prince Siddhartha, son of King Suddhodana and Queen Maya of Kapilavastu (in present-day Nepal).

The story is preceded by 27 panels showing various preparations, in heavens and on earth, to welcome the final incarnation of the Bodhisattva. Before descending from Tushita heaven, the Bodhisattva entrusted his crown to his successor, the future Buddha Maitreya. He descended on earth in the shape of white elephants with six tusks, penetrated to Queen Maya's right womb. Queen Maya had a dream of this event, which was interpreted that his son would become either a sovereign or a Buddha.

While Queen Maya felt that it was the time to give birth, she went to the Lumbini park outside the Kapilavastu city. She stood under a plaksa tree, holding one branch with her right hand and she gave birth to a son, Prince Siddhartha. The story on the panels continues until the prince becomes the Buddha.

Prince Siddhartha story (Jataka) and other legendary persons (Avadana)

Jatakas are stories about the Buddha before he was born as Prince Siddhartha. Avadanas are similar to jatakas, but the main figure is not the Bodhisattva himself. The saintly deeds in avadanas are attributed to other legendary persons. Jatakas and avadanas are treated in one and the same series in the reliefs of Borobudur.

The first 20 lower panels in the first gallery on the wall depict the *Sudhanakumaravadana* or the saintly deeds of Sudhana. The first 135 upper panels in the same gallery on the balustrades are devoted to the 34 legends of the *Jatakamala*. The remaining 237 panels depict stories from other sources, as do for the lower series and panels in the second gallery. Some jatakas stories are depicted twice, for example the story of King Sibhi (Rama's forefather).

Sudhana's search for the Ultimate Truth (Gandavyuha)

Gandavyuha is the story told in the final chapter of the Avatamsaka Sutra about Sudhana's tireless wandering in search of the Highest Perfect Wisdom. It covers two galleries (third and fourth) and also half of the second gallery; comprising in total of 460 panels. The principal figure of the story, the youth Sudhana, son of an extremely rich merchant, appears on the 16th panel. The preceding 15 panels form a prologue to the story of the miracles during Buddha's *samadhi* in the Garden of Jeta at Sravasti.

During his search, Sudhana visited no less than 30 teachers but none of them had satisfied him completely. He was then instructed by Manjusri to meet the monk Megasri, where he was given the first doctrine. As his journey continues, Sudhana meets (in the following order) Supratisthita, the physician Megha (Spirit of Knowledge), the banker Muktaka, the monk Saradhvaja, the upasika Asa (Spirit of Supreme Enlightenment), Bhismottaranirghosa, the Brahmin Jayosmayatna, Princess Maitrayani, the monk Sudarsana, a boy called Indriyesvara, the upasika Prabhuta, the banker Ratnachuda, King Anala, the god Siva Mahadeva, Queen Maya, Bodhisattva Maitreya and then back to Manjusri. Each meeting has given Sudhana a specific doctrine, knowledge and wisdom. These meetings are shown in the third gallery.

After the last meeting with Manjusri, Sudhana went to the residence of Bodhisattva Samantabhadra; depicted in the fourth gallery. The entire series of the fourth gallery is devoted to the teaching of Samantabhadra. The narrative panels finally end with Sudhana's achievement of the Supreme Knowledge and the Ultimate Truth.

Buddha Statues

Apart from the story of Buddhist cosmology carved in stone, Borobudur has many statues of various Buddhas. The cross-legged statues are seated in a lotus position and distributed on the five square platforms (the *Rupadhatu* level) as well as on the top platform (the *Arupadhatu* level).

The Buddha statues are in niches at the *Rupadhatu* level, arranged in rows on the outer sides of the balustrades, the number of statues decreasing as platforms progressively diminish to the upper level. The first balustrades have 104 niches, the second 104, the third 88, the fourth 72 and the fifth 64. In total, there are 432 Buddha statues at the *Rupadhatu* level. At the *Arupadhatu* level (or the three circular platforms), Buddha statues are placed inside perforated stupas. The first circular platform has 32 stupas, the second 24 and the third 16, that add up to 72 stupas. Of the original 504 Buddha statues, over 300 are damaged (mostly headless) and 43 are missing (since the monument's discovery, heads have been stolen as collector's items, mostly by Western museums).

At glance, all the Buddha statues appear similar, but there is a subtle difference between them in the *mudras* or the position of the hands. There are five groups of *mudra*: North, East, South, West and Zenith, which represent the five cardinal compass points according to Mahayana. The first four balustrades have the first four *mudras*: North, East, South and West, of which the Buddha statues that face one compass direction have the corresponding *mudra*. Buddha statues at the fifth balustrades and inside the 72 stupas on the top platform have the same *mudra*: Zenith. Each *mudra* represents one of the Five Dhyani Buddhas; each has its own symbolism.

They are *Abhaya mudra* for Amoghasiddhi (north), *Vara mudra* for Ratnasambhava (south), *Dhyana mudra* for Amitabha (west), *Bhumisparsa mudra* for Aksobhya (east) and *Dharmachakra mudra* for Vairochana (zenith).

Restoration

Borobudur attracted attention in 1885, when Yzerman, the Chairman of the Archaeological Society in Yogyakarta, made a discovery about the *hidden foot*. Photographs that reveal reliefs on the hidden foot were made in 1890–1891. The discovery led the Dutch East Indies government to take steps to safeguard the monument. In 1900, the government set up a commission consisting of three officials to assess the monument: Brandes, an art historian, Theodoor van Erp, a Dutch army engineer officer, and Van de Kamer, a construction engineer from the Department of Public Works.

In 1902, the commission submitted a threefold plan of proposal to the government. First, the immediate dangers should be avoided by resetting the corners, removing stones that endangered the adjacent parts, strengthening the first balustrades and restoring several niches, archways, stupas and the main dome. Second, fencing off the courtyards, providing proper maintenance and improving drainage by restoring floors and spouts. Third, all loose stones should be removed, the monument cleared up to the first balustrades, disfigured stones removed and the main dome restored. The total cost was estimated at that time around 48,800 Dutch guilders.

The restoration then was carried out between 1907 and 1911, using the principles of anastylosis and led by Theodor van Erp. The first seven months of his restoration was occupied with excavating the grounds around the monument to find missing Buddha heads and panel stones. Van Erp dismantled and rebuilt the upper three circular platforms and stupas.

Along the way, Van Erp discovered more things he could do to improve the monument; he submitted another proposal that was approved with the additional cost of 34,600 guilders. At first glance Borobudur had been restored to its old glory.

Due to the limited budget, the restoration had been primarily focused on cleaning the sculptures, and Van Erp did not solve the drainage problem. Within fifteen years, the gallery walls were sagging and the reliefs showed signs of new cracks and deterioration. Van Erp used concrete from which alkali salts and calcium hydroxide leached and were transported into the rest of the construction. This caused some problems, so that a further thorough renovation was urgently needed.

Small restorations have been performed since then, but not sufficient for complete protection. In the late 1960s, the Indonesian government had requested from the international community a major renovation to protect the monument. In 1973, a master plan to restore Borobudur was created. The Indonesian government and UNESCO then undertook the complete overhaul of the monument in a big restoration project between 1975–1982. The foundation was stabilized and all 1,460 panels were cleaned. The restoration involved the dismantling of the five square platforms and improved the drainage by embedding water channels into the monument. Both impermeable and filter layers were added. This colossal project involved around 600 people to restore the monument and cost a total of US$ 6,901,243. After the renovation was finished, UNESCO listed Borobudur as a World Heritage Site in 1991.

●●

Index